D1594040

HORACE'S POETIC JOURNEY

HORACE'S
POETIC JOURNEY

A Reading of *Odes* 1-3

DAVID H. PORTER

NEW JERSEY

PRINCETON UNIVERSITY PRESS

1987

COPYRIGHT © 1987 BY PRINCETON UNIVERSITY PRESS
PUBLISHED BY PRINCETON UNIVERSITY PRESS,
41 WILLIAM STREET, PRINCETON, NEW JERSEY 08540
IN THE UNITED KINGDOM: PRINCETON UNIVERSITY PRESS,
GUILDFORD, SURREY

LIBRARY OF CONGRESS CATALOGING IN PUBLICATION DATA WILL BE
FOUND ON THE LAST PRINTED PAGE OF THIS BOOK

ISBN 0-691-06702-3

PUBLICATION OF THIS BOOK HAS BEEN AIDED BY A GRANT FROM
THE ANDREW W. MELLON FOUNDATION

THIS BOOK HAS BEEN COMPOSED IN LINOTRON BEMBO

CLOTHBOUND EDITIONS OF PRINCETON UNIVERSITY PRESS BOOKS
ARE PRINTED ON ACID-FREE PAPER, AND BINDING MATERIALS
ARE CHOSEN FOR STRENGTH AND DURABILITY. PAPERBACKS,
ALTHOUGH SATISFACTORY FOR PERSONAL COLLECTIONS,
ARE NOT USUALLY SUITABLE FOR LIBRARY REBINDING

PRINTED IN THE UNITED STATES OF AMERICA
BY PRINCETON UNIVERSITY PRESS
PRINCETON, NEW JERSEY

IN MEMORIAM

L.D.P.

quis desiderio sit pudor aut modus
tam cari capitis?

CONTENTS

CONTENTS

LIST OF DIAGRAMS

ABBREVIATIONS

A & A   *Antike und Abendland*

AC   *Acta Classica*

AJP   *American Journal of Philology*

CB   *Classical Bulletin*

CP   *Classical Philology*

CQ   *Classical Quarterly*

CW   *Classical World*

G & R   *Greece and Rome*

GB   *Grazer Beiträge*

GRBS   *Greek, Roman, and Byzantine Studies*

HSCP   *Harvard Studies in Classical Philology*

MH   *Museum Helveticum*

REL   *Revue des Études Latines*

RhM   *Rheinisches Museum*

SHAW   *Sitzungsberichte der Heidelberger Akademie der Wissenschaft*

SO   *Symbolae Osloenses*

TAPA   *Transactions of the American Philological Association*

WS   *Wiener Studien*

YCS   *Yale Classical Studies*

Except where otherwise indicated, the text followed has been that of the Oxford Classical Text (OCT). Line numbers refer to Horace's *Odes* unless another work is specified. Full bibliographical information on secondary sources cited more than once will be found in the Bibliography; sources cited only once are not included in the Bibliography.

PREFACE

My debts in the writing of this book are many and substantial. A grant from the National Endowment for the Humanities and a sabbatical leave from Carleton College enabled me to devote the academic year 1983–84 to research and writing. The British Library once more, as on two previous leaves, graciously permitted me to draw upon its incomparable resources and to enjoy the unique ambiance of the Reading Room, with the libraries of the University of Minnesota, Carleton College, and the London Institute of Classical Studies playing valuable supporting roles. A generous grant from Carleton College paid for the typing and duplicating of the manuscript.

Any student of Horace owes an immense debt to earlier studies of Horace. I have tried in my notes always to acknowledge specific points at which I have drawn on the work of other scholars and when possible to mention other studies which bear directly on particular themes or arguments in my study. The bibliography on Horace, and especially that on *Odes* 1–3, is so vast, however, that anyone who attempts to give exhaustive bibliographical coverage runs the risk of drowning his text in a sea of footnotes, and I have tried to skirt this peril by being rigorously selective in my notes. The result is that inevitably many works that might well have been cited have been omitted. In defense of my selectivity I can say only that my first purpose, as I explain in the Introduction, has been to present a reading of *Odes* 1–3 that concentrates on the larger thematic outlines, and this intent has entailed a number of methodological consequences, among them the decision to keep scholarly commentary and controversy to a background hum. I am happy to record in this Preface, however, my general indebtedness to those many Horatian scholars from whom I have learned but whose work I have not been able specifically to acknowledge in this book.

It remains to record a few more personal debts: To Lucius

Shero of Swarthmore College, and to Francis Godolphin and
George Duckworth of Princeton University, who first kindled
my interest in Horace, and whose store of knowledge and
insight still informs my teaching and research on Horace; to
Helen North and Susan Cobbs of Swarthmore College, with-
out whom I would never have entered the field of classics; to
Emilio J. Calvacca of Collegiate School, who introduced me
to Latin and to Latin poetry in a manner that was at once
rigorous and humane; to my colleagues in classics at Carleton
College, Linda Clader, Jackson Bryce, Nancy Wilkie, and
Ronnie Ancona, who have at many points contributed warm
encouragement and wise advice; to Kenneth Reckford,
Charles Babcock, and Michael Putnam, who read the full
manuscript with great care and discrimination and who made
many useful suggestions toward its improvement; to T. James
Luce and Mark Morford, who gave valuable support and en-
couragement to this particular project; to Sherry Wert, Eliz-
abeth Powers, and Peter Andersen of Princeton University
Press, all of whom made invaluable contributions through
their work on this book; to Betty Kendall, who with won-
derful good humor and immense skill transformed a chaotic
jumble into an elegant typescript; to my many Carleton stu-
dents in Horace seminars over the years, and to the Princeton
students in my 1986 graduate seminar, from all of whom I
have learned more about Horace than I can begin to acknowl-
edge; and finally to Laudie Porter, who for years gracefully
endured my addiction to Horace, and without whose en-
couragement and wisdom the present book would never have
been written.

David H. Porter
Northfield, Minnesota

HORACE'S POETIC JOURNEY

INTRODUCTION

The purpose of this study of Horace, *Odes* 1–3 is to present a reading that concentrates on the structure and movement of the collection as a whole—how the parts relate to each other, how one poem leads into another, one section into the next, above all how different themes progress and develop as the collection unrolls. There are many internal indications that Horace intended the collection to be seen as a single architectural entity, among them the obvious balance of its outside poems, 1.1 and 3.30; the clear grouping of certain large sections by metrical principles—1.1–12, 2.1–12, 3.1–6; the special attention paid to marking important beginnings, ends, and middles; and the very way he speaks of his accomplishment in the last poem: *exegi monumentum aere perennius regalique situ pyramidum altius*. Nor does our emphasis on ongoing linear and thematic development need elaborate defense. Ancient books were intended above all for continuous reading or recitation, and the very manner in which they were written, on a *volumen* that was progressively unrolled from one hand, rolled up by the other, invited attention to linear development even in a non-narrative genre.[1]

Our study focuses first on the internal architecture of the collection, the elaborate and largely concentric patterns by which Horace binds its many diverse poems into a unified and organized whole (Chapter I). The next three chapters analyze in considerable detail each of the three books, using the structural analyses of Chapter I as starting point but concentrating less on structure than on linear, sequential development of themes, motifs, moods. Chapter V adopts the same approach but, like Chapter I, concentrates not on individual books but on the collection as a whole. The Epilogue briefly places Books 1–3 into the larger perspective of Horace's total

[1] On the ancient poetry book and its implications for our understanding of Augustan poetry, see esp. the *Arethusa* issue dedicated solely to this topic: *Arethusa* 13, no. 1 (Spring, 1980).

lyric output, contrasting the thematic and tonal character of this collection with those of the earlier *Epodes* and the later *Odes* 4.

Several consequences follow from the approach adopted in the book. My very emphasis on larger structure, overall thematic progression, has, for one thing, largely ruled out detailed analysis of individual poems. Even when I do delve at some depth into a particular poem, the emphasis is less on the poem itself than on the larger context—the balance between this poem and another, how this poem advances the argument or shifts thematic direction, what role it plays in the collection as a whole. The same emphasis has dictated also that my discussion of the thematic threads of the collection— e.g., Horace's view of Augustus, of his own poetic goals, of *virtus*—concentrate not on the themes *per se* but on how they develop in the course of the collection—on how Horace's stance toward Augustus changes as the collection unfolds, on what happens within the theme of *virtus*, on how Horace's concept of his own role develops.

Also following from the same emphasis is the fact that throughout I treat *Odes* 1–3 as an ongoing, temporally unfolding composition with its own internal chronology of "early" and "late" poems—i.e., those which come in the beginning portions of the collection, and those which come in subsequent portions. That this internal chronology in no way represents the actual chronology of composition is absolutely clear. Several poems that come "early" in Book 1 are demonstrably late in chronology of composition, dating probably from not long before the completion of the collection in 23 B.C., while the actual composition of other poems "late" in the collection—i.e., in Book 3—can be reliably dated to earlier years. The actual date of composition is often of great interest and can assume some importance in the interpretation of individual passages and poems, but it is irrelevant to my present purposes. As a composition unfolds, be it these poems of Horace or a set of Beethoven variations, the listener's sense of "early" and "late" is entirely that of what comes first and

Introduction

what comes later in the ongoing life of the performance;[2] the actual chronology of composition for the individual parts is rarely known, and is of little concern, to such a listener.

In the same way, we treat the collection *as if* it were a linear narrative with its own gradually unfolding life. The *as if* is of paramount importance, for I make no claim that the "narrative" developments I shall be following—Horace's changing stance toward Augustus, toward his poetry, toward himself, toward *virtus*—in any way recreate the historical development of his attitudes, or even that the positions he takes on these themes represent his actual beliefs and feelings. It is quite likely that he has breathed into *Odes* 1–3 something of his own actual experiences, his own time-shaped attitudes, but to prove that such is the case is both impossible and unnecessary. What matters, and what can be clearly demonstrated, is that Horace's creation, the poetic construct that is *Odes* 1–3, *does* progress and develop in certain ways, that interesting and mutually complementary changes do occur with respect to all its major themes, that it does display a life of its own, and that we can accordingly talk about these developments in the same way as one talks about what happens to Oedipus or Hamlet in the course of Sophocles' and Shakespeare's plays. Indeed, we are interested in what happens in *Odes* 1–3 for the same reasons that we are interested in what happens in *Oedipus Tyrannus* or *Hamlet*—not because we want or expect to learn what actually happened at a given time and place, to actual people, but because the experiences, personalities, and emotions central to these works concern and involve any thinking human, and their treatment in these works is such as to speak directly to us.

---

[2] Cf. the comment of J.E.G. Zetzel, "Horace's *Liber Sermonum*: The Structure of Ambiguity," *Arethusa* 13 (1980): 63: "The only significant chronology in a *liber* of this sort is that of unrolling the book: that we are to read the first poem before the second, the second before the third. The order of reading creates its own dramatic time. . . ." Cf. the perceptive comments of C. Witke, *Horace's Roman Odes. A Critical Examination* (Leiden, 1983), 57, on the character of a sequential reading of a single ode.

The situation in *Odes* 1–3 is complicated by the fact that Horace himself was a real person, as were many of the people he addresses or writes about, and that many of the events that figure in the poems also were "real"—the civil wars, Horace's participation at Philippi, the gradual development of the Augustan principate, probably even the notorious falling tree incident. The same principle applies here as to chronological matters, however. It is often possible and useful to learn more about the relationship between Horace's poems and the historical figures and events that they concern, but that is not our purpose here. How Horace felt about the civil wars, his part at Philippi, Augustus's developing principate, the falling tree, we can surmise but never know—that "reality" is ultimately closed to us, though we can make reasoned and useful stabs in the direction of finding these things out. What use Horace makes of these events in *Odes* 1–3, what part they play in his unfolding narrative, how his attitudes toward them change in the poetic reality of the collection, *that* we can know, for the work itself is real and complete. That reality is Horace's own creation, and the roles historical events and persons, himself included, play in that unfolding drama are all part of his own construct. It is that construct which throughout is my subject, and my concern is accordingly with the Horace, the Philippi, the tree, the Augustus we meet in that construct. I shall speak about them as real, for real they are in the same way Hamlet and Oedipus are real. And just as in dealing with these heroes one feels no need constantly to emphasize the fact that they are but dramatic creations, so in dealing with *Odes* 1–3 I shall not constantly remind the reader that the progressions we are charting, the attitudes we are exploring, concern the fictive reality of Horace's creation, not the actual facts of his life. Nor is it amiss in this connection to recall Aristotle's comment on the differences between ποίησις and ἱστορία, his reminder that ποίησις can sometimes penetrate to a reality more significant than that probed by ἱστορία:

Introduction

διὸ καὶ φιλοσοφώτερον καὶ σπουδαιότερον ποίησις ἱσ-
τορίας ἐστίν· ἡ μὲν γὰρ ποίησις μᾶλλον τὰ καθόλου, ἡ
δ᾽ ἱστορία τὰ καθ᾽ ἕκαστον λέγει.

(Poetics 1451b5–7)

Aristotle bases his famous statement on the claim that poetry
deals with universals, history with particulars, and this claim
too is eminently applicable to *Odes* 1–3. For not only do the
individual odes, despite their special relation to specific events
and persons in Augustan Rome, regularly reach beyond par-
ticulars to deal with universals, but as a unified series they
create various patterns and progressions that have an even
broader applicability. Viewed from this larger perspective,
Odes 1–3 are a narrative in which the protagonist moves from
a sense of deep insecurity—about Augustus, about his poetry,
above all about himself—to a sense of assurance; from a sense
almost of being stained and wounded to a sense, at the end,
of being truly *integer vitae scelerisque purus*. The narrative also
concerns two different roads toward freedom, one a road that
skirts involvement, the other a road that entails painful con-
frontation with essential but often uncomfortable facts about
Rome, himself, his poetry. It is on this latter road that in Book
2 Horace confronts the flight at Philippi and the falling tree
incident, with both confrontations coming at critical turning
points in the collection. The very placement of these two
confrontations emphasizes again that Philippi and the tree here
belong to *poiēsis* rather than to *historia*, that Horace has taken
what presumably were actual events and given them a special
place and role in the spiritual journey of *Odes* 1–3. And it is
that larger journey which in its broad outlines, its universal
configurations, so clearly τὰ καθόλου λέγει. For it is the story
not just of "Horace"—the Horace of *Odes* 1–3—but of all who
have felt inadequate for a particular task or role, have initially
sought an easy way out, but have eventually plunged in and
in confrontation and even despair unexpectedly found re-
newal.

The presence of larger underlying patterns in *Odes* 1–3 also effectively complements the other more obvious qualities of the collection. In no way do these patterns detract from the wit, the irony, the sense of play that abounds in so many poems and that can burst forth even in the most serious contexts, but they add a thematic weight, depth, and scope that are sometimes judged lacking in Horace. The presence of these larger patterns makes Horace no less the master of the *tenue*— the refined, the delicate, the slender, the exquisitely crafted— but they stand as evidence also that he is more capable of the *grande* than he—or we—will usually admit. Like everything else in Horace, these contrasting sides of the collection remain perfectly in balance: each poem retains its absolute individuality—self-contained, expressive, with its own unique radiance—and yet each is a functioning, integral part of a larger organism. The interpenetration of these qualities assures that Horace's attention to the *tenue* will never become inconsequential and merely glittering, his concern for the *grande* never ponderous and self-important. Perhaps only Chopin's Preludes approach the perfection of this balance, for there too, as in *Odes* 1–3, dazzling multiplicity combines with expressive unity, absolute individuality with absolute coherence, lyric intensity with epic sweep.[3]

It remains only to emphasize the degree to which my interpretation, like all interpretations, is also to a degree necessarily "fictive reality." The great work of art is itself a completed entity, an unchanging creation given a particular form by its creator—*exegi monumentum*. But one of the qualities of the greatest works seems to be that a given *poiēma* has the capacity to evoke different responses in different persons—indeed, different responses in the same person at different times.[4] The critic's task is twofold: first, to point out the

[3] On Chopin's Preludes, see the provocative comments of Claudio Arrau in J. Horowitz, *Conversations with Arrau* (London, 1982), 158–162.
[4] Cf. Charles Ives's comment in his concluding performance notes on the Concord Sonata (New York, 1947): "The same essay or poem of Emerson

Introduction

significant features of the unchanging creation itself—no easy
task, given the dazzling complexity of many works, not least
of all *Odes* 1–3; and second, to give one's own reasoned,
thoughtful, and time-honed response to the creation one has
described. In what follows I have tried to honor both obli-
gations. No doubt my interpretation will strike some as way-
ward and idiosyncratic, and even my selection of what features
to emphasize, my narration of "what happens in Horace,"
will necessarily reflect my own predispositions and preoc-
cupations.[5] I have tried hard, however, to describe only what
is actually there, be it in the individual poems themselves or
in their complex network of relationships, and my highest
hope is that this attempt to present a continuous reading of
Odes 1–3 will call attention to features of Horace's creation
that have not been previously appreciated and will hence serve
as catalyst for yet other readings of this remarkable collec-
tion—readings that, beginning from the same many-faceted
artifact, will no doubt focus on different aspects and emerge
with different interpretations.

may bring a slightly different feeling when read at sunrise than when read
at sunset."

[5] My phrase represents a conscious gesture of respect toward J. D. Wilson's
wise book, *What Happens in Hamlet* (Cambridge, 1951).

9

CHAPTER I

THE ARCHITECTURE OF
ODES 1–3

Exegi monumentum . . .

Introduction

Horace begins the final poem of *Odes* 1–3 by speaking of his creation in architectural terms:

Exegi monumentum aere perennius
regalique situ pyramidum altius . . .
(3.30.1–2)

It is accordingly but appropriate that the poetic monument he has built displays an intricate architectural form, a structure at times as straightforward and monumental as that of the pyramids themselves, at other times as subtle and complex as the relationship of the Parthenon to the Erechtheum. All of the Augustan poets arrange their works along architectural lines—one thinks at once of Vergil's *Eclogues, Georgics,* and *Aeneid,* of Propertius's *Monobiblos,* of Horace's own *Epodes* and *Satires,* the works that chronologically precede the composition of *Odes* 1–3.[1] But none of these works, complex as

---

[1] For Vergil see esp. the useful survey in G. E. Duckworth, *Structural Patterns and Proportions in Vergil's Aeneid* (Ann Arbor, 1962), 1–15. For Propertius Book I, see esp. O. Skutsch, "The Structure of the Propertian Monobiblos," *CP* 58 (1963): 238–239; B. Otis, "Propertius' Single Book," *HSCP* 70 (1965): 1–44. On Horace's *Satires,* see W. Ludwig, "Die Komposition der beiden Satirenbucher des Horaz," *Poetica* 2 (1968): 304–325; C. Rambaux, "La Composition d'ensemble du livre I des satires d'Horace," *REL* 49 (1971): 179–204; and esp. Zetzel, *Arethusa* 13 (1980): 59–77. On Horace's *Epodes,* see

Introduction

they are in their network of symmetries and balances, of
echoes and contrasts, approaches the structural subtlety and
control of *Odes* 1–3, perhaps for the simple reason that no
other brings together and organizes into a whole so many
discrete entities—eighty-eight separate poems, each a com-
plete and self-contained entity as well as a functioning part of
a larger organism. The workings of this larger organism, like
those of an animate creature, are too complex to be under-
stood through any one approach, and the approach taken in
the present chapter reveals only part of the total pattern. The
symmetries and balances that are here my topic do exist,
however, and the appreciation of their presence is a necessary
first step toward understanding other, perhaps more signifi-
cant aspects of the creature that Horace calls into life in *Odes*
1–3.

My analysis begins from several givens. One is that the
Augustan poets, and not least of all Horace himself, clearly
devote conscious attention to the significant arrangement of
poems within a collection. A second is that such arrangements
frequently make use of concentric symmetries in which outer
components are arranged in balanced or contrasting panels
around a central core.[2] That such concentric symmetry is one
of Horace's organizing principles in *Odes* 1–3 is readily ap-
parent. The first and last poems of the collection, 1.1 and
3.30, are obviously metrical and thematic counterparts to each
other: both are in the First Asclepiad, a meter used nowhere
else in the collection, and both deal centrally with Horace's

---

R. W. Carrubba, *The Epodes of Horace. A Study in Poetic Arrangement* (The
Hague, 1969). On the topic in general, W. Port's survey is still useful: "Die
Anordnung in Gedichtbüchern der augusteische Zeit," *Philologus* 81 (1926):
280–308, 427–468. Useful recent surveys are in B. Seidensticker, "Zu Horaz,
C.1.1–9," *Gymnasium* 83 (1976): 26–27, esp. note 8; and H. Dettmer, *Horace:
A Study in Structure* (Hildesheim, 1983), *passim*.

[2] Several of the studies cited in note 1 above stress concentric symmetry.
In addition, see, e.g., W. R. Nethercut, "Notes on the Structure of Propertius,
Book IV," *AJP* 89 (1968): 449–464; M.C.J. Putnam, "Propertius' Third Book:
Patterns of Cohesion," *Arethusa* 13 (1980): 97–113; and several of the Horace
studies cited in subsequent notes.

poetic aspirations. 1.2 and 3.29, the poems that come respectively second from the beginning and second from the end, also clearly balance each other: both are lengthy, serious poems addressed to major public figures, Augustus in 1.2, Maecenas in 3.29, and both contain striking pictures of the Tiber in flood (1.2.13–20, 3.29.33–41). We shall see presently that other outside poems in the collection also display elements of this same concentric symmetry, with 1.3 balancing 3.27, 1.5 balancing 3.26, and 1.6 balancing 3.25. Moreover, concentric symmetry is even more apparent at the center of the collection, where *Odes* 2.1–12, the twelve poems that fall at the precise center of the eighty-eight-poem collection, form a unit clearly organized along concentric lines.[3] Horace's use of concentric symmetry is flexible rather than rigid. Thus, for instance, 1.3 balances 3.27 rather than 3.28 in the overall scheme of Books 1–3, and Horace's arrangement of 2.1–12 suggests, as we shall see, both a strict concentric alignment in which the pairs are 2.1 and 2.12, 2.2 and 2.11, 2.10 and 2.3, etc., and also an alternative arrangement in which poems 2.2–5 and 2.8–11 are organized as parallel pairs within an overall concentric framework: 2.2 and 2.10, 2.3 and 2.11; 2.4 and 2.8, 2.5 and 2.9. Such suppleness in the use of concentric symmetry is typical of all the great Augustan poets, and we shall find further examples of it in *Odes* 1–3.

2.1–12 exemplify also a third given in the architecture of *Odes* 1–3—organization of poems along metrical lines. I have already mentioned that the First Asclepiad meter is reserved for the two outside poems of the collection, 1.1 and 3.30. Metrical considerations also suggest the inner cohesion of 2.1–12, for here the poems alternate between two meters, Alcaic and Sapphic, a phenomenon otherwise not found in *Odes* 1–3, until the pattern is broken by the concluding poem, 2.12, a poem that in other respects clearly belongs to this central

[3] See esp. W. Ludwig, "Zu Horaz, C.2, 1–12," *Hermes* 85 (1957): 336–345. For a different analysis, one that views 2.12 as introducing the second section of the book, see H. Eisenberger, "Bilden die Horazischen Oden 2.1–12 einen Zyklus?" *Gymnasium* 87 (1980): 262–274.

group of twelve. If the opening group of Book 2 constitutes
a metrically demarcated unit, so do the opening groups of the
other two books, 1.1–12 and 3.1–6. *Odes* 3.1–6 are all in the
same meter, Alcaic, a phenomenon not repeated elsewhere in
this collection and one that underscores and complements the
tonal and thematic cohesion of the group. While metrical
consistency is the touchstone of 2.1–12 and 3.1–6, metrical
variety is that of 1.1–12, a group often called the Parade Odes
in recognition of the fact that they present ten different meters
(including all seven of the basic meters of the collection—
Alcaic, Sapphic, the five Asclepiads) in twelve poems, a phe-
nomenon again unique in *Odes* 1–3.

A final given is that both in *Odes* 1–3 and in his other
collections Horace frequently marks important beginnings
with poems addressed to his patron, Maecenas. Thus in the
first published collection, *Satires* 1, a Maecenas poem marks
the start of each five-poem half of the book (1.1 and 1.6), and
in the *Epodes* Maecenas poems stand at comparable positions,
with *Epode* 1 marking the start of the collection, *Epode* 9 its
center and the start of its second half. In the same way, Mae-
cenas odes mark the beginning of *Odes* 1–3 (1.1), the begin-
ning of the second half of its first book (1.20), and the be-
ginning of the second half of Book 3 (3.16).[4]

It is from these several givens—the characteristic Augustan
predilection for careful architectural arrangement, the fre-
quent inclination toward concentric symmetry, Horace's pen-
chant (one with many literary antecedents) for grouping
poems by meter, and his tendency to mark important begin-
nings with Maecenas poems—that the following analysis of
the architecture of *Odes* 1–3 begins. In *Odes* 1, I suggest four
groups: 1.1–12 (the twelve Parade Odes), 1.13–19, 1.20–26
(two groups of seven, the second of which corresponds to the

---

[4] Other Maecenas poems in *Odes* 1–3 also come at important points in the
collection. 2.12 and 2.20 mark the ends of the two groups of Book 2, 2.17
the beginning of the second half of the second group. Even 3.8 and 3.29
stand at balancing positions in the second and fourth groups of Book 3, 3.8
second from the start of 3.7–15, 3.29 second from the end of 3.25–30.

first and begins with a Maecenas poem, 1.20), and 1.27–38 (a concluding group of twelve that corresponds to the opening twelve Parade Odes). *Odes* 2 divides into two concentrically organized groups, the metrically and thematically interrelated 2.1–12 and a concluding group of eight poems, 2.13–20, also thematically organized. The structure of *Odes* 3 is similar to that of Book 1: an initial group whose thematic cohesion is underscored by metrical considerations (3.1–6—the Roman Odes), complementary second and third groups, this time of nine poems each (3.7–15 and 3.16–24), again with a Maecenas poem marking the start of the second half (3.16), and a concluding group of six that balances the opening six Roman Odes (3.25–30). The mere numerical symmetries of Books 1 and 3 (groups of 12, 7, 7, 12 in Book 1, of 6, 9, 9, 6 in Book 3) are, of course, far less important than the significant and demonstrable thematic and verbal connections that provide the underpinning for these numerical balances. We shall see that such interconnections both support the grouping I have suggested and further underscore the complex symmetry of Horace's design. Not only are Books 1 and 3 arranged so that the outer and inner groups of each correspond (1.1–12 with 1.27–38, 1.13–19 with 1.20–26, 3.1–6 with 3.25–30, 3.7–15 with 3.16–24), but, in addition, there are clear analogies between the corresponding units of these outside books. Thus the outer groups of Book 1 are in various ways counterparts to the outer groups of Book 3, the inner groups of Book 1 likewise counterparts to the inner groups of Book 3. And, in turn, even these intricate interplays seem static in comparison with the dynamic relationships that will emerge in later chapters.

Odes 1

The pillars of the first group, 1.1–12, are 1.2 and 1.12, two balancing poems dealing with Augustus. Their structural equipoise is underscored by their comparable lengths (52 and 60 lines) and by their common meter (Sapphic). The very fact that they share this meter and that 1.10, the Mercury ode, is also Sapphic, has led some critics to end the Parade Odes at 1.9 (before any meters have been repeated), at 1.10 (after the first repetition of a meter), or at 1.11 (following the introduction of the last Asclepiad meter but before a second repetition of the Sapphic).[5] But the very metrical recurrence that troubles these critics effectively rounds out the group. Prominent at the start of the Parade Odes is a Sapphic poem to Augustus that ends by envisioning Mercury embodied in Augustus, and the group appropriately ends by giving similar prominence to two Sapphic odes dealing with Mercury (1.10) and Augustus (1.12).

More important still in suggesting the inner coherence of 1.1–12 are the numerous motivic links that join these two large outside poems, 1.2 and 1.12. A striking feature of 1.2 is its series of questions asking on what divinity the people should call in their hour of need (1.2.25–30); 1.12 begins with a similar series of questions (1.12.1–16). Jupiter figures prominently in the opening section of both poems, but whereas in 1.2.2 and 19 he is the angry *Pater* whose power is manifest in storm and flood, in 1.12.13–18 he is more benevolent, both as *parens* and as sky god. In the same way, the storm- and river-threatened mortals of 1.2.5 ff. are replaced by Orpheus with his control over rivers and winds in 1.12.9–10, the fish-inhabited *ulmus* of 1.2.9 by the *auritae quercus* of 1.12.11–12. The turning point between the contrasting halves of 1.2 comes at the center of the poem, when Horace asks (1.2.25–30) what divinity will bring an end to the agony of the state, an agony that has been portrayed largely through the imagery of wind,

[5] See, e.g. Seidensticker, *Gymnasium* 83 (1976): 26–34, esp. 28 and note 8 (Parade Odes end with 1.9); F. H. Mutschler, "Beobachtungen zur Gedichtanordnung in der ersten Odensammlung des Horaz," *RhM* 117 (1974): 125–126 (Parade Odes end with 1.10); P. Salat, "La composition du livre I des Odes d'Horace," *Latomus* 28 (1969): 563 ff. (Parade Odes end with 1.11). On the special emphasis given to the Sapphic within 1.1–12, see below, pp. 243 ff.

wave, and sea (1.2.6–20); the central strophes of 1.12 speak
of the Dioscuri through the same imagery:

dicam et Alciden puerosque Ledae,
hunc equis, illum superare pugnis
nobilem; quorum simul alba nautis
    stella refulsit,

defluit saxis agitatus umor,
concidunt venti fugiuntque nubes,
et minax, quia sic voluere, ponto
    unda recumbit.

(1.12.25–32)

Both poems contain catalogues of the divinities with whom
Augustus is associated, and both present Jupiter in two
guises—as a protective figure to whom the state can turn for
assistance (1.2.29–30, 1.12.13–18, 49–52) and as the awesome
hurler of the thunderbolt against sinful mortals (1.2.1 ff.,
1.12.59–60).[6]

Around these two dramatic outer poems Horace organizes
the remaining ten poems of the group along largely concentric
lines. 1.5 and 1.8 obviously balance each other, both in manner
and in content. Both are slight (sixteen lines), both deal with
women who destroy their young lovers, both open with re-
peated questions. The *puer* of 1.5, secluded in Pyrrha's dark
grotto, is an apt counterpart to Sybaris, who has fled from
the sun, from the *campus*, from normal activities. Even the
endings of the two poems are related, albeit as much by con-
trast as by similarity. 1.5 ends with Horace, grateful for his
escape, hanging up his wet togs as an offering to the god of
the sea (*maris deo*, 1.5.16); 1.8 ends with Achilles, the son of
a goddess of the sea (*marinae . . . Thetidis*, 1.8.13–14), donning
woman's dress in the hope that he may find escape.

---

[6] Cf. also *triumphos*, 1.2.49, *triumpho*, 1.12.54; *Caesaris . . . Caesar*, 1.2.44,
52, *Caesaris . . . Caesare*, 1.12.51,52; war vs. Medes, 1.2.51–52, war vs.
Parthians et al., 1.12.53–56.

1.4 and 1.9 similarly balance each other, but whereas 1.5 and 1.8 deal with their erotic subjects primarily in playful terms, entering the imaginary realm of Pyrrha and Lydia in such a way as both to mock its exaggerated perils and simultaneously to abandon the concerns of the real world, 1.4 and 1.9 contrast this erotic world with harsh realities—the cold of winter, the ineluctable passage of time, the ultimate certainty of death itself. Both poems sketch the animation of youth, the warmth of passion, against a backdrop of threatening stillness and icy cold (1.4.14–20; 1.9 *passim*, esp. 17–24). Both poems speak of release from this frozen world (cf. *solvitur acris hiems*, 1.4.1, *dissolve frigus*, 1.9.5), though in neither is there any suggestion that the release can be more than a passing parole, the transitory smiles of a summer night.[7]

1.4 also balances 1.11. Again, as in 1.4 and 1.9, Horace's reminder of the brevity of life is reinforced by references to winter (1.11.4–5), again the tone is melancholy rather than playful, and again close verbal links underscore the relationship between the poems:

vitae summa *brevis spem* nos vetat incohare *longam*
(1.4.15)

. . . et spatio *brevi*
spem *longam* reseces.
(1.11.6–7)

Just as 1.4 corresponds to both 1.9 and 1.11, so other poems in this opening group also have more than a single counterpart. 1.7 picks up elements from both 1.1 and 1.3, while 1.2 has strong links both to 1.12 and to 1.10. The principal role of 1.1, of course, is to introduce the collection as a whole, and its closest counterpart is 3.30, the metrically identical and

---

[7] Note also the white-green contrasts in both poems (*albicant*, 1.4.4, cf. *viridi*, 9; *candidum . . . canities*, 1.9.1 and 17, cf. *virenti*, 17); fire (1.4.3, 1.9.5 ff.) and wine (1.4.18, 1.9.6–8) in both; movement of both from opening general pictures to concluding thoughts of love. On links between 1.4, 1.9, and 1.7, see Dettmer, *Horace: A Study in Structure*, 425–427.

thematically related closing poem of the collection. But 1.1 also plays a role in the opening group of Book 1. For one thing, it unmistakably introduces the sea motif (1.1.13–18) that is to be so prominent throughout the collection and especially in the opening group (cf. 1.2.5–12, 1.3 *passim*, 1.4.2, 1.5.5–16, 1.6.7, 1.7.21–32, 1.8.13, 1.9.10–11, 1.11.5–6, 1.12.29–32). It is accordingly appropriate that its closest counterpart within this opening group should be 1.7, that poem which gives so heroic a twist to the thread of sea imagery in the previous poems: *cras ingens iterabimus aequor* (1.7.32). 1.1 shares with 1.7 also the *priamel* form ("some prefer *a*, others *b*, still others *c*; as for me, I prefer *x*"), and the formal similarity is the more appropriate in that, as we shall see in Chapter II, 1.7, like 1.1, *is* a prelude—a new start, an effort to regain momentum after the decline of aspirations signalled by 1.6.

If the first portions of 1.7 recall 1.1, its later portions are reminiscent rather of 1.3. Both 1.3 and 1.7 concern individuals about to set forth on the terrifying deep, Vergil in 1.3, Teucer in 1.7; both deal with the springs of human courage, and both contain in their second halves prominent mythological *exempla*, Prometheus, Daedalus, and Hercules in 1.3, Teucer in 1.7. These *exempla*, however, point in opposite directions. Whereas Horace cites the mythological *exempla* of 1.3 to argue against human daring and to point out its attendant dangers, his portrait of Teucer in 1.7 takes a more positive stance toward human courage before the unknown.

1.10, finally, picks up not only the Sapphic meter of 1.2 but also, largely with a light touch, the deity with whom that poem ended, Mercury. It thus serves as a bridge between the two dominant poems of this opening group—metrically by using the Sapphic meter common to those poems, thematically by returning to the god so closely associated with Augustus at the end of 1.2 and thus foreshadowing the role Augustus will play at the end of 1.12. This bridge poem, poised as it is between man and god, life and death, laughter and sorrow, divine parody and epic reminiscence, seems to build on the theme of Mercury, the god who so easily passes

from heaven to earth, earth to underworld. As such it aptly
intercedes also between the melancholy, elegiac mode of 1.9
and 1.11, between which it is placed, and the brighter, heroic
measures of 1.2 and 1.12, to which it is thematically and
metrically akin.

Diagram 1 both summarizes the preceding analysis and also
suggests the position in it of the one poem not yet discussed,
1.6.

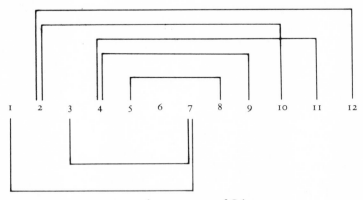

DIAGRAM I. Arrangement of *Odes* I.1–12

The largely symmetrical balances of the remaining eleven
poems highlight the central position of 1.6, that poem in
which Horace sounds his poetic *credo*. This is the first of several
occasions on which Horace gives a central position to a poem
about poetry. It is also one of the most dramatic, for the very
centrality of 1.6 within 1.1–12 underscores its thematic op-
position to the two great outside pillars of the group, 1.2 and
1.12. Here at the center of the group is Horace proclaiming
that he will sing nothing *grande*, that he will eschew songs of
national or epic heroes, songs of that age when men and gods
mingled. And here at the outside of the group is Horace
singing two odes decidedly *grande* in character, odes in which
he celebrates both national heroes and the heroes of legend,
and in which he focuses on the interplay between the human
and the divine (a theme touched on, albeit lightly, also in 1.10,

CHAPTER I

that light companion piece to 1.2 and 1.12). This blatant the-
matic clash between 1.6 on the one hand, 1.2 and 1.12 on the
other, a clash that Horace underscores by the structural ar-
rangement of this opening group, has clear affinities with
other dissonances in this opening group—with the tonal con-
trast between 1.5 and 1.8 on the one hand, 1.4, 1.9, and 1.11
on the other, or with the contrasting attitudes toward daring
that are projected by 1.3 and 1.7. It is such disjunctions in the
opening group that help generate the thematic movement of
the collection as a whole, as we shall see in later chapters.

The structure of the second group, 1.13–19, is less com-
plex—and even more symmetrical. At the outside are two
balancing poems, both in the Second Asclepiad meter and
both dealing with love's agonies. 1.13 paints in Sappho-like
tones the torments of jealousy, while 1.19 describes with equal
vividness the onset of all-consuming passion. The movement
of the two poems is strikingly similar—from forceful depic-
tion of the physical symptoms of passion, the accompanying
sense of total possession in the bulk of the poem, to gentle
closing stanzas that look to some release, some vision of
peace—the longing for a mutually shared love in 1.13.17–20,
the hope for some abatement of the disease in 1.19.13–16.
Not surprisingly, Venus figures prominently in both poems
(1.13.15, 1.19.1, 9), and additional verbal links further em-
phasize their close thematic ties (note especially the fire im-
agery of both—1.13.4, 8–9 [*uror*], 1.19.5–7 [*urit . . . urit*]).

The central poem of this second group, 1.16, is of the same
type, though more substantial both in its actual magnitude
and in its implications. Again the focus is on the incursion of
violent, irresistible passion, this time anger, and again the
poem moves to a gentle concluding stanza that holds out the
hope of better things (1.16.25–28). Verbal ties to both 1.13
and 1.19 reinforce the association of the central 1.16 with these
two outside poems:

O matre (1.16.1)   *mater* (1.19.1)
saevus (1.16.11)   *saeva* (1.19.1)

20

ignis (1.16.11)	*ignibus* (1.13.8)
ruens (1.16.12)	*ruens* (1.19.9)
fervor (1.16.24)	*fervens* (1.13.4)
furentem (1.16.25)	*furens* (1.13.11)
animumque reddas (1.16.28)	*animum reddere* (1.19.4)

In 1.16, however, the ramifications of passion are wider than they are in 1.13 and 1.19, for here the poet explores the impact of wrath not only on the individual but also on the state and even on the race (1.16.13–21). And although on the surface the concluding stanza concerns only Horace's own personal affairs, the public implications of the previous stanzas lend to its move toward reconciliation a weight and seriousness it would otherwise have lacked.

These public ramifications of 1.16 respond to the public dimension implicit in the two poems that immediately precede it, 1.14 and 1.15. These poems function as a pair. Both deal with ships on the sea, both with the theme of imminent danger (though 1.14, in keeping with the pattern of 1.13, 1.16, and 1.19, moves in its final stanza toward some hope of release, while 1.15 ends with the wrath and fire of judgment day—an apt prelude to 1.16). In addition, both poems inescapably suggest larger political overtones, 1.14 by its firm links to earlier ship of state poems and by the language of its last stanza, 1.15 by the hints of Antony and Cleopatra that hover around its Paris and Helen. It is these enigmatic—and ultimately impenetrable—larger, public implications of 1.14 and 1.15 that render the enlarged scope of 1.16 so appropriate.

Balancing 1.14–15 is another pair of poems, 1.17–18, which are similarly intertwined. Both concern escape—in 1.17 Horace offers a haven to Tyndaris, in 1.18 he discusses the escape afforded by wine. Both deal with the potential violence of lovers (1.17.24–28, 1.18.8–9), both with the partnership of wine and love, both with wine's capacity to call forth savagery as well as peace (1.17.21–24, 1.18.8 ff.).[8]

The relationship of these two pairs of poems, as so often

---

[8] Cf. also *vitreamque Circen*, 1.17.20, *perlucidior vitro*, 1.18.16.

in *Odes* 1–3, combines motivic connection with thematic and tonal contrast. Common to all four poems is the theme of danger and violence, but while 1.14 and 1.15 focus on threatened doom with only the end of 1.14 holding out the possibility of haven, 1.17 and 1.18 focus on the joy of escape only to take a darker turn at the end of 1.18. *vites aequora* (1.14.20) corresponds to *vitabis aestus* (1.17.18—cf. also *vitabis* in 1.15.18), the songs of Paris, falsely confident of his safety, in 1.15.14–15, to the songs of Horace and Tyndaris, rejoicing in a safer haven, in 1.17. Paris, the abductor, is recalled by both the Cyrus of 1.17.24–25 and the violent Centaurs of 1.18.8–9, the Helen of 1.15 by the Tyndaris to whom 1.17 is addressed,[9] the *Laertiaden* of 1.15.21 by the Penelope and Circe *laborantis in uno* of 1.17.19–20. And while the public overtones of 1.14–15 lead into the larger compass and implications of 1.16, the lighter, more personal character of 1.17–18 prepares for the personal theme and reduced scope of 1.19.

The structure of the third group of the book, 1.20–26, is closely analogous to that of the second—seven poems in which the first, fourth, and seventh frame two related and balanced pairs (see Diagram 2).

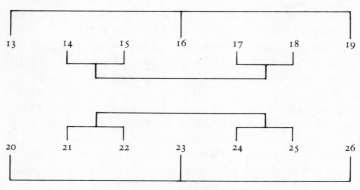

DIAGRAM 2. Arrangement of *Odes* 1.13–19 and 1.20–26

[9] 1.16 is not a true palinode, but certainly Horace seems to be playing with

1.20 and 1.26 are obvious counterparts. Each is twelve lines long, each a warm address to a distinguished but close friend. In 1.20 Horace celebrates Maecenas's recovery from a dangerous illness and refers to the "jocose" echo that hailed his return to public life (1.20.6–8); in 1.26 he bids sadness and fear farewell and expresses both his joy in his friend's presence and his friend's joy in poetry. In 1.20 he offers Maecenas wine which he himself has lovingly nurtured; in 1.26 he offers to Lamia, instead of wine, his own lovingly crafted poetry, not without reference to the untouched springs that are its source.[10]

1.23, like 1.16, both resembles and contrasts with the outside poems of the group in which it stands. It shares with 1.20 and 1.26 its slight twelve-line compass and its theme of freedom from concern. For just as Maecenas's recovery dissipates worry in 1.20 and the Muses' inspiration precludes fear in 1.26, so Horace in 1.23 assures Chloe that she need not fear him. 1.23 differs from these poems, however, both in its erotic theme and Greek addressee—appropriate sequels to 1.22—and in the undercurrent of melancholy that suffuses it— an appropriate introduction to the darker poems that follow. For Chloe's anguish, like the anguish of Vergil in 1.24 and Lydia in 1.25, remains real despite Horace's assurances, and time's passing will soon touch Chloe, just as it has touched Quintilius in 1.24 and Lydia in 1.25.

1.21 and 1.22 show several thematic links. Most important, perhaps, is the fact that 1.21's concluding prayer that Rome and Caesar may escape war and pestilence (lines 13–14) leads directly into 1.22's persistent emphasis on escape and invulnerability. Both poems dwell lovingly on the delights afforded by woodland places (1.21.5–8, *silvis*, 8; 1.22.9–12, *silva*, 9); both speak of archery (cf. *pharetra* in 1.21.11, 1.22.4) and of

---

the idea of Stesichorean recantation as his bridge between the disaster-bound Helen of 1.15 and the haven-bound Tyndaris of 1.17.

[10] Cf. also *plausus* and *laudes* for Maecenas, 1.20.4 and 7, *flores* and *coronam* for Lamia, 1.26.7 and 8; *fluminis ripae*, line 6 of 1.20, *fontibus integris*, line 6 of 1.26; *tu . . . mea* contrast, 1.20.10, *te mei*, 1.26.9.

song (1.21.12, 1.22.9 ff.), and of Jupiter (1.21.4, 1.22.20); and both are unusually rich in expressive anaphora.[11]

1.24–25, which like 1.21–22 together comprise forty lines, are as closely related. Both concern time's ravages, both fruit-less anguish and unallayed grief—cf. *flebilis . . . flebilior*, 1.24.9–10, *flebis*, 1.25.10. The Thracian wind of 1.25.11–12 recalls Thracian Orpheus in 1.24.13; the closed door of Lyce's house (1.25.3–4), the fates that once and for all close in the dead (1.24.17); Lyce's unbroken sleep (1.25.3), the *perpetuus sopor* of Quintilius (1.24.5).

As with 1.14–15 and 1.17–18, the relationship between 1.21–22 and 1.24–25 is one both of similarity and of contrast. The kindly, caring gods of 1.21 and the airy, ironic touch of 1.22 form a striking contrast to the stern, unyielding divinities of 1.24 and the harsh, vindictive scorn of 1.25, but numerous motifs link these contrasting pairs to each other. The young men and women who are to celebrate Apollo and Diana in 1.21 are recalled by the heartless young of 1.25, the happy songs of Horace in 1.22 by the despairing songs of 1.24. But while 1.22 ascribes Orpheus-like powers to Horace's casual love ditties, 1.24 denies the power even of Orpheus's songs (1.24.13 ff.).[12] In 1.22 Horace's high-sounding moral integrity (1 ff.) proves to be merely the prelude to a love song, but it protects him; in 1.24 Quintilius's moral integrity (5 ff.) is real—but it helps him not. And while the youths of 1.25.17 ff. revel in their passing delight (*laeta*, 17) in the green leaves of youth, Diana's delight (*laetam*, 1.21.5) in the greens of her forest is eternal.

The relationship of the two central seven-poem groups of Book 1 is also one of both similarity and contrast. The framing poems of the first group, 1.13, 1.16, and 1.19, deal with incursion, passion, possession, and only in their final stanzas breathe of release, while the framing poems of the second

---

[11] Note esp. *dicite . . . dicite* at the start of 1.21, *dulce . . . dulce* at the end of 1.22. Also *vos . . . vos*, 1.21.5 and 9, *hic . . . hic*, 1.21.13, *sive . . . sive*, 1.22.5–6, *pone . . . pone*, 1.22.17 and 21.

[12] Cf. also Apollo's lyre in 1.21.12, Orpheus's lyre in 1.24.14.

group, 1.20, 1.23, and 1.26, focus on escape, innocence, and joy, with only Chloe's needless fears casting a shadow. In the two linked pairs of the first group the progression is from the dark and serious 1.14–15, where all is danger, threat, and violence, to the relative peace and escape of 1.17–18, while the movement in the pairs of the second group is in many respects the opposite—from hope, escape, and delight in 1.21–22 to death, danger, and despair in 1.24–25. We shall shortly see that the final group, 1.27–38, in many respects bears a similarly contrasting relationship to its counterpart, 1.1–12.

The demarcations that set off this final group of Book I are less clear than in the case of the preceding groups. Here there is neither a sharp contrast (such as that between 1.12 and 1.13) nor a Maecenas poem (as with 1.20) to mark the start of a new section. The reasons for grouping 1.27–38 together are more subtle, though scarcely insignificant. For one thing, 1.26, with its strong ties to 1.20, clearly completes and rounds off the previous section, a fact which, especially when combined with the tonal break between 1.26 and 1.27, leads the reader to take 1.27 as a new beginning. There is also the numerical scheme of the book—12, 7, 7, . . . , which leads the reader to look for a concluding group of twelve. Above all there are the internal links within 1.27–38, which, at least in retrospect, reveal the essential cohesiveness of this concluding section.

The opening poem, 1.27, balances both 1.37 and 1.38 (cf. the way 1.2 is linked to both 1.10 and 1.12). With 1.38 it shares the theme of drinking (cf. *bibam*, 1.27.13, *bibentem*, 1.38.8), and like 1.38 it creates the dramatic illusion of an actual party. And just as 1.27 shies away from Thracian or Median violence, so 1.38 begins by eschewing Persian *apparatus*: a certain gentle decorum will mark both parties, though neither is free of its disturbing cross-currents—the erotic tangles uncovered at the end of 1.27, the *rosa . . . sera* (erotic also?) of 1.38.3–4.[13]

---

[13] On the melancholy connotations of 1.38.3–4, see K. J. Reckford, *Horace* (New York, 1969), 11–13.

The links with 1.37 are even clearer. Again the poems share the theme of drinking (cf. *bibam*, 1.27.13, *bibendum*, 1.37.1, *combiberet*, 1.37.28), and again they both create the dramatic illusion of real parties. Common also to 1.27 and 1.37 is a sharp shift of emphasis midway through the poem—in 1.27 from Horace's general address to the party at large to his close questioning of *Opuntiae frater Megillae*, in 1.37 from the wild communal celebration of victory to a sober sympathy for the flawed but noble Cleopatra. Even the two individuals on whom the concluding focus narrows share certain characteristics: both are "perishing" (cf. *pereat*, 1.27.12, *perire*, 1.37.22), both are victims of *venenum* (1.27.22, 1.37.28) and of *ignis* (1.27.16, 1.37.13), and both arouse Horace's sympathy. One final point of contact between the two poems: while in 1.37 Horace deliberately urges what he had warned against in 1.27, namely wild and excessive drinking, the poem revolves around the same opposition between Roman civilization and barbaric license that was central to 1.27 (see 1.37.5–17, esp. the emphasis on Cleopatra's drunken delusion, 11–12, 14).

1.28, with its theme of death by sea, also has certain affinities with 1.37, but its real counterpart is the ode to *Fortuna*, 1.35. These two poems are of comparable length (36 and 40 lines) and have many points of contact—their emphasis on the equality of all before the power of death (1.28.15–20) or fortune (1.35.1 ff., esp. 5–12); their movement from philosophical generalization at the start to the plight of a single individual at the end (the speaker in 1.28, Caesar himself in 1.35);[14] the emphasis on salvation and release near their conclusions (the release of the shipwrecked speaker and the safety of his benefactor in 1.28, the safety of Caesar in 1.35—cf. *te sospite*, 1.28.27, *serves*, 1.35.29); the theme of past sins plaguing later

[14] I follow Nisbet-Hubbard (and others) in believing that "the poem is a monologue, spoken by the corpse of a drowned man" (*A Commentary on Horace: Odes, Book I* [Oxford, 1970], 317). For a different interpretation, and one that suggests interesting links between 1.28 and 1.29, see B. Frischer, "Horace and the Monuments: A New Interpretation of the Archytas Ode (C. 1.28)," *HSCP* 88 (1984): 71–102.

generations, also near the end of both poems (1.28.30–31, 1.35.32 ff.); and the desperate, threatening hopes with which both poems conclude (1.28.31–36, 1.35.38–40).[15]

The clear counterpart to 1.29 is 1.34. In 1.29 Horace mocks Iccius for abandoning philosophy for military adventure (13–16); in 1.34 he laughs at himself for his own abandonment of philosophy (1 ff.). The poems are of identical length (sixteen lines) and meter (Alcaic), and both focus with apparent incredulity (note 1.29.10 ff. and *cogor*, 1.34.5) on change (cf. *mutare*, 1.29.15, *mutare*, 1.34.13)—appropriate preludes to 1.30, which encourages Venus to change her abode, and 1.35, which deals with the cataclysmic changes *Fortuna* can work.

1.30 and 1.33 are even more obvious companion pieces, both revolving around Glycera, Venus, and a lover's cry of need. These two love poems in turn enclose another even more closely linked pair, 1.31–32. These poems, although of different meters and slightly different lengths, share a remarkable number of thematic and verbal ties, of which the clear link between the *poscit* of 1.31.1 and the *poscimus* of 1.32.1 is only the most obvious.[16] Both poems concern Apollo, both deal with Horace's own verse, both focus on what it is that, above all, the poet should request of the god, and both appropriately give prominent place to the lyre in their concluding prayers (cf. *cithara*, 1.31.20, *testudo*, 1.32.14).

1.36 has links to several poems in this final group. Its closest counterpart is 1.29, with Numida's return from foreign wars balancing Iccius's unexpected departure for just such campaigns. It also neatly joins 1.35 to 1.37, picking up from 1.35 the theme of divinely-given safety in distant wars and closely foreshadowing in its second half the theme of joyous

[15] Among other links, note the emphasis in 1.35 as well as in 1.28 on unexpected danger from the sea: 1.28.18, 21 ff., 1.35.6–8.

[16] I follow Nisbet-Hubbard and Kiessling-Heinze in believing that *poscimus* must be the correct reading in line 1. For the arguments, see these commentaries. On the close links between 1.31 and 1.32, see C. L. Babcock, "Horace *Carm.* 1.32 and the Dedication of the Temple of Apollo Palatinus," *CP* 62 (1967): 190 ff., esp. note 6.

celebration with which 1.37 is to begin.[17] But its clearest counterpart, as we shall shortly see, lies outside this group entirely.

Diagram 3 both summarizes our analysis of this final group and also suggests its essential similarity to the structure of 1.1–12.

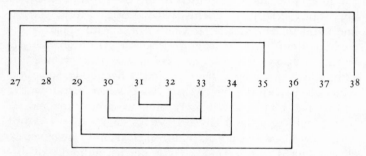

DIAGRAM 3. Arrangement of *Odes* 1.27–38

Again the construction is largely concentric, and again the central position of honor belongs to Horace and his poetry—1.31–32 (cf. the theme and position of 1.6 in the opening group). There are, however, important differences. The concluding group lacks the huge national poems that dominated the first—neither 1.35 nor 1.37, the two poems that clearly touch on national themes, approaches the size or the extravagance of 1.2 and 1.12. Partly because of the absence here of anything like 1.2 and 1.12, partly because 1.31–32 state Horace's poetic *credo* in less absolute terms than does 1.6, the concluding group lacks also the first's sharp and disturbing clash between 1.2 and 1.12 on the one hand, 1.6 on the other. The modulation in 1.27–38 of the dissonance that marked 1.1–12 finds support in other aspects of the final group as

---

[17] Between 1.35 and 1.36, cf. the god who is to guard Caesar (*serves iturum Caesarem in ultimos orbis Britannos*, 1.35.29–30) with the gods who have guarded Numida (*custodes Numidae deos, qui nunc Hesperia sospes ab ultima* . . . , 1.36.3–4). Between 1.36 and 1.37, cf. the similar references to drinking, dancing, the Salii, etc., in 1.36.11–12, 1.37.1–6, with several close verbal links.

well—in the way poems frequently prepare for and flow into
each other,[18] in the less abrupt contrasts in lengths (there is
nothing approaching the disjunction between the tiny 1.11
and the vast 1.12, for instance), the less extravagant array of
meters (six of the twelve poems are Alcaic, and only one poem
is not Alcaic, Sapphic, or Asclepiad). We shall return later to
the significance of these changes; for now we need merely
note their presence and point out that they foreshadow the
next group, 2.1–12, where there is even greater thematic con-
tinuity, even greater consistency of length and of meter.

It remains to comment briefly on the larger concentric sym-
metry of Book 1. There are obvious links between 1.2 and
1.37, 1.3 and 1.36. Both 1.2 and 1.37 concern danger to the
state, and both dangers are associated with water and the sea,
both with unnatural portents and activities (cf. *nova monstra*,
1.2.6, *fatale monstrum*, 1.37.21), both with violent overthrow
of sacred Roman buildings (1.2.3–4, 15–16, 1.37.6–8) and
with civil war (though Antony's part in the war with Cleo-
patra is left unmentioned in 1.37), and, in the end, with
triumphs (cf. *triumphos*, 1.2.49, *triumpho*, 1.37.32). 1.3 prays
for a safe return for Vergil, "the half of my soul," who is
setting out on a journey (. . . *reddas incolumem precor, et serves
animae dimidium meae*, 1.3.7–8). 1.36, in response as much to
this plea of 1.3 as to the similar plea on Caesar's behalf at
1.35.29 ff., reverses the movement of 1.3, bringing home
Numida from his long journeys and in so doing restoring him
to Lamia, who is, in effect, "half of his soul" (1.36.1–9, esp.
7–9).

Similar mirror images characterize the relationships of other
poems at opposite ends of the book. In 1.5 Horace makes an
offering to Poseidon for his escape from the sea (13–16); in
the balancing 1.34 Horace, in response to Jupiter's omen, is

[18] Cf. our previous analysis, and note the following specific links: *quis te
solvere . . . poterit*, 1.27.21–22, *piacula nulla resolvent*, 1.28.34 (note corre-
sponding positions); the demise of the philosopher Archytas in 1.28, of the
philosopher Iccius in 1.29; Iccius *to* East in 1.29, Venus *from* East in 1.30;
Glycera's shrine and ceremonies in 1.30, Apollo's in 1.31; etc.

obliged to set sail once more (3–5). In 1.6 Horace proclaims his intention to sing of the battles of lovers (17–20); in the balancing 1.33 he somewhat fretfully twits Tibullus for his incessant singing of lovers' woes (1 ff.). Even the other poems at the start and end of the book cohere roughly with this concentric pattern. In both 1.1 and 1.38 Horace expresses, albeit in different forms, his sense of his own identity, his notion of what distinguishes him from others; and while the close of 1.1 finds him hoping for the noble garlands of the Muses (29), 1.38's second and final stanza finds him happy in his wreaths of simple myrtle (5–8).[19] Whereas the image of death's footstep (*aequo . . . pede*) powerfully evokes our mortality in line 13 of 1.4, the same image (*iniurioso . . . pede*) suggests the sway of fortune at line 13 of 1.35.[20] Diagram 4 summarizes these relationships.

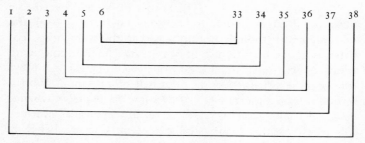

DIAGRAM 4. Arrangement of *Odes* 1.1–6 and 1.33–38

In addition, the balances, previously mentioned, of the dark 1.14–15 with the dark 1.24–25, the lighter 1.17–18 with the lighter 1.21–22, are also part of this same extensive symmetry; in particular, the Tyndaris and Lalage odes, in many ways so

[19] On the balance of 1.1 and 1.38, see W. Wili, *Horaz und die Augusteische Kultur* (Basel, 1948), 154; J. V. Cody, *Horace and Callimachean Aesthetics* (Brussels, 1976), 34–35. On that between 1.2–3 and 1.36–37, see Mutschler, *RhM* 117 (1974): 111–116.

[20] Professor Charles Babcock has pointed out the following additional links between 1.4 and 1.35: cf. *carinas* (1.4.2), *carina* (1.35.8); *pauperum . . . regum* (1.4.13–14), *pauper . . . regum* (1.35.5, 11); *regumque turris* (1.4.14), *potentis . . . domos* (1.35.23–24).

similar, are precisely poised against each other in the structure of this remarkable book, 1.17 the seventeenth ode from the beginning, 1.22 the seventeenth from the end.

Odes 2

The construction of Book 2 is dominated by symmetrically balanced pairs of linked poems (cf. the pairs just mentioned in Book 1). In the first group of twelve, 2.2–3 balance 2.10–11, 2.4–5 balance 2.8–9, with the two linked pairs enclosing the closely interrelated 2.6–7 and being enclosed by the similarly intertwined 2.1 and 2.12. In the final eight poems, 2.13–14 balance 2.19–20, 2.15–16 balance 2.17–18 (see Diagram 5).

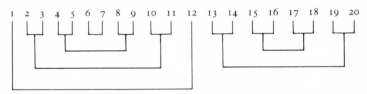

DIAGRAM 5. Arrangement of *Odes* 2.1–12 and 2.13–20

With this clear symmetry of the central book, and the prevalence of balancing linked pairs in it, we may compare the analogous symmetry and balancing of the two central groups of Book 1; a comparable degree of clarity shapes also the balanced symmetry of the two central groups of Book 3, 3.7–15 and 3.16–24.

The outside poems of the opening group, 2.1 and 2.12, establish the mode for the links and balances which characterize the five pairs of poems that they enclose.[21] Both are addressed to major public figures (Pollio in 2.1, Maecenas in 2.12), both focus on the historical writings of their addressee, and both conclude by pointing a contrast between these weighty national subjects and the more frivolous topics of Horace's lyric poetry (2.1.37–40, 2.12.13 ff.). Motivic links

---

[21] On the numerous correspondences within 2.1–12, see Ludwig, *Hermes* 85 (1957): 336–345; Dettmer, *Horace: A Study in Structure*, 203–238.

include the balance between the polysyndeton (*et* and *-que*) at
the start of 2.1 and the comparable sequence of connectives
(*nec, et, -que*) at the start of 2.12, the similar references to the
blood-stained sea near the close of 2.1 (lines 34–36) and the
beginning of 2.12 (lines 2–3), and the following verbal sim-
ilarities:

periculosae (2.1.6)	*periculum* (2.12.7)
minaci (2.1.17)	*minacium* (2.12.12)
fulgor (2.1.19)	*fulgens, fulgentis* (2.12.8, 15)
iocis (2.1.37)	*ioco* (2.12.18)

The balancing pairs 2.2–3 and 2.10–11 contain poems of a
serious cast (cf. the lighter character of the poems they enclose,
2.4–5 and 2.8–9), and in both pairs the first poems, 2.2 and
2.10 (both Sapphic and both twenty-four lines long), em-
phasize a balanced philosophical stance while the second
poems, 2.3 and 2.11, true to the more agitated Alcaic meter
that they share, passionately juxtapose the certainty of death
with the beauty and brevity of life. Verbal and motivic links
abound both within each pair and also between the members
of the two pairs, and the following are merely representative
examples:

2.2 and 2.3:

temperato (last word of 2.2.3)	*temperatam* (same position in 2.3.3)
heaped-up lucre (2.2.23–24)	heaped-up lucre (2.3.19–20)

2.10 and 2.11:

ingens pinus (2.10.9–10)	*sub alta vel platano vel hac pinu* (2.11.13–14)
non . . . neque semper (2.10.17–19)	*non semper . . . neque* (2.11.9–10)
Apollo and his lyre (2.10.18–20)	Lyde and her lyre (2.11.22–24)

2.2 and 2.10:
latius regnes (2.2.9)   rectius vives (2.10.1)

2.3 and 2.11:
Falernian wine (2.3.8)   Falernian wine (2.11.19)
pine and poplar (2.3.9–11)   pine and plane (2.11.13–14)
rose, wine, perfume (2.3.13   rose, wine, perfume
ff.)   (2.11.13 ff.)
ocius (2.3.26)   ocius (2.11.18—same place
    in stanza)

2.2 and 2.11:
splendeat usu (2.2.4)   trepides in usum (2.11.4)

2.3 and 2.10:
preservation of calm atti-   preservation of calm atti-
tude, whether in good   tude, whether in good
times or bad (2.3.1 ff.)   times or bad (2.10.13–15,
    21–24)
rebus in arduis (2.3.1)   rebus angustis (2.10.21)
pinus ingens (2.3.9)   ingens pinus (2.10.9–10)

2.4–5 and 2.8–9 are related by a similarly tight tonal and
thematic network. All four are erotic poems, all four some-
what lighter in tone than the pairs that enclose them. 2.4 and
2.5 concern love affairs in their anxious early stages, with
Horace in both breathing assurance that all will be well: Xan-
thias need not fear reproach on account of his love for a slave
girl (2.4), and, given time, Lalage herself will seek the lover
she now avoids (2.5).[22] 2.8 and 2.9, in contrast, look more to
the past, to erotic situations well past their prime, and both
strike a somewhat worldly-wise, sardonic tone. At Barine's

[22] I follow Kiessling-Heinze and Nisbet-Hubbard in reading *petet* rather
than *petit* in line 16 and in identifying the *maritum* of line 16 with the *te* of
line 3. For a different view, see the sensitive interpretation of Reckford,
Horace, 104–106. On the possibility that the addressee of 2.5 may be Horace
himself, see below, pp. 117–118.

ability to become ever more stunning as the trail of wronged
and jilted lovers grows behind her, Horace, like Venus herself
(cf. 2.8.13), can only laugh. To Valgius, whose grief for his
lost love Mystes is inconsolable (cf. the tears at the center of
2.9, the laughter at the center of 2.8), Horace offers sympathy
and advice, but his whole poem subtly suggests that Valgius's
grief is a bit overdone, with the irony reaching its peak in the
concluding suggestion that love elegy be replaced by national
song![23] As with 2.2–3 and 2.10–11, there is a certain parallelism
between the two pairs. 2.4 and 2.8, both Sapphic and both
twenty-four lines long, deal, albeit from radically different
viewpoints, with the discrepancy between character and fate.
The lovely Phyllis, a woman whose actions reveal her true
moral fineness (2.4.17–20), is unfairly reduced to slavery (13–
14), while Barine, a woman whose whole history bespeaks
blithe disregard of any moral considerations, triumphantly
pursues her devastating rampage through the male ranks, un-
touched by retribution human or divine![24] 2.5 and 2.9, both
Alcaic and both twenty-four lines long, focus—again from
contrasting vantage points—on lovers who are separated from
their loves. In 2.5 an unnamed lover, perhaps Horace himself,
looks forward to the time when Lalage will return his affec-
tion, while in 2.9 Valgius laments the love he once had but
now has lost. Again, however, verbal links among the four
poems extend beyond the parallelism of 2.4 with 2.8, 2.5 with
2.9. Thus the white color of Chloris in 2.5.18 recalls the snowy
color of Briseis in the previous poem (2.4.3), the *non semper
. . . semper . . . semper* of 2.9.1, 9, 17 recalls the emphatic
semper of 2.8.15. The Trojan *exempla* in 2.9.13–17 recall the
Trojan references of 2.4.2–12, the *iuvencis* of 2.8.21, the *iu-
vencae* of 2.5.6.

At the center of these twelve poems, and at the center of

---

[23] Cf. Nisbet-Hubbard, *A Commentary on Horace: Odes, Book II* (Oxford,
1978), 137: "[Horace] maliciously proposes that Valgius should join him in
writing about the settlement of the Eastern frontier."
[24] Note in particular the contrast between *sic fidelem*, 2.4.18, and *perfidum
. . . caput*, 2.8.6.

the collection, are the highly expressive, deeply personal 2.6
and 2.7 (cf. the central position of the highly personal 1.6 and
1.31–32 within their groups in Book 1). 2.6, like 2.5, looks
largely to the future, 2.7, like 2.8–9, largely toward the past.
The verbal ties that link this central pair of poems are so
striking that they would be apparent even if the poems did
not lie side by side:

Septimi . . . mecum (2.1.1)	*O saepe mecum* (2.7.1)
aestuat unda (2.6.4)	*unda . . . aestuosis* (2.7.16)
lasso . . . militiae (2.6.7–8)	*fessum militia* (2.7.18)
vatis amici (last words of 2.6)	*. . . amico* (last word of 2.7)[25]

The eight remaining poems of Book 2 also fall into con-
centrically balanced pairs, 2.13–14 balancing 2.19–20, 2.15–
16 balancing 2.17–18. The relationship between the two out-
side pairs is especially interesting, consisting as it does again
of a combination of close motivic and verbal ties with sharp
tonal and thematic oppositions. We shall see in later chapters
that the concluding portion of Book 2 represents a crucial
turning point in the collection, and the mirror-like inversions
of its outside pairs is one of the means by which Horace
emphasizes and embodies the important thematic shifts that
occur within the short compass of these eight poems.

The most basic opposition between these pairs is that while
2.13–14 concentrate on death, 2.19–20 emphasize life. 2.13 is
the first of several poems in which Horace mentions that
occasion on which he was nearly killed by a falling tree, while
2.14, the Postumus ode, is perhaps the greatest of his several
poems on the theme of mortality. 2.19, in contrast, has as its
theme Bacchus, a god associated with aliveness in all its
forms,[26] and 2.20, the concluding poem of the book, applies

[25] For further links between 2.6 and 2.7, see W. Ludwig, "Horaz, c. 2, 6—
eine Retractatio," *WS* 83 (1970): 101–104.

[26] Cf. Plutarch's familiar association of Dionysus with the moist element
in nature (πασῆς ὑγρᾶς φύσεως κύριος, *Is. et Os.* 35). Horace in 2.19 similarly

to Horace and his poetry this theme of surging, irresistible life, as Horace, not without irony, imagines himself turning into a swan, flying free of the earth, and leaving behind an empty tomb and an immortal reputation. While 2.13–14 focus on human helplessness, our inability to escape our mortal bonds, 2.19–20 suggest instead the boundless range of human capacity, our power to rise above our apparent limitations.

This frontal thematic opposition is woven into the two pairs of Alcaic poems by means of an intricate web of verbal and motivic links. 2.13 and 2.14 emphasize their theme of death and human impotence through imagery of rivers, the sea, and sailing (13.13 ff., 14 *passim*); 2.19–20 respond by using the same imagery to emphasize their theme of life and power (2.19.17, 2.20.8, 13–14, 20). Underworld scenes and images emphasize human mortality in 2.13.21 ff. and 2.14.6 ff., 17 ff.; similar motifs suggest the power of Dionysus in 2.19.29 ff., of Horace himself in 2.20.8. Images of drinking appear in the underworld scene of 2.13 (line 32) and at the end of 2.14 (the heir drinking—and spilling—the priceless wine left by his father); in contrast, passing allusions to wine and to drinking are associated with Bacchic power at 2.19.10 and with Horatian immortality at 2.20.20. The despairing *quam paene . . . vidimus* of 2.13.21–22 yields to the triumphant *vidi* of 2.19.2 (cf. *vidit*, 2.19.29), the grim *visendus* of 2.14.17 to the proud *visam* of 2.20.14. The Orpheus-like Alcaeus of 2.13.29 ff., whose poetry enchants his silent audience and charms even Cerberus, prepares for the similar description of Bacchus at 2.19.1 ff. and 29 ff. (Cerberus again).[27] A tree almost kills Horace at line 11 of 2.13, while trees are associated with Dionysiac liquids at line 11 of 2.19.[28] The Wailing River

---

identifies Bacchus not only with orgiastic ecstasy and with poetic inspiration but also with the whole world of nature—cf. 9–12, 17–20.

[27] Cf. also the contrasting snake-hair associations in 2.13.35–36, 2.19. 19–20.

[28] One might even compare the honey that flows from trees, *truncis lapsa*, at 2.19.11–12, with the *truncus illapsus* by which Horace describes the infamous tree at 2.17.27.

(Cocytus) awaits us all at 2.14.18, but in 2.20.14 we find Horace flying over the shores of the groaning Bosphorus[29] as the poet takes to the "liquid aether" (2.20.2) and leaves behind the dire liquids of 2.14. And for the *Eheu* with which Horace opens the despairing 2.14, we have the *Euhoe* with which he hails Bacchus at 2.19.5 and 7.[30]

The central 2.15–18 also consist of two contrasting pairs, though the network of links and oppositions within these four poems is less fully elaborated than in 2.13–14 and 19–20. In 2.15–16 Horace moves from a shorter to a longer poem (twenty to forty lines), and this movement repeats in the second pair as he moves from the thirty-two-line 2.17 to the forty-line 2.18.[31] In addition, the concerns introduced in general philosophical terms in 2.15–16 find more personal applications in 2.17–18, two poems that, respectively, are addressed to Maecenas (2.17) and clearly have Maecenas in mind as the unnamed addressee (2.18). Thus 2.15's general contrast between extravagance and simplicity is more fully developed in 2.18 and is focused specifically on the relationship between Horace and his wealthier, more extravagant addressee; and 2.16's general observations on the nature and origins of peace of mind provide an appropriate backdrop for Horace's attempts in 2.17 to assuage Maecenas's anxieties about death.

Various specific links again join the poems into pairs aligned both chiastically and in parallel. 2.15 and 2.17 share the ref-

[29] Note also *Bosphorum*, 2.13.14, at precisely the same place as *Bosphori* in 2.20.14. For various links between 2.13 and 2.19–20, see Dettmer, *Horace: A Study in Structure*, 342–349.

[30] Note also the unusually expressive anaphora in all four poems: *ille et . . . illum et . . . ille* (1 ff.), *te . . . te* (11), *dura . . . dura . . . dura* (27–28) in 2.13 (cf. *rapuit rapietque* in the central line 20); *frustra . . . frustra* in 2.14.13 and 15; *parce . . . parce* (7–8), *fas . . . fas* (9, 13), *tu . . . tu . . . tu . . . tu* (17–21) in 2.19; *non ego . . . non ego* (5–6), *iam iam . . . iam* (9, 13), *me . . . me* (17, 19) in 2.20.

[31] It is perhaps not accidental that the number of lines in 2.13–16 is the same as the number in 2.17–20 (128 in each instance). The center clearly falls between 2.16 and 2.17, with the Maecenas poem (2.17), as so often, marking the start of the second half.

erences to temple-building in their last stanzas (2.15.20, 2.17.31); 2.16 and 2.18 share their contrast between gold, on the one hand, which gives neither happiness nor security (2.16.7–8, 2.18.36), and poetry and the simple life, on the other, which render Horace both happy and secure (2.16.37–40, 2.18.9–14). 2.16 and 2.17 are both explicitly addressed to important and affluent friends, and both end with sharp contrasts between Horace and his addressee (2.16.33–40, 2.17.30–32),³² while the surrounding poems, 2.15 and 2.18, both lack a named addressee and both specifically condemn the current fashion for building lavish homes out into the waters (2.15.2 ff., 2.18.20 ff.). Other verbal links between 2.16 and 2.17 include their common references to the whirr of fateful wings (2.16.11–12, 2.17.24–25) and to the signs of the heavens (2.16.2–4, 2.17.13 ff.).

These interlocking relationships within these four poems underline the fact that, despite their significant differences, they share a common emphasis. Unlike 2.13–14 and 2.19–20, which deal in apocalyptic—or at least mock-apocalyptic—terms with ultimate realities, 2.15–18 deal on a more mundane level with the here and now. The mode of 2.13–14 and 2.19–20 is heroic, 2.13–14 confronting head-on the fact of our mortality, 2.19–20 boldly asserting man's kinship with the gods and the immortalizing power of poetic genius. 2.15–18, in contrast, face death less as an eschatological certainty than as a given of everyday existence, and the answers they propose are similarly realistic—reminders of the simple and good life of early Romans, of the marbled texture of human life, of the power of friendship, of the present satisfactions of poetry. To the *leti vis* of 2.13.19–20 Horace counterposes the earthshaking force of Bacchus in 2.19; to the underworld waters of 2.14, the soaring poetic flight of 2.20: *non . . . obibo nec Stygia cohibebor unda* (2.20.6–8). 2.16–18 too have their references to death's power, but their responses are more modest: *nihil est*

³² Cf. also the *te . . . me* contrast of 2.17.22 and 27, the *te . . . tibi . . . te . . . mihi* contrast of 2.16.33–37.

ab omni parte beatum (2.16.27–28); *ibimus, ibimus . . . supremum carpere iter comites parati* (2.17.10–12); *satis beatus unicis Sabinis* (2.18.14); *vivitur parvo bene* (2.16.13).

Odes 3

In keeping with the overall symmetry of the collection, Book 3, like Book 1, consists of four groups of poems chiastically organized, with the 12, 7, 7, 12 division of poems in Book 1 being replaced here by a 6, 9, 9, 6 division (see Diagram 6). In addition, the arrangement within these four groups is again largely along concentric lines.

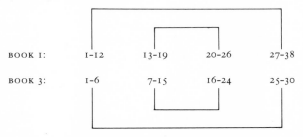

BOOK 1:	1–12	13–19	20–26	27–38
BOOK 3:	1–6	7–15	16–24	25–30

DIAGRAM 6. Corresponding Patterns of *Odes* 1 and *Odes* 3

Such is the case in the opening group, the Roman Odes, with 3.1 corresponding to 3.6, 3.2 to 3.5, and the closely related pair, 3.3–4, standing at the center (cf. the central position of the related pair 1.31–32 within 1.27–38, the central position of 2.6–7 within 2.1–12). 3.1 and 3.6 share not only the same length and numerous close thematic similarities but also a basic parallelism of movement. Both poems open with two stanzas that concentrate on man in relationship with the gods, 3.1 beginning with Horace as *Musarum sacerdos* (1–4), 3.6 with the need to rebuild the temples of the gods (1–4); both move in their second stanza to the necessity of recognizing the gods' supreme position (lines 5–8 of both). The two succeeding stanzas of each concern the impact of super-human forces on human life—the absolute power of *Necessitas* in 3.1.9–16, the punishments wrought by the gods on the

Romans in 3.6.9–16. The central sixteen lines contain each poem's central theme—the contrast between the serenity of the simple life and the fruitless anxiety of the extravagant in 3.1.17–32, the vivid portrayal of contemporary moral depravity in 3.6.17–32. The final sixteen lines of each poem underscore the theme of the central stanzas by brief contrasting vignettes—in 3.1 the contrast between Horace's peaceful Sabine refuge and the fashionable but care-fraught villas of the wealthy, in 3.6 the contrast between the simple and pure life of earlier times and the degenerate life of the present. Both of these final sections begin with a reference to Rome's impact on the sea—the extending of land into the sea in 3.1.33–37 (*aequora*, 33), the dyeing of the sea with Punic blood in 3.6.33–34 (*aequor*, 34)—and both poems end with a dark but sonorous line consisting of a four-syllable noun plus a six-syllable comparative—*divitias operosiores* in 3.1.48, *progeniem vitiosiorem* in 3.6.48 (no other poems in *Odes* 1–3 end in such a line).[33]

3.2 and 3.5 share an emphasis on *virtus*, with this word appearing emphatically in the opening line of the second half of each poem (3.2.17 [also 21], 3.5.29—these are the only occurrences of the word in the Roman Odes). Both poems approach *virtus* through scenes that pit Roman against barbarian (3.2.3–12, 3.5.5–12), albeit in radically different contexts. Both poems emphasize courage in the face of death, both the folly and ignominy of flight (3.2.13–16, 3.5.31 ff.); both move from the largely martial cast of their openings (3.2.1 ff., 3.5.2 ff.) to an exploration of *virtus* as an inner quality of spirit rather than merely as courage in combat; and both move from grandiloquent and sonorous openings to quiet falling closes (3.2.25 ff., 3.5.41 ff., esp. 50–56). Among the verbal and motivic links, note *per medias . . . caedis*, 3.2.12, *sine caede*, 3.5.20; *virtus* in 3.2.17–24 resisting public pressure, spurning the vulgar mobs, finding its lonely way, and fleeing

[33] On the thematic and structural links between 3.1 and 3.6, see Witke, *Horace's Roman Odes*, 67. On the arrangement of the Roman Odes in general, see G. E. Duckworth, "*Animae Dimidium Meae*: Two Poets of Rome," *TAPA* 87 (1956): 300 ff.

the earth (*humum*, 3.2.24), compare Regulus in 3.5.41–56, an
exemplum of *virtus*, fixing his gaze on the earth (*humi*, 3.5.44),
leaving behind the mourning crowds and the relatives that
would detain him, and going his lonely way.

3.3 and 3.4, the two central and longest (seventy-two and
eighty lines) Roman Odes, have numerous points of contact.
After an extended introduction, the bulk of 3.3 consists of a
lengthy speech of Juno (18–68) in which she renounces her
quarrel with the pro-Trojan Olympians; the second half of
3.4 focuses on Jupiter's victory in another divine dispute, the
battle with the Titans (42–80). As so often in Horace, the
center of each poem marks an important turning point—
Juno's relinquishing of her wrath, on certain conditions, in
3.3.30–44; the rapid transition from poetry to Caesar to Jupiter
in 3.4.37–44, a transition marked by the *vos . . . vos* of 37 and
41 (cf. the emphatic *dum . . . dum* of 3.3.37 and 40). The
emphasis in these same central lines of 3.4 on *lene consilium*[34]
and on peace won at long last (cf. 37–40) not only looks ahead
to lines later in 3.4 itself (65–68) but also recalls 3.3's emphasis
on longed-for reconciliation among the gods (cf. 3.3.17–18,
29–30). The focus on Roman *imperium* in 3.3.41 ff. corre-
sponds to that on Jupiter's power in 3.4.42 ff.; Juno's impor-
tant proviso at 3.3.57 ff., sixteen lines from the end of 3.3,
relates to the similar limitations on *vis* at 3.4.65 ff., sixteen
lines from the end of 3.4; and the concluding portions of both
myths appropriately include poignant reminders of grief for
those who fall in conflict (3.3.67–68 [*ploret*], 3.4.73–75 [*dolet,
maeret*]).[35] Finally, both poems deal explicitly with the poet
and his verse, with the sudden address to the Muse at the end

[34] The emphatic placement of *lene consilium* in the first line of the second
half of 3.4 has parallels in the similar placement of key words and phrases in
other Roman Odes: *desiderantem quod satis est*, 3.1.25, *virtus*, 3.2.17, *vera virtus*,
3.5.29. Cf. the importance of the poems that begin the second halves of
Books 1 and 3 (1.20, 3.16) and the second half of the collection (2.7), and
of 2.17 within 2.13–20 (see note 31, above).

[35] Cf. also Minerva and Juno in 3.3.22–24, 3.4.57–60; Apollo in 3.3.65–
66, 3.4.60–64; *alite lugubri* in 3.3.61, *ales* in 3.4.78.

of 3.3 leading into the lengthy passage on Horace and the Muses with which 3.4 begins.

Their common Alcaic meter, their sustained magnitude, and their shared seriousness of tone clearly stamp 3.1–6 as a self-contained group. The three remaining groups of the book show less inner consistency than do the Roman Odes, but the reasons for grouping them as we have are clear. The placement of the important Maecenas poem, 3.16, at the start of the second half of the book clearly marks the beginning of a new group, and the nine poems that begin with 3.16 fall into a coherent pattern that is closely analogous to that of the nine-poem group (3.7–15) which comes between the end of the Roman Odes and the start of the second half. In the same way, the concluding six-poem group both balances the opening six-poem group in a number of respects and also displays a high degree of inner unity. In addition, the lengthy 3.24 is an appropriate poem with which to conclude the third group, while 3.25, with its note of anticipation and of new vistas unfolding, is an effective prelude to the final section of the collection.

The nine poems 3.7–15 fall into a clear concentric pattern. 3.7 and 3.15 are both addressed to wives, and both offer sage and sober advice to their addressees. 3.7 urges Asterie, the (we presume) young wife of the young *mercator* Gyges, to beware of the attentions of her neighbor, while 3.15 urges the aging Chloris, the wife of poor Ibycus, to cease her absurd and lascivious cavorting with the young. Horace tells Asterie to shut her doors at dusk and to pay no attention to the wail of the flute (3.7.29–32), while he admonishes Chloris to leave to others the storming of lovers' doors and the playing of the lyre (3.15.8–9, 14).[36]

---

[36] It would seem accidental that Gyges (3.7) and Chloris (3.15) both appear in 2.5 (and nowhere else in *Odes* 1–3). But is it accidental that Gyges is up against *sagaces hospites* in 2.5.21–24, a *sollicita hospita* in 3.7.9, and that Chloris is related to imagery of the night sky both in 2.5.18–20 and in 3.15.5–6? Note also that both Gyges and Chloris seem clearly older in 3.7 and 3.15 than in 2.5. The much-discussed question as to whether Gyges and Asterie

The similarities that link 3.8 and 3.14 are many and striking. Both are twenty-eight lines long, both Sapphic, and both place the name of their focal figure, Maecenas in 3.8, Caesar in 3.14, in the central stanza (3.8.13, 3.14.16).[37] Both concern preparations for a celebration (3.8.1 ff., 3.14.17 ff.), and both promise wine whose aged fineness they document by reference to historical events earlier in the century (3.8.9–12, 3.14.17–20). Both set their invitations against a backdrop of recent successful national campaigns (3.8.18–24, 3.14.1–4), both urge freedom from cares (3.8.17 [*curas*], 3.14.13–16 [*curas*]), and both express gratitude for escape from dangers that threatened (3.8.6–8, 13–14; 3.14.9–10). The many verbal links include *hic dies* (3.8.9, 3.14.13); *sospitis* (3.8.14), *sospitum* (3.14.10), at the same place in their respective stanzas; *Hispanae . . . orae* (3.8.21), *Hispana . . . ab ora* (3.14.3–4).[38]

While the links between 3.9 and 3.13 are less clear than those between other members of this group, the two poems nonetheless form an appropriate pair. Both are brief Asclepiad pieces, and both create unforgettable poetic worlds in which a peaceful idyll is first shattered, then restored. 3.9 opens up the prospect of a rift between Lydia and her lover only to close the breach charmingly in its concluding stanzas; 3.13 bloodies the clear waters of Bandusia in a manner that many have found acutely disturbing, but by the end the blood seems purged and we are aware only of the *loquaces lymphae*.[39]

---

are man and wife or lovers does not materially affect our interpretation of 3.7: cf. F. H. Mutschler, "Kaufmannsliebe. Eine Interpretation der Horazode 'Quid fles Asterie' (c. 3, 7)," *SO* 53 (1978): 126 n. 3.

[37] On Horace's tendency to give such central placement to people of particular importance, see L. A. Moritz, "Some 'Central' Thoughts on Horace's *Odes*," *CQ* 18 (1968): 116–131.

[38] Cf. the hieratic prohibition against ill-omened words at 3.14.11–12 with the similarly hieratic (and similarly placed) *procul omnis esto clamor et ira* at 3.8.15–16.

[39] Possible verbal and motivic links: cf. the crucial comparatives that end 3.9 (*pulchrior, levior, iracundior*) with the crucial *splendidior* at the start of 3.13; the *venerem et proelia* of 3.13.5 with the whole theme of 3.9; and the death-life by-play of 3.9.9–16 with the emphasis on death and immortality in 3.13.

3.10 and 3.12 are ideal counterparts, the first a somewhat satiric picture of a man immobilized by love, the second a truly poignant poem on a young woman immobilized by love. The frozen posture of the *exclusus amator* in 3.10 is juxtaposed with the wild dance of the elements (3.10.5 ff.), the miserable enslavement of Neobule with the vigorous activity of the young man she loves (3.12.7–12). The lover of 3.10 seems more likely to contrive his own release (cf. 19–20) than does the young girl of 3.12, but the focus of both poems is on the plight of a lover whose passionate affection is unreciprocated. These two brief poems respectively on the misery of a man and a woman in love appropriately enclose a third poem, the central poem of the group and a crucial poem in the collection, which concerns both the unrequited love of an *exclusus amator* (3.11.1–12) and the rather different miseries of a loving woman (3.11.33–52).[40]

In both construction and theme the third group of Book 3 is reminiscent of the second. Its outer components are two large and serious poems, both of Asclepiad meter, the one addressed to Maecenas (3.16), the other concerning Augustus (3.24—cf. the balance of 3.8 [Maecenas] and 3.14 [Augustus] in the previous group). In both poems the focus from the start is on the theme of wealth, though the beginning of 3.16 stresses what wealth *can* do while that of 3.24 emphasizes what it *cannot* do. The insatiability of greed is a key point in both poems (cf. *multa petentibus desunt multa*, 3.16.42–43, *tamen curtae nescio quid semper abest rei*, 3.24.63–64), as is the inability of wealth to provide an escape from anxiety (3.16.17–18, 3.24.1–8). As so often, verbal links underpin thematic connections: cf. the similar opening words of the two poems, *Inclusam Danaen* (3.16), *Intactis opulentior* (3.24); the critical *si* clauses that begin in line 5 of each; *pretium* in 3.16.8 and 3.24.24; *aurum* in 3.16.9 and 3.24.48; *crescentem . . . pecuniam*

---

[40] Note in 3.11, as so often, the central position accorded to a poem on poetry (cf. the central positions of 1.6 and 1.31–32 in their respective Book I groups, of *vatis amici* [2.6.24] within 2.1–12, of 3.3.69 through 3.4.36 within 3.1–6).

in 3.16.17, *crescunt divitiae* in 3.24.63; and *pauperies* in 3.16.37
and 3.24.42. Finally, both poems contrast the cares that wealth
cannot dispel and may even increase with the serene con-
tentment of those not preoccupied with gold (3.16.21 ff.,
3.24.9 ff.).

Typically, Horace juxtaposes these two large poems (forty-
four and sixty-four lines) with two much shorter odes, 3.17
and 3.23 (sixteen and twenty lines, respectively). Both of these
shorter poems are Alcaic, both place their addressee in a rustic
setting, and the ceremonial sacrifice on which 3.23 begins
recalls that on which 3.17 ends (cf. *avida . . . porca*, 3.23.4,
porco bimestri, 3.17.15). Though the addressees are strikingly
different, with the nobly-descended Aelius (3.17.1–9) stand-
ing in sharp contrast to *rustica Phidyle* (3.23.2), the movement
of the poems is in the same direction—toward each person
finding a simple and satisfying stance toward other humans
and toward the gods. Phidyle is to recognize that her humble
but sincere offerings are all that she need proffer, while Aelius
is to celebrate his birthday not with pomp and circumstance
but with a simple gathering in which his whole household,
slaves included, will participate (3.17.16). This emphasis in
3.17 and 3.23 on the satisfaction afforded by simple pleasures
accords nicely with the similar emphasis in the two larger
poems that enclose them (cf. 3.16.21–44, 3.24.9–24).[41]

3.17 and 3.23 are in turn associated with the poems they
enclose, for both 3.18 and 3.22 are addressed to woodland
divinities (Faunus and Diana) very much of a piece with the
rustic ceremonies described in 3.17 and 3.23.[42] Both of these
brief Sapphic poems (sixteen and eight lines, respectively)
promise in their second stanzas a sacrifice in honor of the
divinity to whom they are addressed (cf. the sacrifices of 3.17
and 3.23), and both endow this sacrifice with a certain pathos

---

[41] Cf. in particular *cui deus obtulit parca quod satis est manu*, 3.16.43–44, with
the outstretched, giftless hands of Phidyle, "the sparing," in 3.23.1 and 17.
With my analysis of 3.17–23, compare that of Dettmer, *Horace: A Study in
Structure*, 418–420.

[42] Note esp. the similarity between 3.17.16 and 3.18.11–12.

(3.18.5, 3.22.7–8). The similarities in their opening stanzas are even more marked. Both address the deity in an opening line that includes a vocative, an appositive, and two genitives (*Faune, Nympharum fugientum amator*, 3.18.1; *Montium custos nemorumque, Virgo*, 3.22.1), and both proceed then to emphasize the deity's protective power—Faunus's special association with the young nurslings of the flock (3.18.3–4), Diana's assistance to young women in labor (3.22.2–3). And the tri-form, *ter vocata* goddess of 3.22.3–4 echoes the triple-beat of the celebration of Faunus on which 3.18 ends:

> gaudet invisam pepulisse fossor
> ter pede terram.
> (3.18.15–16)

3.19 and 3.21, like 3.8 and 3.14 in the previous group, are both drinking songs.[43] The two poems share many similarities beyond their comparable lengths (twenty-eight and twenty-four lines). Both, like the drinking songs of the previous group, concern important public figures, and both celebrate special occasions. 3.19 honors the augurship of Murena (10–11),[44] 3.21 a holiday spent with Messalla (note the *bono die* of line 6). Both poems explore both the violent and the gentle side of wine, its capacity to inspire quarrels (cf. *rixarum*, 3.19.16, *rixam*, 3.21.3) and madness (cf. *insanire*, 3.19.18, *insanos*, 3.21.3) as well as gentler pleasures (cf. 3.19.15–17, 26–28, 3.21.4, 8, 13 ff.). Both love (*amor*, 3.19.28, *amores*, 3.21.3) and the Graces (3.19.16, 3.21.22) find their place in these songs, and the simile of the evening star in the last lines of 3.19 nicely balances the reference in the concluding line of 3.21 to the flight of the stars at sunrise. These two drinking

---

[43] Cf. the dating of the wine by a historical reference with the similar procedure in 3.8.11–12 and 3.14.18–20.

[44] On the occasion being celebrated in 3.19, see G. Williams, *The Third Book of Horace's Odes* (Oxford, 1969), 110–111. Williams follows K.M.T. Atkinson, "Constitutional and Legal Aspects of the Trials of Marcus Primus and Varro Murena," *Historia* 9 (1960): 469 ff., in rejecting the usual identification of the Murena of 3.19 with the conspirator executed in 22 B.C.

songs, with their suggestion of wine's potential both for in-
citing violence and for conferring peace, appropriately enclose
3.20, a haunting vignette that hovers suspended between the
threat of violence with which it begins and the note of in-
souciant detachment on which it ends (3.20.11 ff.).[45]

The concentric symmetries of the first three groups of Book
3 give way in the final group to an arrangement that combines
interlocking and concentric elements. The outside poems,
3.25 and 3.30, balance each other, but the four inner poems
interlock, with the short 3.26 and 3.28 forming one pair, the
lengthy 3.27 and 3.29 another (see Diagram 7).

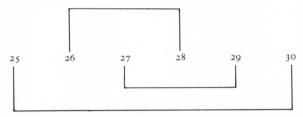

DIAGRAM 7. Arrangement of *Odes* 3.25–30

While it is clear that the prime structural role of 3.30 is to
balance 1.1, the opening poem of the collection, 3.30 also
corresponds in a number of respects to 3.25, the opening poem
of this final group. The two poems are Asclepiad in meter,
and both focus on Horace's poetry, its power and its im-
mortality (3.25.5, 18, 3.30 *passim*). Both stress the magnitude
of Horace's accomplishment (cf. *nil parvum*, 3.25.17, *regalique
situ pyramidum altius*, 3.30.2) and its newness (3.25.7–8,
3.30.13), and both end with wreaths:

cingentem viridi tempora pampino. (3.25.20)

lauro *cinge* volens, Melpomene, comam. (3.30.16)

---

[45] Compare the movement from the large and passionate 3.11 (central
within 3.7–15) to the small and delicate 3.20 (central within 3.16–24) with
the similar movement from 1.16 (central within 1.13–19) to 1.23 (central
within 1.20–26).

The clear verbal similarities between these two last lines are reinforced by several other verbal links between the poems:

dicam (3.25.7)	*dicar* (3.30.10)
recens (3.25.7)	*recens* (3.30.8)
potens (3.25.14)	*potens* (3.30.12, cf.
	impotens, 3)
humili modo (3.25.17)	*ex humili* (3.30.12)
nil mortale loquar (3.25.18)	*non omnis moriar* (3.30.6)

3.26 and 3.28 are as closely linked. Both are brief songs that mask or even abjure Horace's love interest until the last stanza.[46] The first stanzas of both contain prominent military metaphors (3.26.1 ff., 3.28.3–4), and the last stanzas of both focus on Venus's association with particular sites (Cyprus and Memphis in 3.26, Cnidos, the Cyclades, and Paphos in 3.28; cf. *quae . . . tenes*, 3.26.9, *quae . . . tenet*, 3.28.13–14). The *Venus marina* of 3.26.5 appropriately balances Neptune in 3.28; the lyre Horace pretends to abandon at the start of 3.26 (line 4) balances the lyre and song he mentions at the end of 3.28 (lines 11–16).

The comparable lengths of 3.27 and 3.29 (seventy-six and sixty-four lines, respectively) are themselves sufficient to associate the poems within this closing group, but in addition these two poems exhibit a number of verbal and thematic affinities. Both begin with passages that prove to be but introductions to the main matter of the poem: thus the address to Galatea (3.27.1–24) is almost forgotten once we are plunged into the tale of Europa, which occupies the remainder of the poem, and the dinner invitation to Maecenas with which 3.29 opens (1–28) merely provides the occasion for the dramatic philosophical and personal musings that fill out the remainder of the poem. The sea setting of both the Galatea and Europa stories in 3.27 leads to the memorable river and sea imagery that dominates the center and end of 3.29 (lines 33–41, 57–

---

[46] On the erotic implications on which 3.28 ends, see Williams, *Third Book of Horace's Odes*, 143.

64),[47] while the grandiose future promised Europa after her anxiety-fraught sea voyage (3.27.73–76) contrasts with the *probam . . . pauperiem sine dote* which Horace seeks at the end of 3.29 (55–56). The laughter of the gods figures in both poems (3.27.67, 3.29.31), as does their play (*lusit*, 3.27.69 [cf. also 40], *ludum . . . ludere*, 3.29.50). As is so often the case, the links between the two poems emphasize contrast as well as similarity. While much of 3.27 is given over to Europa's pathetic (and at times bathetic) complaints over the injustices done her (cf. *querenti*, 66), the Horace of 3.29 abjures any recourse to *miseras preces* (58).[48] And while 3.27 ends with Venus assuring Europa of the ultimate benefits that will accrue to her from her association with Jupiter (73–76), 3.29 ends with Horace charting a course that will render him immune to the unpredictable whims of the *Pater* (43 ff.).

Conclusion

It remains briefly to review our findings thus far and to comment on some of the larger structural patterns of Books 1–3 as a whole. Let us begin with the book we have just analyzed, Book 3. The book consists of four chiastically arranged groups, groups of six at the outside, nine at the inside. The two inner groups are strikingly parallel to each other in pattern and construction, with each arranging four concentrically organized pairs around a central poem that deals with love (3.11 and 3.20). Each has poems to or about Maecenas and Augustus in corresponding positions, though in the first group 3.8 and 3.14 are of modest length only and occupy the next-to-outside positions, while in the second group 3.16 and 3.24 themselves occupy the emphatic outside positions and are by far the largest poems of the group. The outside pieces of 3.7–15 are two

---

[47] Cf. the roar of the storm in 3.27.23, the din of the flood in 3.29.38–39.

[48] On some of the absurdities of Europa's speech, see Williams, *Third Book of Horace's Odes*, 139. Cf. also *fortuna* in 3.27.75, 3.29.49, *fugiens* in 3.27.41, 3.29.48. Given the many other links between the poems, it is even tempting to hear in the *mugiat* of 3.29.57 a reminiscence of Europa's bull in 3.27!

poems that give frank and sensible advice to two contrasting women (3.7 and 3.15); roughly corresponding to these are two poems that stand next to the outside poems of 3.16–24 and that again offer frank and sensible advice (3.17 and 3.23). The balancing 3.8 and 3.14 of the first group are drinking songs; so are the balancing 3.19 and 3.21 of the second group, two poems that, like 3.8 and 3.14, concern significant occasions in the lives of important public figures.[49]

In addition, the two central poems of these groups, 3.11 and 3.20, share a number of significant similarities. Both are Sapphic, both concern young men whose erotic involvements are carrying them into a danger that they fail to perceive (3.11.38–39 [*non times*], 3.20.1–2 [*non vides*]), and the female danger that threatens each is compared to a lioness (*leaenae*, 3.11.41, 3.20.2—the only appearances of the word in Horace).[50]

Similarly related are 3.13 and 3.18, the balancing poems that stand third from the end of the first group and third from the beginning of the second. Both are sixteen lines long, both mark rural festivals, both promise libations of wine, and both poignantly describe the *haedus* that is to be sacrificed (3.13.3–8, 3.18.5). The cool solace that Bandusia offers the flocks (3.13.10–12) corresponds to Faunus's special association with the flocks (3.18.3–4, 9), the *ilex* of 3.13.14 to the *silva* of 3.18.14, and the talking, leaping waters of Bandusia (3.13.15–16) to the ditch-digger's festive dance (3.18.15–16).[51]

If the relationship of 3.7–15 and 3.16–24 is largely one of

[49] Note even the balancing vintages of 3.8 and 3.21—66 B.C. and 65 B.C.

[50] Other possible links, and ones that reflect the tonal gulf between 3.11 and 3.20: Lynceus's *pedes* and the winds (*aurae*, last word of the fourth line from the end of 3.11) are to snatch (*rapiunt*) him to safety; the sought-for boy of 3.20 sits with the palm of victory *sub pede*, his hair blowing idly in the wind (*vento*, last word of the fourth line from the end of 3.20), like Nireus, who was *raptus* from Ida.

[51] Note the parallel placement of the passages in the two poems. Another such is the parallel between the flocks refreshed from their labors in lines 11–12 of 3.13 and the vacationing people and cattle (*otioso cum bove*) in the same lines of 3.18.

Conclusion

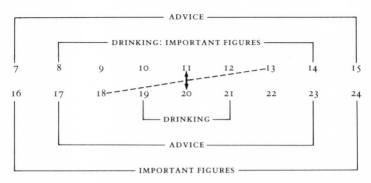

DIAGRAM 8. Arrangement of *Odes* 3.7–15 and 3.16–24

similarity, that of the outside groups, 3.1–6 and 3.25–30, is primarily one of contrast. Both groups are of six poems, of course, both include among their emphases both poetry and national concerns, and the two long poems that dominate the last group (and especially the Alcaic 3.29) recall the lengthy poems with which the book began. But these modest similarities pale beside the striking differences. In character, meter, and tone 3.1–6 are more homogeneous than any other group in the collection; 3.25–30, in contrast, are perhaps more heterogeneous than any section other than the Parade Odes. The focus of 3.1–6 is on a variety of national issues, with personal concerns occasionally coming to the fore; that of 3.25–30 is on a variety of personal concerns, with national issues pushed very much to the background. Horace's poetic activities become focal only at the center of the Roman Odes (from 3.3.69 through 3.4.36); they hold the outside position in the last group—3.25 and 3.30. The significance of these differences is considerable, and the thematic and tonal movement from 3.1–6 to 3.25–30 is one of the shaping rhythms that will be our subject in later chapters.

This review of the structure of Book 3 paves the way for considering a further element in the elaborate organization of the collection, namely the parallelism of Books 1 and 3. Not only does the *a-b-b-a* grouping of Book 1 (12, 7, 7, 12) cor-

CHAPTER I

respond to the *a-b-b-a* grouping of Book 3 (6, 9, 9, 6), but
the parallelism of these outside books extends also to details
of theme, tone, and language. The emphasis on national mat-
ters is most marked in the first group of each book (1.1–12,
3.1–6), while philosophical matters loom large in the last
group of each (1.27–38, 3.25–30); the two central groups of
each book focus on more personal concerns.[52] Both in Book
1 and in Book 3 the two central sections also move from the
more Greek cast (seen most easily in the names of the ad-
dressees) of the first group (1.13–19, 3.7–15) to the more
Roman cast of the second (1.20–26, 3.16–24), a phenomenon
that also contributes to the overall movement of the collection
and to which also we shall return.

The parallelism between Books 1 and 3 frequently extends
even to minute details, and the following are merely repre-
sentative instances of a quite remarkable pattern of corre-
spondences. The penultimate poems of both books are drink-
ing songs that end with a brave and resolute individual daring
to face the blows of fortune and to turn defeat into victory—
Cleopatra in 1.37, Horace himself in 3.29 (cf. the nautical
setting of both passages, the *quaerens* of Cleopatra's choice in
1.37.22 with the *quaero* of Horace's choice at 3.29.56). The
close relationship between the balancing Lalage and Tyndaris
odes, poems respectively third from the end of the second
group and third from the beginning of the third group in
Book 1, is paralleled by the close relationship between the
Bandusia and Faunus odes, which hold precisely analogous
positions in the second and third groups of Book 3. This
relationship is underscored by the fact that these four poems
themselves share a number of similarities. Thus Faunus is
associated with the safety of flocks in both 1.17 and 3.18, and
1.22 ends with *Lalagen . . . loquentem*, 3.13 with Bandusia's
loquaces lymphae. Similarly, 1.17 offers Tyndaris the same sort

[52] Note the philosophical focus both of the two longest poems of 1.27–38,
1.28 and 1.35, and of the most substantial poem (though not the longest) of
3.25–30, 3.29.

52

of cool haven that Bandusia affords the flocks in 3.13;[53] 1.22 gives us a Horace rendered bold (see lines 17 ff.) by his encounter with a Sabine wolf, 3.18.13 a (presumably) Sabine wolf who wanders harmless *inter audaces . . . agnos*.[54]

Yet another link between these two outside books is the extensive concentric symmetry that joins their outside poems—1.1 to 3.30, 1.2 to 3.29, 1.3 to 3.27, 1.5 to 3.26, and 1.6 to 3.25. Of the familiar metrical and thematic links between 1.1 and 3.30 I have already spoken. I need merely add here that while 1.1 looks somewhat anxiously toward future poetic goals, 3.30 proudly hails the creation that is now complete. Both emphasize Horace's connection with Aeolic song (1.1.34, 3.30.13–14), and both conclude by laying claim to the garlands of the Muses (1.1.29 ff., 3.30.15–16). 1.2 and 3.29 also have many points of contact—their comparable grandeur of conception; their dominant images of the flooding Tiber and of the sea, with these coming in the first half of 1.2, the second half of 3.29; their common references to the angry Sky Father (1.2.2, 3.29.44), to the easy laughter (1.2.33, 3.29.31) and cruel play (1.2.37, 3.29.50) of the gods.[55]

The relationships between 1.3 and 3.27 have been less frequently noted but are, if anything, even more marked than those between 1.1 and 3.30, 1.2 and 3.29. Both 1.3 and 3.27 begin with a grim catalogue of the dangers that await an embarking seafarer, and both pray for safe passage to attend the voyage at hand. Both speak of the awesome monsters of the deep (1.3.18, 3.27.26–27), both tell of the sights the seafarer must face (cf. *vidit* in 1.3.19, 3.27.32 [also *vides* in 3.27.17]), of the boldness of the adventurer (cf. *audax* in 1.3.25 and 27, 3.27.28), and of the link between *scelus* and *culpa* and

---

[53] With the *vitro* of 3.13.1, cf. the *vitream* of 1.17.20. Aside from the *vitro* that ends the poem that follows 1.17 (1.18.16), these are the only appearances of these words in *Odes* 1–3.

[54] Cf. the same motif in the Tyndaris ode, 1.17.9.

[55] Cf. also the similarly located *aura tollat*, 1.2.48–49, *aura feret*, 3.29.64. On ways in which 3.25–30 balance 1.1–6, see the extensive analysis in Dettmer, *Horace: A Study in Structure*, 140–161.

death (1.3.38–40, 3.27.37–38). Among the many other links the following are noteworthy:

Iapyga (1.3.4)	*Iapyx* (3.27.20)
quae tibi creditum (1.3.5)	*credidit tauro latus* (3.27.26)
impiae (1.3.23)	*pietas* (3.27.35)
fraude mala (1.3.28)	*mediasque fraudes* (3.27.27)
Iovem (1.3.40)	*Iovis* (3.27.73)

Despite these numerous verbal links, it is important also to remember one crucial difference between 1.3 and 3.27: in 1.3 the outcome of Vergil's voyage is left uncertain, and the poem ends on a note of despairing, almost hysterical anxiety. 3.27, however, climaxes in Europa's safe arrival in Crete and in prophecies of her glorious future, so much so that any anxiety that may have hovered over Galatea's imminent departure is effectively dispelled (and probably quite forgotten). The manner in which 1.3 looks ahead to an uncertain future, 3.27 back to a completed journey, closely and significantly parallels the contrasting stances taken by 1.1 and 3.30 with reference to Horace's poetic ambitions.

1.5 and 3.26 share not only their *tenuis* manner—refined, elegant, witty, slender—but, once more, a number of specific verbal and thematic connections. Both deal with the warfare of love, though the metaphor is central in 3.26, only implicit in 1.5 (e.g., in the *urget* of line 2); both associate love closely with the sea, and the *maris deo* with which 1.5 ends is an apt counterpart to the *marinae . . . Veneris* of 3.26.5; in both poems Horace speaks of hanging on the wall (cf. *paries* in 1.5.14, 3.26.4) the accoutrements of his abandoned preoccupation—his lyre and armor in 3.26, his sea-soaked garments in 1.5.[56] The last stanzas of both poems contain significant shifts—the sudden shift of focus from the lovesick *puer* to the love-free

[56] On the balance between 1.5 and 3.26, see Wili, *Horaz und die Augusteische Kultur*, 182. If, as Nisbet-Hubbard strongly argue, Zielinski's *deae* at 1.5.16 is correct, the relationship between 1.5 and 3.26 is even closer. Cf., however, E. A. Fredricksmeyer's reply, "Horace *Odes* 1.5.16: God or Goddess?" *CP* 67 (1972): 124–126.

Horace in the final stanza of 1.5, the equally swift shift from the renunciation of love to the revelation of new love in the final stanza of 3.26.

Finally, 1.6 and 3.25 also form a pair. Both are of Asclepiad meter, both are twenty lines long, and, most important, both focus on poetry. Here as elsewhere, however, the numerous specific links between the poems serve above all to underscore their basic thematic divergence. 1.6 proclaims that Horace will abandon the *grande* for the *tenue* (cf. 9), while 3.25 proudly proclaims *nil parvum aut humili modo, nil mortale loquar* (17–18). 1.6 backs off from singing the praises of Caesar (10–12); 3.25 explicitly takes on this task (3–6). The *Musa* of 1.6.10 is *imbellis . . . lyrae potens*; Bacchus, the divine force with which Horace associates his verse in 3.25, is *Naiadum potens Baccharumque valentium proceras manibus vertere fraxinos* (14–16). Horace in 1.6.19 speaks of himself as *vacui*, the devotee of inconsequential convivial and erotic poetry; the Horace of 3.25.13 speaks of the *vacuum nemus* that inspires his lofty verse. And while the Horace of 1.6.13–16 shies away from heroic songs that deal with the interplay of humans and gods, the Horace of 3.25 sings of his own productive encounter with a god. The thematic gulf between these two poems is yet one more of the many dissonances that help generate the thematic movement of the collection.[57]

[57] Might one even forge a balance between 1.4 and 3.28? Both celebrate festivals of gods, both speak of Venus, of nymphs, and of wine, and both lightly sound the *carpe diem* theme. Cf. also the *visit* of Vulcan in 1.4.8, of Venus in 3.28.15. On the possible links between 1.4 and 3.28, see Dettmer, *Horace: A Study in Structure*, 158–161.

CHAPTER II

BOOK 1: THE RESTORATION
OF COURAGE

nil mortalibus ardui est

Introduction

The balanced symmetries that were our subject in Chapter I suggest a static architectural quality in *Odes* 1–3 that is only part of the story. These symmetries are there, and they are the necessary underpinning for the more dynamic relationships that are our subject in the remainder of this book. But just as in a Bach fugue or a Beethoven sonata the listener's (or the performer's) attention is less likely to focus on the underlying structure, integral as that structure is to the composition, than on the ongoing surge and flow of the music, the accompanying sense of progression and development, so the reader of Horace's *Odes*, and still more the listener at a recitation, will almost certainly be less aware of the symmetries we have just discussed than of the linear progressions, thematic movements, tonal variations that occur as the work gradually unfolds. This is as it should be. Horace not inappropriately speaks of himself as a *vir Mercurialis* (2.17.29–30), and the mercurial quality of his verse (to use a pun that is quite in keeping with Mercury himself) is one of his most striking poetic qualities. Like mercury, Horace's verse moves and flits with lightning speed, constantly changing direction, pace, and configuration.[1] This quality is present in all of his

[1] Cf. Horace's comparison of himself to a bee at 4.2.27–32. On Horace and Mercury, see esp. C. Neumeister, "Horaz und Merkur," *A & A* 22 (1976): 185–194.

56

poetry—think, for instance, of the manifold surprises of *Satires* 1.9 or 2.6, of the jarring shifts of mood throughout the *Epodes*, of the dazzling narrative flow of the *Ars Poetica*, of the infinite tonal and thematic variations of *Epistles* 1—but nowhere is it more marked than in *Odes* 1–3. Indeed, the very swiftness and violence of the thematic disjunctions in *Odes* 1–3 are what require as underpinning the architectural symmetries analyzed in Chapter I; and, in turn, the disjunctions between corresponding units within this seemingly static edifice are often what create the vivid sense of thematic movement and development. In this way the collection's linear movement and architectural symmetry, qualities that might seem to work against each other, prove complementary aspects of the total design.[2]

Such is clearly the case in Book 1. We have seen that the opening group of twelve poems structurally corresponds in many ways to the closing group of twelve. Just as striking, however, are the ways in which these two groups diverge from each other, a divergence especially marked in the relationship between the first six poems and the last six, two groups that, as we have seen, balance each other concentrically. Thus 1.1 faces the uncertain future in hopes of receiving the legendary garlands of the Muses and of storming heaven itself, while 1.38, its counterpart at the end of the book, remains resolutely bound to the earth and expressly favors the simple myrtle over any more esoteric garlands. 1.2 and 1.3 likewise look to the uncertain future: What god can save us from the storms unleashed by civil war (1.2.25 ff.)? What will be Vergil's fate? In contrast, 1.36 and 1.37 joyously celebrate *faits accomplis*. Thus fearsome anxiety over the fate of Rome (1.2) yields to wild joy at her salvation (1.37), near-paranoia over the divine wrath man courts by his daring (1.3) to thanksgiving for the gods' protection of the returning Numida (1.36)

---

[2] On the complementarity of static and dynamic patterns in *Odes* 1–3, cf. M. S. Santirocco, "Horace's *Odes* and the Ancient Poetry Book," *Arethusa* 13 (1980): 50–53.

and admiration for the courage of Cleopatra (1.37). Both 1.4 and 1.35 confront our subservience to more powerful forces—to death (1.4) and to fortune (1.35)—but whereas 1.4 ends in resignation and acceptance, 1.35 ends on a note of positive action (1.35.29–32, 38–40). 1.5 ends with Horace metaphorically abandoning the sea, while 1.34 begins with him metaphorically setting sail once more; in 1.6 he proclaims that he will concentrate on love's insignificant squabbles (17–20), while in 1.33 he expresses impatience over Tibullus's endless obsession with erotic misfortunes. The following analysis will suggest that similar thematic progressions characterize the movement of Book 1 at every point.

Odes 1.1–12

If in its architectural configurations and its motivic links 1.1–12 falls into a largely concentric pattern with 1.6 as its focal point, in its linear progressions it falls rather into two groups of six poems, 1.1–6 and 1.7–12, each of which displays something of the same tonal and thematic progression. The character of this progression is especially apparent in the opening six poems. From the lofty poetic aspirations of 1.1, its sweeping review of human occupations, and from the dramatic plunge into the agony of the civil wars in 1.2, its grandiose visions of divine succor, Horace moves within six poems to an express declaration in 1.6 that he is the poet solely of the *tenue*, that his lyre is unsuited to the *grande*, a word that well describes 1.1's lofty aspirations, 1.2's magnitude of theme and conception. From the far-reaching philosophical excursions evoked by Vergil's departure in 1.3, the probing into basic questions about human ambition, our relationship to the gods, the perplexing gulf between our brave strivings and our mortal blindness, Horace descends to the exquisite but limited 1.5, where Vergil's seafaring is replaced by the *puer* adrift on the sea of love, the serious moral questionings of 1.3 by the uncertainties associated with the fickle Pyrrha, 1.3's profound but pessimistic exploration of our ambivalent relationship to the gods by the easy and conventional act by which Horace thanks Poseidon for his escape from Pyrrha.

In one sense, the movement within 1.1–6 is a movement from the real world to the world of poetic escape. The various occupations sketched in 1.1 share the fact that all are the stuff of real life, activities that absorb the serious attentions of the human race.[3] Nor can the reality of the issues at stake in 1.2 be questioned. The poem may speak through the language of image and portent, but it deals with events and emotions that were all too real for Horace and his contemporaries. 1.3 and 1.4 also face harsh realities. 1.3 confronts human daring, a quality at once majestic and repellent, dangerous and benef-icent, allied both to the courage that civilizes the world and to the blind folly that calls down the wrath of the gods. 1.4, developing an image introduced in 1.3.32–33 (*semotique prius tarda necessitas leti corripuit gradum*), confronts the grim tread of death, the fact that death comes to humans as surely as spring follows winter:

> pallida Mors aequo pulsat pede pauperum tabernas
>   regumque turris.
>
> (1.4.13–14)

The concluding lines of 1.4 emphasize the point by reminding us of the youthful loves and joys that death will obliterate. These same lines also, however, provide a natural transition to the poem that follows, a poem in which Horace in effect abandons those very realities upon which he has insisted in 1.4 to slip into the world of youthful love evoked in 1.4.17–20. 1.5 ends with Horace celebrating his own escape from the sea of passion that threatens Pyrrha's current *puer*, and the image aptly captures what happens in the poem. For in 1.5 Horace leaves behind the real world—the *mercator*'s struggle with the sea (cf. 1.1.13–18), the flood of civil strife (cf. 1.2.5 ff.), 1.3's daring challenge to the deep, even 1.4's springtime

---

[3] The one possible exception is the figure described in lines 19–22. On this passage, see below, pp. 241 ff.

return to the sea (cf. 1.4.2)—and escapes into the exquisite artificialities of the Alexandrian love lyric, into a world of impossibly beautiful women in perfumed grottoes, a world as glittering as glass—and as fragile, as distanced from every-day realities in Horace's time as it is in our own. 1.5, where implicitly Horace turns from harsh reality to elegant artifice, leads easily into 1.6, where he expressly renounces poetry about the heroic and the serious in favor of songs in which, fancy-free and lighthearted (*vacui* and *leves*, 1.6.19 and 20), he will sing of that imaginary world where passion alternates with levity, parties with lovers' tiffs, and where the most fearsome weapon is a well-honed fingernail.

All of this is in no way to suggest that 1.5 and 1.6 are poor poems, or to deny the potential seriousness, magnitude, and reality of the theme of love. Horace himself, however, em-phasizes in 1.6 both the essential *levitas* with which he here approaches this theme and also the fact that for him this theme here represents a deliberate turning away from more serious affairs of the world. This same lightness of treatment, and this same emphasis on artifice, obviously characterize 1.5, and these very qualities both account for its inimitable grace and render it a sharp retreat from the weighty issues, the serious world, of 1.1–4. Moreover, this sense of retreat in 1.5 and 1.6, far from being a flaw in the poems, is itself a function of the role these poems play in the larger design of the collection.

Using this contrast between 1.1–4 and 1.5–6 as starting point, we may also characterize the movement within 1.1–6 as a movement away from human initiative and involvement. 1.1 makes clear that Horace is not attracted by most of the occupations that others pursue, but his description of these several occupations leaves no doubt about the seriousness with which humans, himself included, immerse themselves in their chosen callings. 1.2 by its very emphasis on Rome's desperate straits, her urgent need for purgation, suggests Horace's in-volvement in Rome's plight and points toward the need for action and initiative. The bulk of the poem locates this po-

tential for initiative in the hands of the gods, but at the end
it circles briefly back to the human realm in its concluding
mention of Augustus (1.2.49–52).

Human initiative, our willingness to act and to take re-
sponsibility, is at most a secondary theme of 1.1, and in 1.2
it figures more as a quality that Rome implicitly needs than
as one that the poem actually explores. In 1.3, however, this
theme is central, and much of the apparent strangeness of this
puzzling poem results from the fact that in it for the first time
in Books 1–3 Horace focuses squarely on a theme that by its
very nature is troubling and ambivalent. Horace's uncom-
promising confrontation with human involvement, initiative,
and aspiration hides none of the less attractive features of
these qualities, and the negative associations he explores have
led many to find this poem awkward, tactless toward his
closest friend, and unworthy of the place of importance it
receives in this collection.[4] In fact, however, Horace's decision
to associate Vergil with the whole range of human aspiration
and daring, with the willingness to tackle hard and hazardous
tasks, a theme that is central to the whole collection, is perhaps
the highest compliment he could pay to the man he calls *animae
dimidium meae* (1.3.8).

Equally complimentary, and typical of the candor with
which he approaches Vergil in other poems, is the fact that
in exploring this theme Horace masks none of its inherent
ambivalence. 1.3 reveals both the glory and the folly of cou-
rageous enterprise, both its allurements and its dissuasions.
nil mortalibus ardui est (1.3.37): who would not wish, like Pro-
metheus and Heracles, to amend the human lot, like Daedalus
to escape one's earthly tether (cf. 1.3.27–37)?[5] Who does not
admire the *aes triplex* of those brave enough to dare great deeds
(cf. 1.3.9)? And yet:

[4] See, e.g., Nisbet-Hubbard, *Commentary on Horace, Odes I*, 44–45.
[5] Note that in 1.3 Prometheus and Heracles, like Daedalus, are treated as
examples of *human* ambition (cf. the *gens humana* of 26, which introduces the
mythological examples).

CHAPTER II

caelum ipsum petimus stultitia neque
per nostrum patimur scelus
iracunda Iovem ponere fulmina.
(1.3.38–40)

Who can deny that great daring often unleashes great evils upon the world? Who when faced with awesome undertakings does not shrink and, like Horace confronting Vergil's voyage, cry out at the folly of the undertaking?[6] What great explorers of the unknown have totally escaped that *hubris* which is so often the corollary of powerful will, talent, and intellect?

One suspects that the ambivalence that emerges in 1.3 in association with human initiative has particular reference to poetic initiative, the more so in that there was a long tradition of speaking of poetic undertakings through nautical metaphors.[7] The magnitude of the poetic journey on which Horace had embarked in *Odes* 1–3 was all too apparent to him, and the fact that by 1.6 he is already radically trimming his sails (cf. his escape from the sea in 1.5.13–16) merely underscores his own ambivalence toward the undertaking. One suspects also that this same ambivalence has some reference to Vergil's

[6] In a poignant example of such ambivalence toward high and daring goals, Pablo Casals tells of a mountain-climbing accident that occurred on his first United States tour, when he was already an established concert artist: "The boulder hit and smashed my left hand—my fingering hand. My friends were aghast. But when I looked at my mangled bloody fingers, I had a strangely different reaction. My first thought was 'Thank God, I'll never have to play the cello again.' " (*Joys and Sorrows* [London, 1970], 105.)

[7] See W. Wimmel, *Kallimachos in Rom* (Wiesbaden, 1960), 228 ff.; W. S. Anderson, "Horace *Carm.* 1.14: What Kind of Ship?" *CP* 61 (1966): 91; Cody, *Horace and Callimachean Aesthetics*, 82 ff. Both Anderson and Cody see 1.3 as referring to the composition of the *Aeneid*, as do C. W. Lockyer, "Horace's *Propempticon* and Vergil's Voyage," *CW* 61 (1967–68): 42–45; D. A. Kidd, "Virgil's Voyage," *Prudentia* 9 (1977): 97–103; and R. Basto, "Horace's *Propempticon* to Vergil: A Re-examination," *Vergilius* 28 (1982): 30–43. On the possibility that the nautical send-off 3.27, which balances 1.3 in the composition of *Odes* 1–3, may also refer to poetic endeavor, see R. S. Kilpatrick, "Remember Us, Galatea: Horace, Carm. 3.27," *GB* 3 (1975): 191–204, esp. 200 ff.

poetic activities as well, for he too at this time had embarked on an awesome poetic voyage, the writing of the *Aeneid*, a task that was leading him, like Horace in *Odes* 1–3, toward fearful obstacles and into uncharted waters. The very fact that on his deathbed Vergil still felt the *Aeneid* too flawed to be published poignantly suggests the ambivalence that this greatest of Roman poets could feel about the fruits of human endeavor.[8]

That 1.3 relates indirectly to the poetic voyages undertaken by Vergil and Horace in the 20s B.C. must remain in the realm of conjecture, but two points about 1.3 are certain. It is clear, first, that early in the collection this poem dramatically brands human courage, initiative, and aspiration as qualities that at once repel and attract the doer, that arouse both admiration and disapproval in the onlooker. The ambivalent character of these qualities will be a central theme of the collection, and the strong emphasis upon this theme in this early poem is both appropriate and necessary. Second, in 1.3 Horace associates Vergil, the man who had the courage to embark on the *Aeneid*, with qualities that are notable more by their omission than by their presence in the preceding poem. For while 1.2 identifies a desperate need for human courage and initiative— the origins of the stain, after all, are in human *scelus* (1.2.21– 24, cf. 29–30), the response given in 1.2 itself largely skirts the issue by turning to the gods (25 ff.). Even when the poem finally comes around to Augustus, it approaches him via his identification with Mercury and says virtually nothing of his distinctively human qualities. To 1.2, with its puzzling detour away from human capacities, 1.3, with its full-scale confrontation of these capacities, stands in stark contrast. For 1.3 not only portrays human endeavor in all its ambivalence, as a quality noble and positive as well as one potentially foolhardy

---

[8] The fact that Horace in 1.1.36 expresses his poetic ambitions through a clear allusion to Vergil, *Eclogue* 9.29, and that 1.2 alludes heavily to *Georgics* 1, establishes a context in which it seems more plausible to take 1.3 as referring to the composition of the *Aeneid*: see Santirocco, *Arethusa* 13 (1980): 51. On the Vergilian character of 1.2, see below, Chapter V, note 24.

and dangerous, but the examples it adduces in its second half—
Prometheus, Daedalus, Hercules, figures normally known as
benefactors of civilization—leave no doubt that we are to un-
derstand the poem as dealing with courage, with the human
will toward achievement, in the broadest sense. 1.3 indeed
portrays these qualities as deeply marbled, but it also em-
phasizes their distinctive humanness, and this very focus on
human strivings stands out in 1.3 the more boldly after the
notable absence of any such focus in 1.2.[9] And what better
bearer of this theme than the Vergil who at that very time in
the *Aeneid* was daring to portray both the grandeur and the
tragedy of great endeavor, both its nobility and its inevitable
failings?

As the opening group moves from the harsh realities of 1.1–
4 to the graceful artifices of 1.5–6, human initiative also suffers
diminution, with the pessimism of the second half of 1.3
paving the way for the decline. For while 1.3 captures some-
thing of the potential grandeur of human initiative, it ends up
suggesting that such initiative is self-defeating. In the same
way, the initial burst of activity in 1.4 gives way to resignation
and helplessness by the end of that poem. Lines 1–12 depict
a world of vigor, renewed life, energy, lines 13–20 the do-
minion of death and the negation of warmth and vitality.[10]
This movement of 1.4, so parallel to that of 1.3, in turn leads
to the passive, escapist figures of 1.5 and 1.6—Pyrrha's *puer*,
ignorant of where his love is leading him and helpless to

[9] That the contrasts between 1.2 and 1.3 are not fortuitous is suggested by
the fact that the poems share a number of motivic links: cf., for instance,
Jupiter and his thunderbolts, 1.2.1–4, 1.3.38–40; *monstra*, 1.2.6, 1.3.18 (both
times in a marine setting); *scelus*, 1.2.29, 1.3.39; winged Mercury, 1.2.41 ff.,
winged Daedalus, 1.3.34 ff.; Mercury to earth, 1.2.42 ff., diseases to earth,
1.3.30 ff.; *serus in caelum redeas* (of Mercury-Augustus), 1.2.45, *caelum ipsum
petimus stultitia*, 1.3.38.

[10] Note that 1.4 does not capitalize on the possibility of associating public
themes with its addressee Sestius, *consul suffectus* during the year that saw the
publication of *Odes* 1–3. To say this is not to deny that the poem may contain
indirect allusions to its addressee: see E. L. Will, "Ambiguity in Horace *Odes*
1.4," *CP* 77 (1982): 240–245.

control his destiny, and Horace, thankful for his timely escape and resolved in the future to leave important and potentially hazardous themes to others and to limit his own endeavors to matters of slight consequence. The very words he uses in 1.6 to characterize himself and his poetry—*pudor, tenuis, vacuus, levis, culpa ingeni*, albeit givens of the *recusatio*, nonetheless emphasize how far he has moved from the bold enterprise and endeavor of 1.1.29–36, where he speaks of storming the heavens, of striking the stars (cf. 1.3.34–37!), of mingling with the gods themselves, all by the power of his poetry.

1.3 and 1.4 stand midway between these contrasting images of Horace's calling and mediate between them. In 1.3, speaking to a fellow poet, Horace expresses both his admiration for soaring aspiration (cf. 1.1.29–36) and his strong inclination to stand apart from such daring (cf. 1.6). 1.4 looks toward 1.1.29–36 with its opening celebration of the rebirth that comes with spring, the powerful sense of energy released, activity renewed, our kinship with the gods; but it ends in a mood more appropriate to 1.6, with its emphasis on mortal limitations, the brevity and uncertainty of life, the necessary curtailment of any high hopes.

Underscoring the thematic movements we have been charting is the sharp decline in actual magnitude that comes with 1.4–6. 1.1–3 are respectively thirty-six, fifty-two, and forty lines long, 1.4–6 respectively twenty, sixteen, and twenty lines long—from an average length of 42.67 lines in 1.1–3 to one of 18.67 in 1.4–6. This abrupt decline in magnitude from the first three poems to the second three represents a structural enactment of the clash between what is said in 1.6 and what is done in 1.2, a further manifestation of Horace's own uncertainty as to what course he should follow. Shall he be a poet of the *grande*, as in 1.2 and 1.1.29–36? Or a poet of the *tenue*, as expressly stated in 1.6 and implicitly suggested in 1.5? That 1.3, which focuses on the ambivalence attendant upon any journey, any daring enterprise, stands between these polar extremes is no accident, for Horace's ambivalent attitude toward Vergil's voyage is but the reflection of his ambivalence toward his own.

All of this is not, of course, to suggest that size is in any way a measure of excellence in the *Odes*. Some of the greatest odes are among the most slender, and at the end of the collection Horace in effect reaffirms his allegiance to the *tenue*. But Horace himself at many points calls attention to his own vacillation between the poles of the *grande* and the *tenue*—e.g., in 1.6, 2.1.37–40, 2.20.1, 3.3.69–72, 3.4.1–2, 3.25.14–20, 3.30; and in charting his progression along the parameter of magnitude we are doing no more than following his own lead.

Horace's handling of the sea image that runs through the first six poems aptly sums up both his own ambivalent attitudes and also the distinctive thematic progressions within these poems. 1.1.13–18 and 1.3.1–20 portray seafaring as a serious and dangerous human endeavor, and both in these passages and in the apocalyptic vision of 1.2.5 ff. the sea represents an awesome force with which humans must contend. Even in 1.4.2 it remains a challenge to which they return each spring. By 1.5, however, the sea has become merely a metaphor for the vagaries of love, and 1.5's conclusion, in which Horace celebrates his escape from that sea, follows naturally upon his shrinking from Vergil's voyage in 1.3. By the time he reaches 1.6 he is shying away even from songs of nautical exploits, be they Agrippa's (cf. line 3) or Ulysses' (cf. line 7).

The sea motif that helps define the movement of 1.1–6 is of critical importance again in 1.7. At first glance this poem, with its emphasis on escape from care (17–19) and on peaceful havens (1 ff.), seems intent on sustaining the escapist thrust of 1.5 and 1.6. Its concluding section, however, in which Teucer eloquently urges his companions again to face the great sea, sounds a different and more sonorous theme, and what one brings away from the poem is less its avowed theme of the solace of wine than its heroic call to face the unknown with courage. In these concluding lines the poem suddenly rises to a grandeur that is in keeping with its quasi-epic meter, and this epic quality is further underscored by the Vergilian character of these lines[11] and by the fact that they recall the recent Vergil poem, 1.3, a poem also about embarkation and the courage to face the unknown.

The overall effect of 1.7 is to restore some of the momentum and magnitude of 1.1–3 after the decline of 1.4–6. For one thing, the conclusion to which 1.7 rises contrasts sharply with the low-lying promises on which 1.6 ends. No sooner has 1.6 announced that Horace will eschew epic themes and the grand manner than 1.7 gives us a Trojan hero in an epic setting speaking with something approaching Vergilian grandeur, and about the promises a god has made to him (cf. the Trojan themes, the divine-human interchange specifically mentioned in 1.6.5–8, 14–16)! The clash is scarcely less abrupt than that between 1.6 and 1.2. Moreover, the fact that 1.7 not only recalls the heroic figures and themes of 1.3 but also by its *priamel* form recalls 1.1, that poem to which it is parallel in the construction of 1.1–12, further reinforces our sense of a new start. Underscoring the tonal and thematic weight of 1.7's final lines is the fact that even in size—thirty-two lines—1.7 rises well above the slight proportions of the three preceding poems.

If the effect of 1.7 is to regain some of the magnitude with which the book began, the effect of the poems that immediately follow is swiftly to undercut this brief upward surge. The spirit of initiative that rings through Teucer's noble words, the sense that even in the toughest times humans can and should confront great challenges, are rapidly dissipated by 1.8, which concerns a young man whose vigor is sapped by love. 1.8 balances 1.5 in the structure of Book 1, and its Sybaris, like Pyrrha's helpless *puer*, is a figure who is robbed of initiative and for whom the best hope now is that he may

[11] Cf. esp. the similarity of 1.7.25–32 to *Aeneid* 2.198–207. It is not certain, however, which passage comes earlier: cf. J. Vaio, "The Unity and Historical Occasion of Horace *Carm.* 1.7," *CP* 61 (1966): 172–173.

escape relatively unscathed (cf. Horace in 1.5). In contrast to the heroic Teucer at the end of 1.7 stands the Achilles at the end of 1.8, a heroic figure temporarily immobilized and emasculated, the image of what Sybaris has become. About all that remains in 1.8 of the heroic stance of 1.7.25–32 is the underlying assumption that humans *should* be involved in the real activities of the real world.

With 1.9 and 1.11 we return to the bleak world of 1.4, that poem which both balance in the plan of 1.1–12, a world where human agency is thwarted by powers beyond our control. In place of Teucer's bold confrontation of the future—*cras ingens iterabimus aequor*—we have deliberate avoidance of such confrontation: *quid sit futurum cras fuge quaerere* (1.9.13, cf. 1.11.1–3). For Teucer's Tennysonian summons for men to be their own masters (cf. *Ulysses* 45 ff.), we have capitulation to the gods: *permitte divis cetera* (1.9.9, cf. 1.11.3–6). Again, however, not all is yet surrendered, at least in 1.9. In contrast to the bleak resignation of 1.4.17–20, which simply accepts as inevitable the loss of warmth and love, 1.9 ends with a passionate summons to action and involvement (18–24), and even the *carpe diem* of 1.11.8 presupposes some measure of human agency and initiative.

Appropriately set between 1.9 and 1.11, with their emphasis on the limitations humans face, is 1.10, a poem in which divine initiative replaces human. It is a god who receives credit for the early civilizing of humans (lines 2–4), a god who leads Priam on his nighttime visit to the Greek camp (13–16), a god who guides our footsteps on our own last journey (17–20).

Accompanying the decline in human initiative from 1.7 through 1.11 is again a decline in length. From the thirty-two-line 1.7 we move to the twenty-line average of 1.8–10 (sixteen, twenty-four, twenty lines respectively) and thence to the minuscule 1.11 (eight lines)—no steady progression, to be sure, but clear in its larger outlines. More important than these mere numbers is the fact that there is a decline also in magnitude of conception. From the heroic dactyls of 1.7 we turn to the somewhat exotic Greater Sapphic in 1.8, from the large resonances of Teucer's words to the exquisite but limited compass of Sybaris and Lydia.[12] It is clear that already we are back in the Alexandrian world of 1.6.17–20 and 1.5. 1.9 recaptures something of the magnitude of 1.7, partly through its dark theme, partly through its use of the Alcaic (the first appearance in *Odes* 1–3 of the meter that will later in the collection consistently accompany Horace's most serious utterances), but the range of human action suggested at the close (18–24) falls far short of the heroic scope of 1.7.25–32 and in fact embraces the very sort of erotic pastimes spurned in 1.8.[13]

1.10, with its hymnic character and the Sapphic meter that Horace used for the stately 1.2, seems to promise a return to grandeur, but the sonorous phrases with which it begins serve mainly to set off the light and even humorous character of lines 7–12. The fourth and fifth stanzas, with their dark echoes of the *Iliad* (13–16) and their reminder of Mercury *psychopompos* (17–20), capture a measure of the anticipated gravity, but the poem remains, both in size and in thematic scope, predominantly lightweight. The same is true of 1.11, which, exquisite as it is in craftsmanship and dark as it is in theme, is *tenue* in length and *humile* in its portrayal of human potential: seize what you can, avoid trying to probe the future, match your ambitions to the small compass of your life—a far cry from Teucer's *o fortes peioraque passi . . . viri* (1.7.30–31), or from the questing ambitions associated with Vergil in 1.3.

All five of these poems, 1.7–11, touch upon serious themes, basic concerns, but in all of them there is the pull toward the frivolous or at least the escapist. Erotic obsession effectively removes Sybaris from the world of action in 1.8, Apollo's laughter and Mercury's delight in theft sound the dominant notes of 1.10; 1.9 and 1.11 poignantly counterpose human

---

[12] Note esp. *vitat*, 1.8.10, the first appearance in *Odes* 1–3 of a word that in the next groups, 1.13–26, will frequently appear in connection with the theme of escape and avoidance (see 1.14.20, 1.15.18, 1.17.18, 1.23.1).

[13] Cf. *latet*, 1.8.13, *latentis*, 1.9.21 (in analogous positions in the fourth line from the end of both poems). Note also that *campus*, which in 1.8.4 refers to the exercise field, in 1.9.18 refers to the lovers' trysting place.

warmth and animation against the cold and immutable fact of our mortality, but there is no suggestion that the release they recommend can be more than a passing interlude. Even 1.7 itself foreshadows the escapist mode of the poems that follow by setting its heroic Teucer in the context of a poem ostensibly dealing with wine's power to grant momentary oblivion and peace. One notices also that none of these five poems in any way touches on national issues, though Plancus as addressee in 1.7[14] and Mercury in 1.10 offer obvious entrées to such issues.

1.12 seems intended to stop this steady decline, and on the surface it appears to offer what the preceding poems lack—magnitude, range, an emphasis on serious public issues and courageous solutions. In fact, however, these promises prove largely hollow. So far as constructive human initiative is concerned, it offers little. Aside from the passing reference to celebrating a triumph over various Eastern enemies (1.12.53–56—cf. the similar passage at 1.2.51–52), it consists mainly of a resounding list of gods and heroes, an impressive catalogue but one quite devoid of content so far as current needs are concerned. The poem recalls a host of past heroes, but even here it says curiously little about what they were or what they did—one need merely compare the portrait of Regulus in 3.5 to perceive the shallowness of the figures we meet in 1.12. And of Augustus himself—what he is, what he has done, what he must do—the poem says virtually nothing. Moreover, while 1.2, the companion piece to 1.12, at least projects in its first half a powerful and gripping sense of genuine crisis, acute need, even this is lacking in 1.12. The series of questions with which 1.12 begins has its close analogue at 1.2.25–30, but in 1.2 these questions are set against a backdrop of real urgency

---

[14] Cf. the reference to Plancus in 3.14.28. On Plancus and the background of 1.7, see Vaio, *CP* 61 (1966): 168–175; on the possibility that the ode subtly recalls Plancus's alleged murder of his brother, see C. F. Kumaniecki, "De Horatii carmine ad Plancum (Hor. *carm.* I.7)," *Eos* 42 (1947): 5 ff.; D. West, *Reading Horace* (Edinburgh, 1967), 115 ff.

created by the opening six stanzas, a portion of 1.2 that has no counterpart in 1.12.

What is analogous in 1.2 and 1.12, and what is the crux of the matter, is that the answers to their series of questions effectively evade the real issue, namely the need for positive human action at a time of grave human crisis. This is not to deny for a moment that Horace, Augustus, and their contemporaries may have thought that appeals for divine succor and emulation of great Romans of the past were relevant to the current needs of the state. The point, however, is that no intelligent person then or now, let alone persons of such acute good sense as Augustus and Horace, could have any illusions that pious prayers and reverent gestures alone would solve the problems Rome was facing. What was needed was pragmatic action by intelligent and determined humans. One need merely look at odes that come later in this collection or in Book 4—at the specific moral qualities associated with Augustus and Rome in 3.1–6, 3.24, and the *Carmen Saeculare*, for instance, or at the lists of Augustus's accomplishments cited in 4.5.17–24 and 4.15.4–24—to perceive by contrast once again the essential emptiness of 1.12 with respect to qualities and accomplishments such as these. Many readers have sensed that 1.12 rings hollow, and the actual content of the poem justifies this instinctive response.[15] Large in bulk the poem surely is, and undeniably grandiloquent in tone, but in terms of serious confrontation of moral or national issues, serious human involvement and initiative in the solving of Rome's problems, it is but a hollow hulk. Surely Horace, if anyone, knew that defeating the Parthians and voicing high-sounding hopes for divine assistance were no answer to the realities of the present and the horrors of the recent past.

Even the brief and limited poems that precede it touch more on real human issues than does 1.12—on the uncertainties of

[15] See, e.g., K. Quinn, ed., *Horace. The Odes* (London, 1980), 145: "The ode . . . seems oddly stilted and pointless." Cf. Nisbet-Hubbard, *Commentary on Horace, Odes I*, 145–146; G. W. Williams, *Tradition and Originality in Roman Poetry* (Oxford, 1968), 274.

life, the inevitability of death, the power of passion, the possibility of humans courageously facing the unknown or at least resourcefully seizing the present. The juxtaposition of the large 1.12 with the petite 1.11 is especially telling. Weighed against the pithy directness of 1.11, the sprawling mass of 1.12 is found wanting, as if a large balloon were placed in the balance against a dense, dark gemstone. While 1.12 may appear to counter and reverse the decline in substance that stretches from 1.7 through 1.11, in terms of genuine human or moral content it provides not the stopping point for that decline but its natural conclusion.

In addition, one's realization that the magnitude of 1.12 is a matter more of extent than of weight, more of sound than of substance, in retrospect inclines one more clearly to perceive the hollowness of the second half of 1.2, that poem which in so many ways resembles 1.12 and which is its obvious counterpart within 1.1–12. For in response to the agony of real need identified in 1.2.1–24, the second half of 1.2, like the whole of 1.12, offers future promises, recourse to the gods, and chauvinist trumpetings with scarcely a trace of the solid human initiative that is really needed—and that will be emphasized in other national poems later in the collection.

Again, this is not to say that 1.2 and 1.12 are bad poems or that they do not deserve the crucial positions Horace assigns them in *Odes* 1–3. In fact, they perform their given roles to perfection. Their positive contribution is to serve as the defining pillars of the opening group, and this they clearly accomplish by their obvious preeminence of size and manner and by their unmistakably parallel relationship. They also serve, however, what we might call a negative function. The very fact that they raise expectations which they do not fulfill creates in the audience an alertness toward the satisfaction of these unfulfilled expectations later in the collection, just as an incomplete harmonic or thematic progression early in a composition makes the listener the more eager for the resolution that is to come, the more satisfied when it eventually does occur. The opening of 1.2 creates an expectation that its hu-

man and moral dilemmas will find human and moral re-
sponses. The remainder of 1.2 and the whole of 1.12 purport
to bring such responses, but what they offer, as we have seen,
contains little of honest moral quest, of determined human
initiative—little, in short, that relates to real contemporary
needs. The sense of incompleteness, of expectations unsatis-
fied, that is thus created—and most readers of 1.12, and many
even of 1.2, have felt it—is acute and troubling, but this seem-
ing defect, this suspicion that these poems are less than they
might be, is part of Horace's larger design. For when later
poems in the collection—1.35 and 1.37, 2.15, 2.16, and 2.18,
3.1–6, 3.14, and 3.24—begin to offer more satisfying reso-
lutions, we respond to them with an alertness and an eagerness
that would not have been there but for the very lack of such
resolutions in 1.2 and 1.12.

In addition, as we have noted in Chapter I, the placement
of 1.6 at the fulcrum of the group dominated by 1.2 and 1.12
further sharpens our response to these two large poems. The
fact that this central poem expressly denies Horace's ability
to do what 1.2 and 1.12 obviously attempt openly invites
skepticism: either 1.2 and 1.12 are in some way untrue to what
Horace really feels, or in 1.6 he is grossly exaggerating his
limitations. In fact, of course, both of these perceptions are
in some way true. 1.2 and 1.12 do indeed, as part of Horace's
design, fall short of what a national poem can and should be,
and 1.6 does materially overstate Horace's alleged unsuita-
bility for the heroic style. Again, though, the distortion is
more than a bit of typical Horatian fooling, for the contra-
dictions established between 1.6 and the two large odes that
enclose it alert the reader to the significant ways in which 1.2
and 1.12 are deficient,[16] while 1.2 and 1.12 suggest that Horace

---

[16] In *Odes* 4 Horace sets the large and Pindaric 4.4 and 4.14 between two
passages that declare his unfitness to write such poems, 4.2.1–32 and 4.15.1–
4. As in 1.6 there is obvious irony in Horace's self-depreciation, irony under-
lined by 4.3.19–20, *o mutis quoque piscibus donatura cycni, si libeat, sonum* (cf.
4.2.25–27). Nonetheless, the thematic rift thus established between 4.2.1–32
and 4.15.1–4 on the one hand and 4.4 and 4.14 on the other is strikingly

CHAPTER II

is more capable of the grand manner than he admits in 1.6, a suggestion that will find fruition later in the collection.

In yet another respect 1.12 itself foreshadows what is to come. The list of Roman heroes that begins at line 33 offers little of substance itself and does not speak to present needs, but the contexts in which the heroes are placed subtly introduce thematic threads that will become important later in the collection. The first stanza of the catalogue, lines 33–36, mentions four Roman heroes—Romulus, Numa, Tarquinius, and Cato. Horace's uncertainty as to which of these he first should sing follows a familiar poetic tradition, but it also tersely, if subtly, suggests two themes that will later become focal. The outside figures of the quartet, Romulus and Cato, are firmly associated in Horace's poetry with the civil wars,[17] while the inner pair suggest two alternative styles of leadership, the temperate wisdom of a Numa (*quietum . . . regnum*) or the harsh autocracy of a Tarquinius (*superbos . . . fascis*). 1.12.33–36 offers no more than passing allusions, but these allusions serve notice that later Horace will have to face the fact of the civil wars—the lasting stain of the *scelus* of Romulus (cf. 1.35.33–34), the implications of the *Catonis nobile letum* (cf. 2.1.23–24), and the role he himself played in those wars (cf. the references to Philippi at 2.7.9–12, 3.4.26). He will also have to face a central question about Augustus: Is the *princeps* to be a leader who embodies *lene consilium, vis temperata*, or one who relies primarily on naked *vis* (cf. 3.4.41–42, 65–68)? This choice facing Augustus is only suggested here in the contrast between Numa and Tarquinius, but it will emerge as central in the Roman Odes.

---

similar to that established in the earlier collection between 1.6 on the one hand and 1.2 and 1.12 on the other. In both cases the effect of the rift is to make us look with some skepticism at the large poems, which seem so clearly to contradict Horace's avowed intentions. On the tension throughout *Odes* 1–3 between *recusatio* and praise of Augustus, see E. T. Silk, "Bacchus and the Horatian *Recusatio*," *YCS* 21 (1969): 195–210.

[17] Cf. Cato in 2.1.23–24, Romulus in *Epode* 7.17–20, *Odes* 1.35.33–34; cf. 3.3.15 ff., where divine civil war is the theme.

The second stanza of the catalogue, 1.12.37–40, also hints at a theme that will later loom large. Common to Regulus, the Scauri, and Paulus is the fact that all displayed their courage by dying in a losing cause, Regulus by his refusal (at great personal cost) to accept the terms offered by the Carthaginians in the First Punic War, M. Aurelius Scaurus by his defiant bravery (which cost him his life) when captured by the Cimbri,[18] and Paulus by his choice to die nobly, *animae . . . magnae prodigus*, on the battlefield of Cannae. These passing references in 1.12 point ahead to Horace's full treatment of this same theme in 3.2 and 3.5, the latter, of course, in connection again with Regulus. In addition, both 3.2 and 3.5 contain hints of Horace's own action at Philippi, where he chose flight and safety over death on the battlefield, and other poems in the second half of the collection suggest that the theme of bravery in war held for Horace, because of Philippi, a very personal— and very troubling—relevance. 1.12.37–39's glancing references to death on the battlefield thus not only point ahead to important public themes in 3.2 and 3.5 but also introduce Horace's own concern with this particular theme.

The heroes mentioned next, Fabricius, Curius, and Camillus (1.12.40–44), also point ahead. For while Horace introduces them in a military context, he moves thence to the *saeva paupertas et avitus apto cum lare fundus* that nurtured them. Like everything else in 1.12's catalogue, these allusions to the life-style of early Rome are brief and unemphatic, but they foreshadow the increasing emphasis that will be placed on staunch simplicity and sturdy family life in later poems such as 2.15, 2.16, 2.18, 3.1–6, and 3.24.

Moreover, it is worth noting that several of the Greek heroes mentioned in the first half of 1.12 will also return with increased significance in subsequent poems. The Orpheus of

[18] On the reference in 1.12.37 to M. Aurelius Scaurus, see Nisbet-Hubbard, *Commentary on Horace, Odes I*, 158, and authorities cited there. On the intentional ambiguities within 1.12.37–40, see R. Merkelbach, "Augustus und Romulus (Erklärung von Horaz carm. I 12, 37–40)," *Philologus* 104 (1960): 149–153.

1.12.7–12 will lead first to the ineffective Orpheus of 1.24.13, then to the Orpheus-like Alcaeus and Bacchus of 2.13.29 ff. and 2.19.29 ff. The Alcides of 1.12.25 points ahead to the Hercules of 3.3.9 and of 3.14.1, both closely associated with Augustus himself, and the *pueros . . . Ledae* of 1.12.25 will lead ultimately to the benevolent Dioscuri who attend Horace's climactic voyage in 3.29.62–64. Indeed, in the manifold roles it plays in the larger pattern of *Odes* 1–3, 1.12, by grace both of what it contains and of what it significantly lacks, is a superb application on the structural level of the principle of *lucidus ordo* which Horace enunciates in the *Ars Poetica*:

> ordinis haec virtus erit et venus, aut ego fallor,
> ut iam nunc dicat iam nunc debentia dici,
> pleraque differat et praesens in tempus omittat . . .
>   (*Epistles* 2.3.42–44)

We can now briefly review the movements within 1.1–12. The twelve poems fall into two groups of six, and within each of these six there is a clear sense of decline in actual magnitude, in emphasis placed on human initiative, and in the degree to which poems relate to the realities of human existence. The two movements are parallel, but they are far from identical. 1.1–6, with its weighty line-up of 1.1–3, both begins higher and, at least apparently, ends lower—in the lovely but escapist 1.5 and 1.6. 1.7–12, which opens with nothing comparable to the national scope of 1.2, the philosophical explorations of 1.3, begins less high, moves less far into the realm of pure escape (1.9 and 1.11, in contrast to 1.5 and 1.6, still deal with serious issues), and ends with an apparent return to grandeur in 1.12. But the theme of our inability to shape our fate sounds even more emphatically in this second group than in the first— at least in 1.3 humans contrive their own downfall; and the sprawling hollowness of 1.12 in its own way represents an even greater denial of human initiative than does the mere avoidance of serious topics in 1.5 and 1.6. The overall movement toward decline is reflected also in our sense that 1.2, with its powerful first half, towers far above the windy rhetoric that marks the whole of 1.12. Even the very size of 1.12, in the end, contributes to one's sense of decline: that it looks so substantial renders more acute one's discovery that it is largely without substance. Its emptiness of real human issues strikes me as profoundly despairing—a despair no less powerful for being implicit rather than explicit, and a despair that aptly builds upon 1.11's dark recognition of human impotence.

Odes 1.13–19

This emphasis on the inefficacy of human agency becomes a dominant theme in the group that follows, 1.13–19. Poem after poem emphasizes the forces with which humans must contend, forces that we cannot control and that assault us from without. Such is the character of passion in the three similar "framing" poems, 1.13, 1.16, and 1.19. Whether the passion be jealousy (1.13), rage (1.16), or love itself (1.19), it rushes upon its victim (note *ruens* in 1.19.9, cf. 1.16.12), burning and torturing the body (1.13.3–4, 8, 1.19.5 and 7, cf. 1.16.24) and maddening the spirit (1.13.5–6, 1.16.5–8, 25, cf. 1.19.4, 9–12), an irresistible force possessed of animal savagery (cf. 1.16.13–16) and daemonic power (cf. 1.16.5–12, 1.19.1–4). The ship of 1.14 is pitted against similarly awesome forces, as are the hapless Helen and Paris of 1.15, and the same sort of imagery depicts their predicaments—fire (1.15.35–36) and flood (1.14.1 ff.), the assaulted, wounded body (1.14.3–6) and the raging mind (1.15.12, 27), the sense of being but a pawn in the hands of superior powers (note especially the *timidus navita* of 1.14.14, the terrified Paris of 1.15.29–32).[19] Even 1.17 and 1.18, where the focus is on escape rather than on

---

[19] Note also the close relationship between 1.13 and 1.14, both twenty lines long, both in Asclepiad meter, with many words used of 1.14's ship recalling the language of love poetry—e.g. *saucius* (5), *gemant* (6), *taedium* (17), *desiderium* (18), *cura* (18). On the language of love used to describe the *navis* of 1.14, see Anderson, *CP* 61 (1966): 92 ff.; N. K. Zumwalt, "Horace's *Navis* of Love Poetry (*c.* 1.14)," *CW* 71 (1977–78): 250 ff.

incursion, include references to raging, violent lust (1.17.22–28, cf. 1.18.8–11) and the maddening power of wine (1.18.13–16, cf. 1.17.22–24).

Indeed, it is this vivid and ubiquitous panorama of the irrational forces against which humans struggle that lends particular poignancy to the other recurrent motif within the group, the search for escape, respite, haven. Four of the seven poems circle around to this one motif in their concluding stanza (1.13.17–20, 1.14.17–20, 1.16.25–28, 1.19.13–16), and 1.17 is one long variation on this same theme. Whether in its praise of Faunus, of wine, of Horace's protected vale, or of poetry itself, the motif that resonates in 1.17 is that of protection, safety (cf. *defendit*, 3; *impune, tutum*, 5; *nec . . . metuunt*, 8; *tuentur*, 13; *vitabis*, 18; *innocentis*, 21; *nec metues*, 24). 1.18 similarly stresses the escape offered by wine (3 ff.), and 1.15 juxtaposes the lovers' illusions of safety with the reality of their impending doom (19 ff.).

If 1.13–19 is a section in which humans strive to escape forces too powerful for them to control, it is also a section in which the poet himself for the most part shies away from larger themes. The group abandons any explicit reference to national themes such as those of 1.2 and 1.12, touching on national issues only through the impenetrable indirections of 1.14–15, poems that seem both unmistakably to suggest larger frames of reference and obstinately to resist any attempt to pin down these larger implications. Along the same lines, the largely Roman addressees of the first six poems (Maecenas, 1.1; Caesar, 1.2; Vergil—actually his ship, 1.3; Sestius, 1.4; Agrippa, 1.6) are also absent here except for Varus in 1.18 (the intervening group, 1.7–12, occupies an intermediate position in this respect: 1.7 is to Plancus, 1.12 clearly has Augustus in mind, and 1.10 is to Mercury; the other three have Greek addressees). The actual magnitude of poems falls still farther in 1.13–19, to an average of 23.43 lines after the averages of 30.67 and 26.67 in the first two groups. This prevailingly slight compass of the poems—only 1.15 exceeds thirty lines—accords well with the character of the whole group, in which virtually all of the poems display the exquisite refinement and something of the artificiality that we associate with Alexandrian verse and with the *tenue*.[20] Four poems, 1.13, 1.16, 1.17, and 1.19, clearly belong to the type described by Horace in 1.6.17–20; a fifth, 1.18, is a drinking poem of the same ilk (cf. the *convivia* of 1.6.17); and even 1.14 and 1.15, despite their larger resonances, remain above all exquisite imitations of Greek originals. If the structure of the opening section highlights Horace's indecision as to his poetic course—whether he is to be a poet of the *grande*, as in 1.2 and 1.12, or a poet of the *tenue*, as in 1.6—the second group clearly casts him, at least for the time being, in the latter role.

The overall effect of this group, an effect that complements the poems' recurrent emphasis on escape, is to draw us away from the real world and into an enchanting but unreal poetic universe. We must again stress that to say this is in no way to denigrate these poems. 1.17 is unquestionably among Horace's greatest poems, and others of the group are almost as fine. But just as Horace in 1.17 invites Tyndaris to retreat from the harsh world into his secluded haven, so these poems collectively take us into a retreat where we forget the larger concerns raised earlier in the book—the crisis Rome faces (1.2), the ambivalence of human aspiration (1.3), the certainty that we shall die (1.4, 1.9, and 1.11).[21] These issues are scarcely touched upon in 1.13–19, and to recognize this fact is only to recognize that these superbly crafted and deeply affecting poems have their limitations, and again that these limitations are part of a larger design. For the retreat into the secluded world of 1.13–19 is but the necessary preparation for the return

[20] 1.14 is based on Alcaeus, 1.15 imitates Bacchylides, 1.16 has some glancing connection with Stesichorus, and 1.17.18 expressly alludes to Anacreon, but the prevailing feeling of the group remains Hellenistic, a feeling well supported by the numerous Hellenistic touches identified in Nisbet-Hubbard's commentary on these seven poems.

[21] 1.15 and 1.16 have their grim allusions to death, but the focus is on specific sources of death—e.g., the downfall of Troy (1.15.10, 33–36), the force of anger (1.16.17–21)—not on the general fact of our mortality.

to the real world later in the book, the avoidance of certain
basic issues but a means of whetting our appetite for the
confrontation of these issues that is to come.

We should recognize also that not all is avoidance and escape
in 1.13–19. There are undercurrents present that already are
drawing us back toward the real world and its serious con-
cerns. For one thing, 1.14 and 1.15 carry a genuine depth of
concern and tantalizing hints that this concern has larger ram-
ifications. Horace leaves unclear the specific significance of
these poems, and as with all such "problem poems" in Horace,
one is best advised to assume that had Horace wished his
reader to take away a particular message, he would have made
the poems less opaque and enigmatic. What *is* abundantly
clear in both poems, however, is that what is at stake is more
important, more public, than is the case in purely personal
poems such as 1.5, 1.8, or 1.13. The final stanza of 1.14, as
well as the whole tradition of ship of state poems, makes it
inevitable that we attach to the storm of that poem some larger
implications, and our inclination in that direction receives
reinforcement when in the next poem Horace explicitly as-
sociates the voyage of Helen and Paris with public danger on
a large scale—with, in fact, the destruction of a great civili-
zation and race. The opening lines of this final stanza of 1.14,
*nuper sollicitum quae mihi taedium, nunc desiderium curaque non
levis*, breathe an aura of passionate caring that we have not
heard since the opening of 1.2. And the description of the
devastation of war wrought by Helen and Paris again touches
the reality of recent Roman experience and again recalls the
opening of 1.2. If Horace in these poems uses allegory to
avoid direct consideration of the issues that surfaced in 1.2,
that very allegory which is his escape is so cast as both to
suggest the depth of his concern and also to presage his even-
tual open confrontation of these issues.[22]

Moreover, the erotic poetry of this group, another avenue

[22] Note how the *imbellisque lyrae Musa potens* of 1.6.10, a phrase used of
Horace's own verse, is recalled, with decidedly negative connotations, in the
imbelli cithara carmina divides of 1.15.15, a phrase here used of the cowardly
Paris.

by which apparently to escape dealing with the "real world," itself exhibits a depth of feeling that 1.6, his "program" for such pieces, had seemed to rule out. And in contrast to the Horace of 1.5, who revels in his escape and in his ironic observer stance, the Horace of 1.13, 1.16, 1.17, and 1.19 is himself involved, himself taking the initiative, himself seeking to make things better. The contrast is immediately apparent from a comparison of the Lydia poems of 1.1–12 and 1.13–19. Both concern a young person helpless in the grip of passion, but in 1.8 Horace stands aside, a somewhat cynical bystander in the manner of 1.5, while in 1.13 he himself is a participant, the prey to emotions that seem both more intense and more real. The same is true of 1.13–19 as a whole. Both the depth of feeling that animates them and the fact of Horace's own involvement represent steps ahead from the dispassionate detachment of 1.5 and 1.6, and both foreshadow the active and passionate involvement in larger issues that will come later in the book.

Yet another positive undercurrent within this group is the fact that moral concerns are implicit at several points in a way that we have not met since early in Book 1. Horace's catalogue of the sufferings that will come from the folly of Helen and Paris in 1.15, his eloquent exploration of the far-reaching consequences of anger in 1.16.17–21, his reference to *pietas* in 1.17.13, his condemnation of the excesses of drink in 1.18.8 ff., even his praise of the felicity of happy love in 1.13.17–20—all these, slight touches though they be, carry an implicit moral concern that will lead to important developments later in the collection.

Finally, the very poetry of this section, *tenuis* though it be in form and scope, begins to belie the limitations Horace had placed upon his verse in 1.6.17–20:

nos convivia, nos proelia virginum
sectis in iuvenes unguibus acrium
cantamus vacui, sive quid urimur
    non praeter solitum leves.

The poetry of 1.13–19 rises far above, and probes far deeper, than the ironic frivolity of these lines, and Horace himself in the beautiful central lines of 1.17 captures the different quality of this section:

> di me tuentur, dis pietas mea
> et musa cordi est. hic tibi copia
>   manabit ad plenum benigno
>   ruris honorum opulenta cornu;
>   (1.17.13–16)

The secluded vale of poetry, to which Horace invites Tyndaris and into which he for the time draws us, is allied to the gods, to *pietas*, to the fertility of the land itself. The repose it offers is no mere escapism, its serenity no mere lack of caring. 1.13–19 may represent a retreat from reality, but this retreat already betrays an impulse toward return.

Odes 1.20–26

As we saw in Chapter I, 1.20–26 correspond closely to 1.13–19, and in many ways this seven-poem group sustains the thrust and builds on the themes of the preceding seven-poem group. The decline in length continues, with the average of these seven poems descending to 16.57 lines, by far the lowest average of any group in the collection. In accordance with this inclination toward the *tenue*, three of the poems are clearly of the artificial erotic mode that set the tone for the previous group—1.22, which despite the high-sounding morality of its start turns out to be but a love poem about Lalage; 1.23, Horace's exquisite, manifestly Anacreontic ode to Chloe; and 1.25, a nasty but darkly humorous poem gloating over Lydia's loss of youth. Again there are no poems that, like 1.2 and 1.12, focus on national issues or adopt the grand manner; the only references to national affairs are the passing allusion to Rome's enemies at 1.26.3–5 and the prayer at 1.21.13–16 that Diana and Apollo may drive famine and pestilence away from Rome and Caesar and upon the Persians and Britons. Escape

still remains a constant preoccupation, whether in this con-
clusion to 1.21, in the assurance to the skittish Chloe that she
need not fear (1.23.9–10), or in the ecstatic farewell to fear
and sadness and the *unice securus*[23] of 1.26.1–2 and 5–6. The
theme is implicit even in 1.20, which refers indirectly to Mae-
cenas's escape from illness (cf. 1.21.13–16), and in 1.24, which
seeks to assuage Vergil's grief (see especially lines 19–20: *sed
levius fit patientia quidquid corrigere est nefas*); and poetry's pro-
tective power is the central theme of 1.22 just as it is of 1.17,
the poem that balances 1.17 in the overall pattern of Book
1—both are pieces in which poetry "keeps the wolf far hence,
that's foe to men" (cf. 1.17.9, 1.22.9 ff.).[24] Above all, the
world of 1.20–26 remains one in which there seems still a
diminished range of human aspiration, scant faith in the power
of human enterprise and initiative. Humans can, as in 1.13–
19, through poetry carve out a secure haven for themselves,
and the possibility of retreat to this artificial world lies behind
Horace's confidence in 1.22 and 1.26.6–12 (as in 1.17). But
the remainder of human existence remains circumscribed by
powers beyond his control—the passing of time (cf. 1.23 and
1.25), death (cf. 1.24), the gods (cf. 1.21); and passive en-
durance—the *patientia* of 1.24.19—is the only answer.

In other respects, however, 1.20–26 represent a turning
point in Book 1, with the actual fulcrum coming at the di-
vision between 1.19 and 1.20, the precise midpoint of the
book. For with 1.20, addressed to Maecenas, Horace takes a
significant step away from the predominantly artificial world
of the previous group. He returns to that world in 1.22, 1.23,
and 1.25, to be sure, but of the seven poems in 1.20–26, four
have Roman addressees—1.20, 1.22, 1.24, 1.26, a sharp in-
crease from the one Roman addressee of the previous group.
1.20–26 touch the real world in other ways too, and again
1.20 signals the change. Not only is this poem addressed to

---

[23] The only use of *securus* in *Odes* 1–3.

[24] J. Webster, *The White Devil* V.iv. Note that the wolf appears in line 9
of both 1.17 and 1.22.

CHAPTER II

a real person, and one significantly involved in public affairs,
but also it refers to actual recent events in Rome (3–8). Several
of the other poems also touch upon reality in a manner dif-
ferent from that of 1.13–19. 1.21.13–16 and 1.26.3–5, slight
touches though they be, address contemporary national affairs
without the allegory in which such references are cloaked in
1.14–15. Both 1.23 and 1.25 touch on the theme of time's
passing, 1.23 lightly but poignantly, 1.25 harshly and with
some bitterness, and the poem set between these two, 1.24,
deals head-on with the ultimate reality, death. No masking
of real issues in this poem, no recourse to the gods (cf. 1.24.11–
12) or flight to the artificial world of poetry (cf. 1.24.13–14).
The only escape offered is grimly realistic—and eminently
Vergilian: human endurance (1.24.19).

Accompanying this movement back toward reality, both
physical and metaphysical, is an increasing depth of emotional
involvement on the part of the poet, a movement foreshad-
owed in 1.13–19 by the genuine feeling that animates the love
poems, the obvious concern expressed in 1.14.17–20, and the
fact that increasingly Horace himself is an active participant.
But whereas in 1.13–19 Horace's feelings find expression in
the artificialities of erotic poetry or the indirections of allegory,
in several poems of 1.20–26 they wear no such disguises. His
true concern for Maecenas, and his joy at his patron's recovery,
obviously animate 1.20, and their expression is the more tell-
ing in that it eschews the extravagant language with which
Horace addresses Maecenas in 1.1. 1.26, the brief balancing
poem to 1.20, is even more forthright in its expression of joy
and affection. In addition, 1.26, while not abandoning the
artificial mode of Callimachean verse (cf. the telltale *fontibus
integris* of line 6),[25] nonetheless associates poetry's garlands
with a real person, its escape from fears and sadness with real

[25] On the Alexandrian associations of *fontibus integris*, see Wimmel, *Kal-
limachos in Rom*, 222 ff.; S. Commager, *Odes of Horace* (New Haven, 1962),
11 ff.; Nisbet-Hubbard, *Commentary on Horace, Odes I*, 305. On the origins
of the image, cf. W. Clausen, "Callimachus and Latin Poetry," *GRBS* 5 (1964):
189.

84

contemporary issues—a clear step ahead from the imaginary heroines and the erotic preoccupations of 1.17 and 1.22, and a step toward the more active role poetry will play in the next group. In particular, the *Lesbio . . . plectro* of line 11 looks toward the fuller exploration of Alcaean poetry that will come in 1.32, the Alcaic meter, used only here in 1.20–26, toward the predominance of this meter in 1.27–38, where the Alcaean influence implicit in 1.26 becomes more explicit, the confidence briefly limned in 1.26 more fully developed.

Above all, though, it is in 1.24 that Horace touches upon real issues. This should come as no surprise, for just as Vergil calls forth the extraordinary candor of 1.3, so his presence in 1.24 obliges Horace to face harsh realities unmasked—that Quintilius's death cannot be reversed, that his great virtues cannot be replaced,[26] that no poetry can call him back, that the gods are unrelenting and without pity. If the movement of 1.13–19 is from the quasi-tragic 1.14–15 to the escape-oriented 1.17, that of 1.20–26 is from the escape-oriented 1.21–22 to the genuinely tragic 1.24.

There is a change of direction also within Horace's stance toward Vergil. 1.3 and 1.24 (both Asclepiad in meter) are similar in that in each Horace confronts not only a real event, Vergil's departure in the one, Quintilius's death in the other, but also the disturbing themes implicit in that event—the theme of human audacity in 1.3, that of our mortality in 1.24. But whereas in 1.3 Vergil is the active party, Horace a bystander who ultimately shrinks from the bold initiative implicit in Vergil's departure, in 1.24 it is Horace who takes the initiative and who strives to help his friend once more face the world with courage. Indeed, Horace's advice to Vergil here points the way toward his own facing of hard facts in Book 2.

In the same way, Horace also takes the lead in other poems

---

[26] Note that moral considerations of the sort introduced by 1.22.1 ff. but effectively skirted in the remainder of 1.22 come more fully into play in 1.24.6–8, preparation for the greater emphasis placed on ethical themes in 1.27–38.

of this third group, perhaps in no very dramatic fashion, but at least in a manner more directed toward the real world and toward positive ends than was the case in the previous group, where what initiative he took was confined by its allegorical and erotic settings and was almost exclusively aimed at escape. It is Horace who sends an invitation to Maecenas in 1.20, who directs the prayers of the young boys and girls of 1.21, who reaches out toward Chloe sensitively in 1.23 (and toward Lydia insensitively in 1.25), and who takes the initiative toward celebration in 1.26.

Nor must we overlook 1.22, a lighthearted spoof that deftly sidesteps the moral issues broached by its opening lines, but a poem that nonetheless is of central importance to the theme of human initiative. For the source of Horace's safety in *Integer vitae* is Horace's own song; it is this human creation, this product of human initiative, that will protect him wherever he may go and that, metaphorically at least, gives him a measure of autonomy even toward Jupiter himself (cf. lines 19–20)! The theme of 1.22 is similar to that of 1.17, as we have seen, and the tone even lighter, but in one sense 1.22 goes far beyond 1.17. Whereas throughout 1.17, and especially in its crucial central stanza, lines 13–16, Horace associates the haven of poetry with Faunus and the gods, in 1.22 his song and its protective power spring entirely from himself. The ironic lightness of 1.22 keeps one from taking it too seriously, but in retrospect one realizes that it represents an important step forward. The Horace who shrank from Vergil's lonely journey in 1.3 now declares himself prepared to undertake the most awesome of journeys (1.22.5–8, 17–22), a declaration that looks ahead in Book 1 to Horace's willingness to sail in new directions in 1.34.3–5 and, in later books, to the lonely *iter* he is prepared to take with Maecenas in 2.17.10–12 (cf. *iter* in 1.22.5) and to the lonely voyage he blithely sketches at the end of 3.29 (cf. also *negata temptat iter via*, of *virtus*, at 3.2.22). In addition, the power of his poetry to protect him from the Sabine wolf (a step beyond the mere freedom from wolves of 1.17.9–10) looks ahead to the Orpheus-like Alcaeus and Bacchus of 2.13 and 2.19, both figures closely associated with Horace's own poetry (cf. the ineffective Orpheus of 1.24.13 ff.). More immediately, of course, the self-reliant Horace of 1.22, happily strolling alone in his Sabine woods, leads directly to the isolated individuals who inhabit the next three poems—to the lonely Chloe of 1.23, in vain searching the woods for her mother; to the bereft Vergil of 1.24, in vain striving to coax back the dead; and to the aging Lydia of 1.25, in vain trying to recapture her lost youth.

Just how far the slight poems of 1.20–26 advance the argument is apparent if one compares the concluding poems of 1.13–19 and of 1.20–26. 1.19 presents a poet beset by harsh, superior forces, a figure who at best hopes to moderate the impact of the goddess upon himself (13–16) and who is unable to sing what he chooses (10–12). 1.26, in contrast, presents a poet who, *unice securus*, throws fear and sadness to the winds, who revels in his companionship with the Muses, and who is clearly in control of his Lesbian lyre. From 1.13–19, where involvement is troublesome, even dangerous, escape is the highest objective, and the dominant movement is toward retreat, he has progressed to 1.20–26, where he begins actively to court involvement, where he brings a measure of confidence and initiative toward the harsh realities of the world, and where the dominant movement begins to be forward and outward.

Significant also, and again positive in its implications, is the contrast between 1.21 and 1.2, two poems that, despite their obvious differences, are clearly designed as structural counterparts. Both immediately follow the Maecenas poems that open the two halves of Book 1, and both appeal for divine protection of Rome and her leader (1.2.25 ff., note *Caesar* at 44 and 52; 1.21.13–16, note *Caesar* at 14). 1.2 suggests that Rome's foreign enemies would be a more appropriate target for military energies now directed inward (22, 51), and 1.21 voices a similar hope that war, famine, and pestilence may be driven from Rome and Caesar and upon their enemies (13–16). A number of verbal correspondences underscore the parallelism of the two poems. Both poems accord special attention to Apollo as Rome's savior—he is the first to be mentioned in the catalogue that begins at 1.2.30, and he is by far the more prominent of the two divinities mentioned in 1.21 (note the special emphasis on his shoulders in both poems—*umeros*, 1.2.31, *umerum*, 1.21.12). *Persae* in 1.2.22 is picked up by *Persas* in 1.21.15, *Medos* in the penultimate line of 1.2 by *Persas atque Britannos* in the penultimate line of 1.21. The anaphora (*hic . . . hic*) at the start of the final stanza of 1.2 corresponds to the anaphora (*hic . . . hic* again) at the start of the final stanza of 1.21, and both poems end with divine-human cooperation—Mercury taking the form of Augustus at the end of 1.2, Apollo responding to human prayers at the end of 1.21.

As is so often the case, the clear similarities between these poems serve above all to emphasize their significant differences. 1.21 is smaller in scale, less grand in conception, far less imposing than is 1.2, a contrast that closely parallels that between the immediately preceding Maecenas poems. But perhaps for this very reason 1.21 also seems more intimate, more heartfelt, more in tune with Horace's true style and sentiment than does 1.2—a contrast that again mirrors the relationship of 1.20 to 1.1. Most important is the fact mentioned earlier—that in the unassuming 1.21 there is, surprisingly, more room for human agency than there is in 1.2. In contrast to 1.2, where Horace's stance suggests bewilderment, uncertainty, and even despair (note especially the series of questions beginning at line 25), in 1.21 he knows precisely what needs to be done and confidently goes about doing it. Whereas in 1.2 the gods seem to turn a deaf ear to human prayer (*prece qua . . . minus audientem . . . Vestam*, 26–28), Horace concludes 1.21 by assuring his young chorus that their prayer will be heard and heeded (*vestra motus . . . prece*, 16). And whereas in 1.2 hope for improvement seems to begin with the gods above (29 ff.), in 1.21 it begins, albeit humbly, with humans below (16). There is again a close parallel in the contrast between 1.1, where Horace's grandiose hopes for success depend upon Maecenas's approval (35), and 1.20, where Horace himself, in his own simple way, has already taken the initiative.

Before we turn to the final group, 1.27–38, it is worth briefly reviewing the two central groups from a somewhat different perspective. Our emphasis has been on larger thematic movement, on structural juxtapositions and balances, in short, on features that a person reading through the poems *seriatim* may at first overlook. Just as remarkable as these larger structural features, however, is a quality that such a reader is more likely to pick up, and one that materially contributes to the sense of onward movement, namely the way in which thematic and motivic links between poems enable one poem to flow almost seamlessly into the next. Thus 1.13 establishes the pattern for 1.14—four stanzas about incursion, a final stanza about relief, with the two poems sharing the same length, related meters, and numerous motivic links. 1.15 combines 1.14's nautical setting and its theme of impending danger with the erotic focus of 1.13, while 1.16 sustains this erotic emphasis and blends with it something of the city-in-danger theme of 1.15 (1.16.17–21). 1.16 also reverts to the pattern of 1.13–14, in which an emphasis on incursion and danger throughout the poem yields to the hope of escape in the final stanza. This final stanza of 1.16 in turn leads directly into 1.17 and 1.18, where the focus is on escape, while in the same way the concluding references to drunken license in 1.17 lead directly into 1.18. To round out the circle, the *saeva . . . tympana* near the end of 1.18 leads easily into the *Mater saeva* with which 1.19 begins, and this poem, with its last-stanza emphasis on escape, returns to the pattern set by 1.13 and 1.14.

1.19 ends in the search for release and in libations of wine, an apt introduction to Horace's invitation to Maecenas (1.20) to share wine that honors his patron's recovery. Escape from disease is but implicit as the background to 1.20, but this theme becomes explicit and focal in the last stanza of 1.21—an obvious reminiscence of the pattern made so familiar in the previous group. Both the woodland settings associated with Diana and the escape theme at the end of 1.21 lead into 1.22, where a jaunt in the woods provides the setting for Horace's soliloquy on escape. The silvan setting remains in the imagery of 1.23, as does the emphasis on escape, though here the focus is more on Chloe's fears than it is on Horace's assurances that she need not fear him (last stanza again). This undercurrent of panic in 1.23 leads naturally into 1.24, where, like Chloe in her trackless forest, humans are surrounded by forces beyond their ken and control and where, in contrast to Horace's song in 1.22, Orpheus's song, despite its power over the trees (1.24.14—cf. the woodland references of the three previous poems), is of no avail. 1.25 sustains the themes of 1.24—separation, loss, tears, vain laments—with the silvan motifs of the previous poems now providing the imagery by which Horace in the final stanza contrasts Lydia with her youthful tormentors. The undercurrent of macabre humor in 1.25 leads into the pure joy of 1.26, with several motivic links also easing the transition—cf. *vento* (1.25.12), *ventis* (1.26.3); *gaudeat* (1.25.18), *gaudes* (1.26.7); garlands (1.25.17–20, 1.26.7–8). This last represents a final, joyous appearance of the woodland-vegetation motif that has run through the previous poems, while the references in the opening lines of 1.26 to fear and sadness look back to the dominant themes of 1.23 and 1.24. This brief overview may at least suggest the sort of motivic and thematic flow that is present not just within this group but throughout *Odes* 1–3, a constant delight to the reader and a constant reminder of the onward, almost narrative flow of the collection.[27]

Odes 1.27–38

Just as Horace creates in 1.13–26 both a sense of continuous forward movement and also a complex network of contrasts and oppositions, so in the final group of Book 1, 1.27–38, he

[27] On possible links between 1.26 and 1.27, 1.32 and 1.33, pairs that in fact bridge the structural divisions which I propose, see R. S. Kilpatrick, "Two Horatian Proems: *Carm.* 1.26 and 1.32," *YCS* 21 (1969): 215–239.

works simultaneously with two highly contrasting structural arrangements. We saw earlier that the twelve poems of this group are so arranged as to form a concentric pattern in which the related poems 1.31–32 function as fulcrum. We shall shortly see that the same twelve poems are so organized as also to fall into two roughly parallel groups of six poems each, 1.27–32 and 1.33–38. This simultaneous presence of two patterns, one based on concentric symmetry, the other on parallel motion, has, of course, its close analogue in the similarly complex structure of its counterpart in Book 1, 1.1–12, where also parallel motion and concentric arrangement complement each other.[28]

The parallelism of the two inner groups of 1.27–38 is easily seen. Both begin with poems that stress irresistible and often harsh enslavement to love, 1.27 and 1.33. Both poems focus on the domination of Venus (1.27.14, 1.33.10 ff.), the impossibility of escape (1.27.21 ff., 1.33.14–16), and the fact that those Venus binds are often ill-matched (1.27.18–20, 1.33.10–16; cf. esp. *digne puer meliore flamma*, 1.27.20, *ipsum me melior cum peteret Venus*, 1.33.13). The next pairs of poems in each group, 1.28–29 and 1.34–35, are also parallel to each other, but within these pairs the pattern is chiastic, with 1.29 balancing 1.34, 1.28 balancing 1.35, an arrangement that coincides with the concentric pattern analyzed in Chapter I. 1.29 and 1.34, both Alcaic and both sixteen lines long, concern individuals who abruptly abandon philosophy for a new and more active course (cf. 1.29.13 ff., 1.34.1 ff.), while 1.28 and 1.35 are both long serious poems dealing with superhuman forces to which we are subject.[29] The parallelism of the fourth poems in the two groups, 1.30 and 1.36, is not marked, though each is a short poem in which love looms large,[30] but

[28] Vergil too makes use of complementary parallel and concentric patterns: see Duckworth, *Structural Patterns and Proportions in Vergil's Aeneid*, 1–15.

[29] For a fuller analysis of links between 1.29 and 1.34, 1.28 and 1.35, see above, p. 27.

[30] Note also *ture* in both 1.30.3 and 1.36.1; Numida returns from the West to eager friends (1.36), while Venus is to come from the East in response to Glycera's urgent summons (1.30).

that of the fifth and sixth poems, 1.31 and 1.37, 1.32 and 1.38, is clear. 1.31 and 1.37 are both Alcaic poems that mark important national occasions, 1.31 the dedication of the new temple to Apollo, 1.37 the victory over Cleopatra. Both begin with the public event, and both move at their close to the self-sufficiency of an individual, Horace himself in 1.31, Cleopatra in 1.37.[31] This closing emphasis of 1.31 and 1.37 leads naturally into the two final poems, 1.32 and 1.38, both brief and Sapphic, both focusing on Horace himself and, in particular, on the modesty of his expectations.[32]

In thematic movement too these two groups are analogous. Each begins in a light erotic vein reminiscent of 1.6.17–20 but moves thence to weightier poems in which Horace is more personally involved and in which national issues play an explicit part. Thus the light 1.27, with its focus on *convivia* and the *proelia* of love (cf. 1.6.17–20), is followed by the serious 1.28 and, after the lighter 1.29–30, by 1.31–32, two poems where a significant national event, the dedication of the new temple to Apollo, provides an occasion for Horace to make important statements about his own poetic and personal values. 1.31 for the first time in the collection articulates Horace's basic values; one might even see the poem as making explicit what was implicit but playfully obfuscated in 1.22:

> frui paratis et valido mihi,
> Latoe, dones, at, precor, integra
>   cum mente, nec turpem senectam
>   degere nec cithara carentem.
>   (1.31.17–20)

And 1.32, again despite its slender elegance and its seeming emphasis on the lighter side of Alcaean poetry, also contains

---

[31] Note also wine and drinking at the start of 1.37, *novum . . . liquorem* at the start of 1.31; avoidance of shame at the end of 1.37, of shameful old age at the end of 1.31; prominent sea pictures in the center of both poems (1.37.12 ff., 1.31.10–15).

[32] Cf. also *vacui sub umbra*, near the start of 1.32, *sub arta vite*, near the end of 1.38.

a serious core and, like 1.31, marks an important step ahead. As we saw in Chapter I, 1.32, in concert with 1.31, occupies the position held by 1.6 in the first section, and like 1.6 it articulates Horace's poetic credo. But whereas 1.6 emphasizes only Horace's devotion to the *tenue*, his utter unsuitability for larger themes, 1.32 implicitly raises the possibility that Horace, like Alcaeus, can and will work in both styles. The express emphasis of 1.32 is again, as in 1.6, on light erotic poetry, whether Horace's or Alcaeus's, with the *vacui sub umbra lusimus* (1.32.1–2) recalling the *cantamus vacui* of 1.6.19, but several aspects of the poem point also toward more serious poetry of the sort ruled out in 1.6. There is, for one thing, the early emphasis on the lasting quality of Horace's verse (1.32.2–3), an implicit suggestion of its serious worth and one that is echoed in 3.30.[33] The same implication is present also in the poem's final stanza where, in almost hieratic terms (note especially lines 15–16), Horace associates Apollo with his poetry. Above all there is the fact that here for the first time Horace specifically names Alcaeus as his chosen model and that in doing so he not only stresses Alcaeus's lighter verse but also explicitly refers to the civic roles he played. It is a significant step beyond the generalized references of 1.1.34 (*Lesboum . . . barbiton*) and 1.26.11 (*Lesbio . . . plectro*) and one that clearly opens the way for Horace, like Alcaeus, to take on public responsibilities and deal with larger themes—a possibility emphasized by the use of the word *vates* at line 2.[34]

The movement of 1.33–38 is even more apparent. Horace

[33] Cf. 1.32.2–3 and 3.30.1–4, the Latin *carmen* on Alcaeus's Lesbian lyre (1.32.3–5) with *princeps Aeolium carmen ad Italos deduxisse modos* (3.30.13–14). Even though the *Latinum . . . carmen* of lines 3–4 probably does not refer to the Roman Odes, it suggests a gravity that contrasts with the *si quid vacui . . . lusimus* of lines 1–2. Underscoring this implicit contrast is the uncertainty of reference in the *quod* of line 2, which at first seems clearly to refer back to the playful *si quid* of line 1, in retrospect to look ahead to the weightier *Latinum . . . carmen* of 3–4. On the thematic significance of 1.32, see Babcock, *CP* 62 (1967): 191–192.

[34] On *vates* in 1.31.2, see J. K. Newman, *Augustus and the New Poetry* (Brussels, 1967), 130–131.

begins again with the petty squabbles of erotic verse (1.33), moves via a poem on his own "conversion" (1.34) to the obviously weightier national and philosophical themes of 1.35, and then, after a lighter poem (1.36), climaxes the set (and the book) with 1.37, a poem that weaves strongly felt national, personal, and moral considerations into a single piece, after which the light but deeply personal 1.38 (cf. the similar character of 1.32) rounds out the group.

Both groups also move both in their addressees and in their settings from the artificial world of poetry toward the real world of Rome. Despite the presence of Falernian wine in 1.27.10 and of Horace and Tibullus in 1.33, the two opening poems remain essentially Greek in theme and character, as do 1.29 and 1.30 in the first group. But with 1.29 and 1.31 in the first group, 1.34–37 in the second, events and figures from contemporary Rome—Iccius, Caesar, Numida, Cleopatra—begin to flood the canvas. 1.32 and 1.38 conclude this movement by focusing on the Roman poet himself, albeit in poems that harmoniously blend Greek and Roman elements[35] and provide gently falling cadences to their respective groups.

Complementing this movement from the artificial world of poetry to the real world of contemporary Rome is a progression within both 1.27–32 and 1.33–38 from a state of helpless dependence, where the highest goal is to escape, to a condition of self-reliance, where one feels able to deal with the world's problems rather than to flee them. 1.27 and 1.28, both of them monologues from a rather shadowy speaker to an unanswering addressee, create worlds where humans are hopelessly enslaved to superior forces. The only hope for the drowned speaker of 1.28 is that he may be freed from his endless wanderings—from death itself there can be no escape (1.28.15–20); the hapless *Opuntiae frater Megillae* of 1.27 is as

---

[35] In 1.32 note esp. the blending of the *Latinum . . . carmen* with the Lesbian lyre (lines 3–5—note the interlocked word order), in 1.38 Horace's imbuing of his Greek antecedents (on which see Nisbet-Hubbard, *Commentary on Horace, Odes I*, 421–422) with an intensely personal focus.

hopelessly caught in the bonds of love—not a sorcerer, a god, a hero could free him:

quae saga, quis te solvere Thessalis
magus venenis, quis poterit deus?
　　vix illigatum te triformi
　　　Pegasus expediet Chimaera.
　　　　　(1.27.21–24)[36]

In 1.27–28 the gods control all (cf. 1.27.14, 1.28.17, 19–20, 29), and human action consists largely of accepting our role as pawns of these capricious but powerful beings (cf. the world of 1.13–19). By the time we reach 1.31–32, however, the roles are virtually reversed. The initiative now lies with humans, and divine action is shaped by human request. Thus 1.31 and 1.32 begin with the emphatic *quid . . . poscit* and *poscimus:* "What does the poet request of the god? We request. . . ." Even the ends of 1.31 and 1.32, which approach Apollo with genuine reverence, find the poet defining his own *desiderata* (1.31) and voicing his own vision of poetry's role (1.32). The stance taken toward the god is not unlike that taken toward the Muse in 1.26, but there is a greater independence, a fuller articulation of personal values and poetic goals.

The transition from the dependence of 1.27–28 to the considerable autonomy of 1.31–32 comes primarily in the intervening poems, 1.29–30, but 1.28 itself provides important first steps. For while the speaker of 1.28 cannot but accept his death, he at least takes the initiative in trying to better his lot, a step toward Cleopatra's willingness to deal bravely with a desperate situation in 1.37. There is also in 1.28 at least the recognition that the power to free the speaker rests with a human agent, another slight gesture in the direction of human autonomy, another step toward the emphasis on change that will come in the two following poems. And while Horace casts the poem in a form that, with its shadowy, unidentified

---

[36] With the *quis te solvere . . . poterit deus* of 1.27.21–22, cf. the *teque piacula nulla resolvent* of 1.28.34.

speaker, deliberately skirts direct involvement of the poet, the poem confronts with obvious seriousness the theme of death and thus moves toward his bold focus on this theme in Book 2 (cf. the same theme in 1.24). 1.29, albeit humorously, deals quite directly with human autonomy, for unlike the enslaved lover of 1.27 or the dead speaker of 1.28, Iccius can and does alter his life, a point that Horace's incredulity, expressed through the exaggerated *adunata* of 1.29.10 ff., effectively underscores. 1.30, like 1.27, deals with the power of love, but where 1.27 recognizes human helplessness before love's power, 1.30 admits the power of Venus but grants humans the same sort of initiative toward the goddess as Horace will exert toward Apollo in the next two poems. One can perhaps best appreciate the tone of 1.30 by contrasting its "calm detachment"[37] with the grim, almost desperate stance that Horace adopts toward Venus in the earlier Glycera poem, 1.19. 1.30 exudes confidence in human ability to influence the goddess, while 1.19 can but hope that human efforts may lead to some improvement; 1.30 immediately takes the initiative toward Venus, while 1.19 only in its last stanza, almost as an afterthought, considers what action to take.

The theme of divine supremacy and control is strongly reestablished with 1.33:

> sic visum Veneri, cui placet imparis
> formas atque animos sub iuga aenea
>   saevo mittere cum ioco.
>
> (1.33.10–12)

Given these conditions, what can humans do but play the parts assigned them by the goddess? The next poems also stress divine dominance. It is the thunderbolt of Jupiter that provokes Horace's change of course in 1.34, Fortune and Necessity that rule the world in 1.35, the gods who are to be thanked for Numida's return in 1.36. Even 1.37 begins with a nod in the gods' direction (1.37.2–4). The overall emphasis

---

[37] E. Fraenkel, *Horace* (Oxford, 1957), 198.

of 1.37, however, is on human initiative and autonomy. It is human resources that fashion the victory celebrated in the first part of the poem, and still more is it uniquely human qualities that enable Cleopatra to salvage victory from defeat in the second.

It is a vast stride from the helplessness of humans in 1.33 to the human grandeur of 1.37, but it is a step taken not without preparation. In retrospect we can see that the three intervening poems, 1.34–36, all lead up to 1.37. 1.34 may deal with conversion, with human response to divine initiative, but it also, like 1.29, deals with our ability to change course, to move out of patterns in which, like the humans of 1.33, we seem inextricably bound. Moreover, the very fact that the Horace who in 1.3 stood apart from Vergil's sailing is now himself daring the sea represents a step forward. In addition, Horace's change of course here leads not to the conventional piety one might have expected but instead to open and honest confrontation with the unknown powers that shape our lives (1.34.9 ff.).[38] These concluding lines of 1.34, with their marked shift away from the light tone on which 1.34 began, lead naturally into 1.35, the first forty-line poem since 1.12 and the first poem since 1.2 in which Horace openly alludes to the horrors of the civil wars.[39] The very fact that he is now confronting not the incessant tiffs of the erotic universe, as in 1.33, but the looming realities of recent civil strife, not lovers' subservience to the petty laws of Venus but our subjection to the fearsome rule of *Fortuna*, looks ahead to Cleopatra's confrontation with historical and philosophical reality in 1.37. And 1.36, after its gracious acknowledgment of divine assistance, also emphasizes, although on a lower plane than in 1.35, human activity—the friendship of youths who have

[38] On the significance of Horace's "conversion" in 1.34, see K. J. Reckford, "Horace, *Odes* 1.34: An Interpretation," *Studies in Philology* 63 (1966): 499–532. Reckford sees the poem as moving toward adventurousness, commitment, new experiences.

[39] On Horace's indirect allusions to the civil wars in 1.14 and 1.15, see above, p. 80.

grown up together (6 ff.), love whose tight bonds (cf. 18–20) are more voluntary than the oppressive bonds of 1.33.10–16, joyful shared celebration that in its verbal motifs as well as in its theme leads directly into 1.37. Moreover, the safe return celebrated in 1.36 responds both to the *serves iturum Caesarem* of 1.35.29 ff. and to the anxiety over Vergil's departure in 1.3, the poem that balances 1.36 in the overall symmetry of Book 1: humans *can* make the voyage; human initiative is *not* necessarily self-destructive.

The real answer to 1.3, of course, comes in 1.37, a poem that with its Alcaean model and serious theme fulfills the implicit promises of 1.32. The courage of Cleopatra, who seeks no safe harbor (1.37.23–24), is of a piece with that explored in 1.3, and the kinship is emphasized by a number of significant verbal ties:

nec timuit . . . nec (1.3.12–14)	*nec . . . expavit . . . nec* (1.37.22–23)
siccis oculis . . . vidit (1.3.18–19)	*visere . . . vultu sereno* (1.37.25–26)
audax (1.3.25 and 27)	*ausa* (1.37.25)[40]

In both 1.3 and 1.37 human audacity arouses mixed feelings in Horace, but his ambivalence finds strikingly different expression in the two poems. 1.3 in the end seems to suggest that audacity in all its forms is dangerous and to be avoided, be it even the audacity of a Hercules or a Prometheus. 1.37, in contrast, clearly distinguishes between the deluded audacity that fueled Cleopatra's dreams of conquest and the clear-eyed courage that enabled her to win a noble death, a distinction that permits Horace to praise one side of Cleopatra's audacity as warmly as he condemns the other. The movement of the

[40] Professor Charles Babcock has pointed out the following additional links between 1.3 and 1.37: *monstra*, 1.3.18, *monstrum*, 1.37.21 (both associated with the sea); *nefas*, 1.3.26, *nefas*, 1.37.5; *macies et nova febrium . . . cohors*, 1.3.30–31, *contaminato cum grege turpium morbo virorum*, 1.37.9–10. On the place of 1.37 in the collection as a whole, see V. Pöschl, *Horazische Lyrik. Interpretationen* (Heidelberg, 1970), 72–74.

poems is also significantly different, with 1.3 opening with
praise of human courage and ending in condemnation, while
1.37 reverses this movement so as to end on a note of affir-
mation, a shift of emphasis that is all-important and that com-
plements the thematic movement of the book.

If clarity of vision and courage characterize Cleopatra in
1.37, these same qualities become increasingly characteristic
also of the poet himself as he approaches the end of Book 1.
Here for the first time Horace speaks about real persons and
real events with the moral energy and discrimination that we
associate with the poet of the *Satires* and the best of the *Epodes*.
He can in 1.35 voice genuine concern for Augustus's safety,
but he does not mask the fact that any thought of Augustus
inevitably carries with it memories of the civil wars (cf.
1.35.29–38). He can praise Caesar for defeating Cleopatra, but
his praise does not rule out an expression of the admiration
he feels for the defeated queen, and the hawk simile that
provides the fulcrum of the poem implicitly suggests the po-
tential for violence in Caesar.[41] Noteworthy also is the contrast
between 1.37 and 1.14. 1.37, like its Alcaean model, openly
deals with political issues and is appropriately cast in Alcaics,
that meter which Horace will use with ever-increasing fre-
quency as the vehicle for his most heartfelt concerns. 1.14,
on the other hand, clearly imitates Alcaeus but masks its public
concern in impenetrable allegory and does not use the Alcaic
meter. There is still, of course, nothing approaching a probing
examination of what Augustus stands for. 1.35 contains but
a passing reference to him and the by-now familiar cliché that
futilely looks to foreign conquest as the means to purge in-
ternal problems (1.35.38–40, cf. 1.2.51–52, 1.12.53–56,
1.21.13–16); and 1.37 offers little more than a still hyperbolic
account of his military victory. Horace will not really tackle
the substantive issues associated with Augustus until the Ro-
man Odes, but at least here at the end of Book 1 he speaks

---

[41] On this simile, see Commager, *Odes of Horace*, 91.

with a new integrity, a new energy and candor, and largely without the rhetorical excesses that vitiated 1.2 and 1.12.[42]

It is perhaps because the Horace of these final poems is at last confronting the real world and speaking in his own voice that he can end Book 1 on so peaceful a note. The diminutive 1.38 is not without melancholy, not without its wistful glance toward the last rose of summer, but it is the poem of a man who knows who he is and where he stands. For 1.38, slight as it is, is not without moral content. The themes of simplicity, of rejecting luxurious excess, of knowing what one truly needs, both recall the crucial 1.31 and foreshadow key themes of Books 2 and 3. As in 1.37, the focus is on conscious human choice, the decision to act one way rather than another. This theme, handled heroically in 1.37 and with supreme modesty in 1.38, provides the logical conclusion to the thrust toward human initiative in the second half of the book. It also looks ahead to the more developed discussions of moral issues that will come in Books 2 and 3.

The final twelve poems of Book 1 thus function as two sub-groups of six poems each that move in roughly parallel fashion. The effect of these two groups is to extend the positive thrust of 1.20–26 and, further, to counter the essentially negative movement of the first groups of Book 1. The thrust of this final section is toward affirmation of human initiative, toward confrontation of real issues and the real world, toward magnitude of theme and execution. Again the actual lengths of the poems subtly embody this tendency, with the 21-line average of 1.27–38 finally reversing the downward movement that had led to the 16.57-line average of 1.20–26.

The rising movement that characterizes the end of Book 1 is apparent not only in the parallel rising thrusts of 1.27–32

---

[42] Cf. the movement from the formal address to Maecenas in 1.1 to a more informal address to him in 1.20. In the same way, Horace's extraordinary directness toward Maecenas in 2.17 will point the way to a comparable directness toward Augustus in 3.24. On the change of tone between 1.1 and 1.20, see M. S. Santirocco, "The Maecenas Odes," *TAPA* 114 (1984): 244–245.

and 1.33–38 but also in the relationship between these two groups. For while both groups move in similar directions and by analogous steps, the upward surge of the second reaches higher and is far more assured than that of the first, a discrepancy whose magnitude and significance are but inadequately reflected in the modest increase from the 20-line average of 1.27–32 to the 22-line average of 1.33–38. A more valid index of the degree by which the second group outstrips the first emerges from a comparison of analogous poems in the two groups. Contrast, for instance, Horace's impatience with Tibullus's absorption in erotic complaints in 1.33 with his own complete immersion in convivial and erotic concerns in 1.27; Horace's own dramatic change of course in 1.34, the gravity of tone that suddenly infuses the second half of this poem, with his bemusement over Iccius's change of course in 1.29, the distanced levity that characterizes all of that poem; the urgency and immediacy of 1.35, its focused discussion of national, moral, and philosophical issues, with the uncertainty of context, the distanced setting, and the relatively narrow range of 1.28; the celebration of Numida's return, the thanksgiving for the gods' past help, in 1.36, with the prayers that Venus may come, the as-yet-unfulfilled hopes for divine aid in 1.30; the vigor, drama, and passion of 1.37, again with a strong sense of completion and accomplishment, of prayers answered, with the gentler quality and narrower scope of 1.31, again with a sense of a journey that is still beginning, of prayers still to be answered; or even the calm assurance and stability of 1.38, the firm impression that Horace knows where he stands, with the restive, still questing quality of 1.32, the impression that the poet is still charting his course. While the parallel rising movements of 1.27–32 and 1.33–38 both contribute materially to the upward surge on which Book 1 ends, at every point the poems of the second group rise higher than their counterparts in the first, attaining a seriousness and scope, a degree of assured involvement and initiative, a sense even of fulfillment and completion, that are lacking in the earlier group.

It is in the upward surge of this final section that the long arc of Book 1 finds its natural conclusion, in its final poems that thematic movements introduced in the opening poems of the book find at least their intermediate destinations. A brief survey of the contrasting stances taken in the concentrically balanced outside poems of the book suggests, moreover, how far Horace has progressed by this stage of his journey. While in 1.6 he abjures larger themes for smaller, in 1.33 he twits Tibullus for his unceasing obsession with erotic subjects,[43] and in the poems that follow he himself turns to larger themes. In 1.5 he leaves the sea, and the placement of this poem immediately before 1.6 suggests that 1.5's concluding celebration of Horace's freedom from involvement is not unrelated to 1.6's emphasis on his departure from larger themes; in 1.34, by contrast, he again sets his sails for the open sea, and the placement of this poem immediately before the *Fortuna* ode, coupled with the way the second half of 1.34 leads into 1.35, suggests that the change of course signalled in 1.34 is not unrelated to his resumption of larger themes in 1.35 and 1.37. In 1.4 the initial burst of springtime activity yields to resignation before death at the end of the poem, while in the balancing 1.35 initial despair over the power of *Fortuna* gives way at the end to vigorous initiative taken on Caesar's behalf and to hopes for a better future. In 1.3, as we have seen, Horace turns away from bold departures, while in the balancing 1.36 he welcomes the traveler home. In the same way, the modest garlands of 1.38 provide some fulfillment of the hope for the Muses' garlands in 1.1, and the fulfilled prayers of 1.37, the celebration of the defeat of Antony and Cleopatra, correspond to the anxiety of 1.2, its desperate hopes for an end to civil strife. In place of flood waters unleashed (1.2.5

---

[43] On the tone of 1.33 and especially of *miserabilis* . . . *elegos* (2–3), see B. Otis, "Horace and the Elegists," *TAPA* 76 (1945): 186; A. J. Boyle, "The Edict of Venus: An Interpretative Essay on Horace's Amatory Odes," *Ramus* 2 (1973): 173 ("the eternal whine of the elegist"). Along with most modern scholars, Otis and Boyle follow the scholiasts in identifying the Albius of 1.33 with the poet Tibullus.

ff.), *nova monstra* at large (1.2.6), Rome's buildings threatened (1.2.15–16), 1.37 offers a sea purged of its menace, a *monstrum* subdued (21), the threat to the *Capitolium* (6) dispelled (12 ff.); where in 1.2.1 ff. the earth felt the blows of an angry *Pater*, in 1.37.1 ff. it is to be pounded by the joyous dance of free feet. For the desperate *Iam satis* of 1.2.1 Horace can now answer *Nunc est bibendum, nunc . . .* (1.37.1).

Conclusion

The movement within the four groups of Book 1 thus builds upon and complements the chiastic arrangement of the groups. The two outside groups balance each other not only in their similar concentric configuration but also in their superimposed division into two parallel groups of six poems. In both sub-groups of 1.1–12 the dominant movement is away from magnitude, involvement, and initiative, while in both sub-groups of 1.27–38 the movement is back toward such qualities; and just as the movement of 1.33–38 rises to a greater sense of magnitude and assurance than does 1.27–32, so 1.1–6 begins at a higher point than does 1.7–12.

The mirror-like relationship of these outer groups is reproduced in the similar relationship of the two inner groups, 1.13–19 and 1.20–26. In neither of these is there the strong sense of movement found in the outer sections of the book, but the groups clearly complement each other in structure and theme, and the progression from the serious 1.14–15 to the lighter 1.17–18 in the first group is reversed in the movement from the lighter 1.21–22 to the darker 1.24–25 in the second. In addition, the focus on escape in 1.13–19 clearly extends the dominant momentum of 1.1–12, while the involvement and initiative implicit in 1.20–26 prepare for the rising movements of 1.27–38.

The fulcrum of the book comes between 1.19 and 1.20, but not all the changes of direction take place at that point. In terms of actual length the turnabout does not come until the final twelve poems, with all the previous groups showing marked declines:

1.1–6	30.67 lines average length
1.7–12	26.67
1.13–19	23.43
1.20–26	16.57
1.27–32	20
1.33–38	22

It is worth noting in the same connection that while this steady decline is clearly reversed in the final twelve poems, the average length of poems in this final group (21 lines) still falls far short of that in the first twelve (28.67 lines). On the other hand, the poems of 1.13–19 already contain hints of the movement back toward involvement, so that while the actual decline in magnitude is not arrested until late in the book, already at an early stage there are clear signs of the resurgence of initiative and energy that will eventually lead to poems of more substance.

Book 1 represents the first stage of a long journey, and we have suggested that the distance already traversed is considerable. At the same time, Horace still has a long way to go before he fulfills the high expectations raised by the opening poems of Book 1. Not yet is he in a position to claim for himself the sort of energy and daring he associates with Vergil in 1.3. He can admire such qualities in Cleopatra, but as for himself, he chooses still to end on the more reflective, more passive, more withdrawn note of 1.38. Nor has he fully answered the questions so dramatically raised in 1.2. 1.35 voices his heartfelt concern for Caesar, 1.37 his unqualified joy in the defeat of Antony and Cleopatra that in effect ended the civil strife. But neither 1.2 nor 1.37 links Caesar with much other than military victory, while both 1.2 and 1.35 clearly suggest that the task of purgation and restoration will require moral leadership, not just martial force:

Conclusion

audiet civis acuisse ferrum
quo graves Persae melius perirent,
audiet pugnas vitio parentum
    rara iuventas.

· · · · · · · · · · ·

cui dabit partis scelus expiandi
Iuppiter?
      (1.2.21–24, 29–30)

eheu, cicatricum et sceleris pudet
fratrumque. quid nos dura refugimus
    aetas? quid intactum nefasti
      liquimus? unde manum iuventus

metu deorum continuit? quibus
pepercit aris?
      (1.35.33–38)

The answers given in 1.2 and 1.35 to these profound problems, namely recourse to divine aid (1.2) and military exploits against distant enemies (1.2.51–52, cf. 22; 1.35.38–40), both skirt the basic issue and are a far cry from the more substantial (and tougher) answers Horace will offer in Book 3.

Finally, the lofty poetic goals voiced in 1.1.29–36 also seem still largely unfulfilled. 1.31–32, despite their advance over 1.6, still emphasize limited ambitions and light poetry, and even the splendid poems with which the book ends do not in length approach 1.2 and 1.12. These final poems do, however, establish a new course for Horace, as 1.34 metaphorically suggests. The explicit identification of Alcaeus as Horace's model in 1.32, the clear emphasis on moral qualities in 1.31 and 1.35, the admiration voiced for the resolute independence of Cleopatra in 1.37—these are the significant early stages of movements that will gather momentum in Book 2 and will reach their true *telos* in Book 3.

CHAPTER III

BOOK 2: DEATH AND POETRY

nec Stygia cohibebor unda

Introduction

We have seen that the overall pattern of Book 1 contains in its first half a gradual retreat from the great issues raised in the opening poems, in its second half a gradual return toward such issues. National themes, powerfully introduced by 1.2 but merely touched upon in the center section of the book, begin again to become focal in the final poems (1.35 and 1.37). Man's mortality, a theme dramatically sounded in 1.3 and 1.4 but increasingly submerged in subsequent poems of the first and second groups, again emerges as a central concern (1.24, 1.28, 1.35), and basic moral issues of a sort almost totally absent after 1.3 begin also to loom larger (1.31, 1.35, 1.37). From poems set in the artificial world of erotic, sympotic poetry Horace moves back toward poems in which contemporary Roman citizens and Roman issues hold center stage, and an overriding sense of the constraints that limit human aspirations begins to yield to a suggestion of our capacity to initiate action and significantly shape our lives. Horace's image of his own role as poet, grandiosely articulated in 1.1 but severely diminished in 1.6, begins to regain stature in 1.17, 1.22, and especially 1.31–32, and the actual size of his poems, steadily on the decline through most of the book, begins again slowly to build. More important than this numerical lengthening in the final poems of the book, however, is the fact that the magnitude of the larger poems, 1.28, 1.35, 1.37, is now

genuine and not merely apparent. Gone are the lengthy cat-
alogues of divine allies and Roman heroes that characterized
1.2 and especially 1.12. Of empty bombast all that remains
is the chauvinistic touch on which 1.35 ends and the exag-
geration in Horace's account of Actium and its aftermath in
1.37; in other respects these two poems deal with real persons,
issues, and feelings.

Horace has so shaped Book 1 as to suggest that he is now
ready to tackle some of the larger issues raised therein, that
he now possesses in some measure the initiative and assurance
needed for this task. He has also, however, so shaped Book
1 as to leave largely unanswered the substantive question of
what stance he will actually take on these great personal,
moral, and national matters—how, for instance, in handling
national themes, he will push beyond the flattery and bombast
of 1.2 and 1.12; how he will deal with the central issue of the
civil wars, and his own part in them; what stance he will take
toward Augustus; whether he will espouse specific courses of
action that confront Rome's domestic problems, or continue
to fall back on "punish the Parthians" clichés. In the same
way, Horace has not revealed in Book 1 in what directions
he will develop the moral thrust implicit in 1.31 and 1.35, or
whether his confrontation with mortality in 1.24 and 1.28 will
now carry him beyond a shallow *carpe diem* stance that in
effect skirts the issue. Will his poetry now dare the great and
dangerous voyage, or will it revert to cautiously hugging the
shoreline? Such are the sorts of questions that Horace leaves
himself as still having to answer in the remainder of the col-
lection. In particular, the end of Book 1 seems calculated to
leave us guessing. For while 1.34, 1.35, and 1.37 bespeak
Horace's readiness to brave the open sea, the modest scope
and circumscribed claims of 1.38 suggest the continued pos-
sibility of a more cautious approach, so that as Book 2 opens
we still do not know what course he will choose.

What we find in Book 2 is a structure in some respects
parallel to that of Book 1. Again, as in Book 1, the opening
poems confront large issues—the civil war in 2.1 (cf. 1.2),

important philosophical questions in 2.2 (cf. 1.3), death itself
in 2.3 (cf. 1.4); and again subsequent poems turn away to
lighter matters (2.4–5, cf. 1.5–6) and express a sense of im-
potence, withdrawal, loss of initiative (2.6). With 2.7 there
begins a gradual return of initiative and impetus that builds
slowly in 2.7–12, then rapidly accelerates in the final group
of the book, 2.13–20, where Horace starts really to confront
the philosophical issues introduced by 2.2, the issue of mor-
tality raised by 2.3, and where in 2.20, the poem that leads
into the Roman Odes, he in effect declares his readiness to
take on the large national concerns raised by 2.1. The overall
parallelism with Book 1 is clear—an initial decline followed
by a gradually accelerating restoration. Again reflective sym-
metry underscores the reversal of movement that takes place,
with 2.7–12 closely mirroring 2.1–6 in structure as well as in
movement, and again the overall falling, then rising move-
ment of the book finds reflection in the changing length of
the poems. After the weighty 2.1 (forty lines) and the 30.67-
line average of 2.1–3, 2.4–6 fall to an average of 24 lines; the
next six odes (2.7–12) rise slightly to an average of 25.33; the
last eight (2.13–20), a group that contains three 40-line poems,
climb sharply to an average of 32. Also analogous to Book 1
is the way in which the final poems, 2.19–20, give expression
above all to a new sense of confidence, a new courage toward
the hazards of the unknown (cf. 1.37),[1] and the way in which,
as confidence and magnitude grow, the Alcaic meter becomes
increasingly predominant. For just as the Alcaic, used rela-
tively sparingly in 1.1–26, appears in six of the last twelve

[1] Underscoring the parallelism of 1.37 and 2.19 are a number of links
between the poems. Both are Alcaic, 32 lines long, and in the penultimate
position in their book. The centrality of Bacchus in 2.19 recalls the emphasis
on drinking and drunkenness in 1.37, the defeat of the Giants' attack on
Olympus (2.19.21 ff.) recalls the defeat of Cleopatra's threat to Rome (1.37.6
ff.), the women unharmed by the snakes in their hair (2.19.19–20) recall
Cleopatra *fortis et asperas tractare serpentis* (1.37.26–27). Cf. also the crucial *vidi*
and *vidit* of 2.19.2 and 29, the *ausa . . . visere* of 1.37.25; the *ruina* of the
maddened Pentheus (2.19.14–15) and the *dementis ruinas* threatened by Cleo-
patra (1.37.7).

poems of Book 1, so in Book 2 the Alcaic alternates with other meters in 2.1–12 but then appears in six of the final eight poems. In both books this movement toward the Alcaic meter comes in sections that contain poems dealing expressly with Horace's choice of Alcaeus as his prime model (1.31, 2.13). It is, of course, a movement that will climax in the complete dominance of the Alcaic in the first six poems of Book 3.

The parallels with Book 1, clear and significant as they are, should not, however, obscure the important structural differences between the two books. Above all, there is the fact that while Book 1 consists of two halves that closely reflect each other, Book 2 begins with two such correlative sections (2.1–6 and 2.7–12) but then progresses to a dramatic eight-poem closing group. While this final group has certain structural affinities to the opening twelve-poem section and is itself organized along concentric lines, in many respects it represents an anomalous and asymmetrical unit whose function is significantly to advance the argument. While the movement within Book 1 and the opening twelve poems of Book 2 is in a sense merely reflexive, with the second half of each regaining ground lost in the first half, the movement of 2.13–20 surges steadily forward, attaining in 2.19–20 a level of assurance unlike anything approached in Book 1 and relentlessly drawing us upward to the lofty heights of the Roman Odes.

Odes 2.1–12

The magnitude, intensity, and gravity of 2.1 are apparent from the very start. If the end of Book 1 leaves us uncertain as to whether Horace will plunge into the fray or take again to the sidelines, the opening lines of 2.1 seem at once to give us our answer:

Motum ex Metello consule civicum
bellique causas et vitia et modos

ludumque Fortunae gravisque
principum amicitias et arma

nondum expiatis uncta cruoribus,
periculosae plenum opus aleae . . .
(2.1.1–6)

The very first words make clear that Horace will again, as in
1.2, be concerned with national issues, and the lines that fol-
low strengthen the association by recalling both the theme
and the language of 1.2.[2] The impact of these opening lines
is the greater in that not until the *tractas* that begins line 7 do
we discover that it is another person rather than Horace him-
self who is to deal with the themes mentioned in the first six
lines.[3]

In placement and emphasis 2.1 also recalls 1.1. For just as
Horace begins Book 1 with a poem that voices his own soaring
poetic ambitions, so he begins Book 2 with a poem that fo-
cuses on Pollio's high literary aspirations. Horace's descrip-
tion of Pollio's enterprise recalls also 1.3, for just as there
Horace both praises the courage of those who sail the deep
and warns of the hazards of the voyage, so in 2.1.6–8 he both
praises Pollio's daring undertaking and warns of its dangers.
The thematic similarity is the more significant in that the
Vergil of 1.3, like the Pollio of 2.1, was himself at this time
also embarked on a daring literary venture, one to which the
words of 2.1 are as applicable as they are to Pollio's:

periculosae plenum opus aleae,
tractas, et incedis per ignis
suppositos cineri doloso.
(2.1.6–8)

[2] Cf., e.g., *arma nondum expiatis uncta cruoribus*, 2.1.4–5, with 1.2.21–22, 29.

[3] With the deferred *tractas* of 2.1.7, cf. the way *scriberis Vario* (1.6.1) and *nolis* (2.12.1) at once tell the reader that it is not Horace but another who is writing of the matters in question.

Nor must we forget that both 1.3 and 2.1 are themselves but stages in Horace's own poetic voyage and that these words of 2.1 have their applicability to his enterprise as well as to Vergil's and Pollio's.

If in various ways 2.1 takes us back to the high aspirations and lofty themes of 1.1–3, it also obviously builds on themes and motifs introduced at the end of Book 1. Its length, meter, mention of *ludus fortunae* (2.1.3), and emphasis on the horrors of the civil war all recall 1.35, and its vivid and detailed evocation of scenes from the recent wars takes us back to 1.37.[4] The effect of these ties is to create the impression that 2.1 is extending the rising momentum of the end of Book 1, and both in its aura of passionate involvement and in the candor with which it faces the horrors of the recent Roman past it goes beyond anything we have met there. Indeed, it goes farther even than 1.2, for it confronts the civil wars not through omen and image but through extended literal description, and instead of turning to the gods for respite and assistance, as 1.2 does midway through its course, 2.1 resolutely holds its gaze fixed on these harsh realities until the very last stanza.

2.1 also, however, prepares for the movement by which in subsequent poems of this first group Horace will, for the time at least, again turn away from such harsh confrontations. For one thing, the very movement of the poem is from an emphasis on human initiative and courage, whether in Pollio himself (lines 7–16) or in the persons of whom he is writing (17–24), to an emphasis on superhuman forces beyond our control (25–36).[5] And it is this movement from autonomy to helplessness, confidence to despair, that leads to the final stanza, where Horace suddenly declares his unwillingness to

---

[4] Note how the repetition of *iam* in 2.1.17 ff. recalls that of *nunc* in 1.37.1 ff. Cf. also the description of Cato in 2.1.23–24 (a description that has advanced beyond the *Catonis nobile letum* of 1.12.35–36) with the death of Cleopatra, also with spirit unsubdued, in 1.37. On the relationship of 1.37 to 2.1, see Pöschl, *Horazische Lyrik*, 74.

[5] The Cato passage, 2.1.23–24, acts as the crucial turning point.

write poetry of the sort he has just written, a passage that both verbally and thematically recalls 1.6.17–20.[6] The reminiscence of 1.6 is appropriate, for these concluding words of 2.1 serve the same function here as 1.6 serves in Book 1, that of distancing Horace from serious themes such as those of 2.1, casting him once again as the poet of elegant trifles, and setting him apart from those who, like Pollio and Vergil, would dare the hazardous crossing. They also remind us of what we may have forgotten in the course of the poem—that 2.1, like 1.6, has affinities to the *recusatio*, a poem that declares one's own inability, and another's ability, to take on a particular poetic assignment: *Pollio* will sing of the civil wars, *I* of lighter matters.[7]

If in 2.1 Horace probes more deeply into Rome's national trauma only to turn away at the end once more, in 2.2 he turns not to the light trifles one might expect from 2.1.37–40 but once more to serious matters. 2.2, it is true, mentions national issues only through its passing reference to Phraates (2.2.17), nor will Horace confront such topics squarely again in Book 2; but 2.2's emphasis on basic ethical concerns builds on the ethical implications of several poems late in Book 1 in the same way that 2.1 builds on the themes of 1.35 and 1.37. Implicit in 1.31, 1.35, 1.37, and 1.38 is an emphasis on the choices that determine the quality of one's life—the things one chooses to pray for (1.31.15–20, cf. 1.38 *passim*), the qualities that distinguish persons of sense from the foolish mob (cf. 1.35.21–28),[8] the manner in which one chooses to die (1.37.21–32). Such considerations come fully to the fore for the first time in 2.2, an important breakthrough that both

[6] Cf. esp. the concluding words of the two poems: *leviore plectro*, 2.1.40, *non praeter solitum leves*, 1.6.20.

[7] On the affinities of 2.1 to the *recusatio*, see Nisbet-Hubbard, *Commentary on Horace, Odes II*, 29–30; Silk, *YCS* 21 (1969): 206.

[8] Whatever the truth behind the troubled text of 1.35.21–28 (cf. Nisbet-Hubbard, *Commentary on Horace, Odes I*, 396–397), it is clear that the lines somehow point a contrast between the *vulgus infidum* of line 25 and those of more sense.

signals a return to the moral acuity of the *Satires*⁹ and also looks ahead to important thematic developments later in the collection. In particular, the emphasis on using what one has, on living modestly and contentedly within one's capacities, will assume great importance later, both in personal poems such as 2.16 and 3.29 and in public poems such as 3.1 and 3.24.

2.2 also picks up from 1.37 an emphasis on the kingdom within. Just as 1.37 gives us a Cleopatra who remains a queen despite her defeat and death (1.37.21–32, esp. 31–32), so 2.2 stresses that ruling one's spirit is more important than ruling the world (9 ff.) and confers the true crown on that person whose inner virtue remains untainted by greed (21–24; cf. *regnes* in 9, *regnum* in 21).

It is in such a context that Horace in 2.2.19 for the first time in *Odes* 1–3 uses *virtus*, a word that will appear with increasing frequency later.¹⁰ That he here introduces *virtus* in a context that stresses qualities of the spirit rather than of the body, inner victory rather than external success or triumph, is a feature whose full significance will become clear only with his climactic and final use of the word in 3.29.55. For now we need note only two further points. First, here at its first appearance *virtus* carries no military connotations (and is in fact contrasted with the martially-won restitution of Phraates). Second, the context by which the poem implicitly

⁹ The end of 2.2, *quisquis ingentis oculo irretorto spectat acervos*, seems even to recall two vivid passages from the opening satire, the *acervus* passage of *Satires* 1.1.32–44, and the *pictis tamquam gaudere tabellis* of *Satires* 1.1.72.

¹⁰ I follow Kiessling-Heinze in reading *virtus* rather than *Virtus* in 2.2.19, largely because nothing in the text seems unmistakably to suggest that *virtus* here is a divine personification. If those editors who read *Virtus* are correct, there will also be a progression from this superhuman, near-deified abstraction in 2.2.19 toward the increasingly human and personal appearances of *virtus* in subsequent poems of the collection. The other references to *virtus* are in 2.7.11, 3.2.17 and 21, 3.5.29, 3.21.12, 3.24.22, 31, and 44, 3.29.55, a "frequency curve" that moves from no mentions in Book 1 to two in Book 2, three in 3.1–15, and five in 3.16–30. OCT treats the two appearances in 3.2 also as personifications.

defines the *virtus* of line 19 is one that at every point stresses
choices that lie wholly within human powers, deliberate
courses of action that can stand unshaken by the blows of
fortune or the caprice of the "gods"—how one uses what one
has (lines 3–4), how one acts toward other humans (5–8), how
one masters one's own spirit (9–12), how one responds to
greed and the lure of gold (13–16, 21–24).

2.3 maintains the serious thrust of 2.2 and something of its
philosophical cast, with the *temperatam* of line 3 picking up
the *temperato* of line 3 of 2.2, thus drawing attention to a theme
that will become increasingly important later in the collection
(most notably in the *vim temperatam* of 3.4.66). The focus of
2.3 is less on moderation and self-control, however, than it
is on death, a theme that was prominent early in Book 1 and
that surfaced several times in its second half (1.24, 1.28, 1.35,
1.37). It is on this foundation that 2.3 builds. From the somber
moriture of the first stanza, through the dark thread of the
three sisters in the central stanza, to the doleful *ur* and *um*
sounds of the final stanza, the emphasis is everywhere on
death, Book 2's powerful first sounding of a theme that is to
be central throughout the book.[11]

This focus on death in 2.3 reveals a poet still willing to
confront significant issues rather than to flee them, but this
focus also leads him away from 2.2's emphasis on human
choice and self-reliance and toward an attitude of resignation.
The movement of 2.3 underscores this shift. Its first half leaves
room for human activity and initiative and leads up to the
emphatic *ferre iube* of line 14. Its direction shifts, however,
immediately thereafter, precisely at the center of the poem,
with the dark *dum . . . atra* of lines 15–16, and from these
lines on, the emphasis is everywhere on the superior forces
that shape human destiny. Instead of the imperatives that en-
close the first half (*memento*, 1; *iube*, 14), we have verbs that
increasingly suggest passivity and resignation—*patiuntur* (16),
cedes . . . cedes (17, 19), *potietur* (20), *nil interest* (22), *moreris*

[11] The death theme is, of course, implicit in 2.1.

(23), *cogimur* (25), *versatur* (26)—until by the end all vestiges have been erased both of that impulse to action which sounded in the first half of 2.3 and of that solid faith in human *virtus* which characterized 2.2:

omnes eodem cogimur, omnium
versatur urna serius ocius
    sors exitura et nos in aeternum
    exsilium impositura cumbae.
(2.3.25–28)

Just as in 2.1 Horace in despair takes momentary refuge in lighter topics (2.1.37–40) when confronted with the depth of horror inherent in the civil war past (2.1.25–36), so here, when confronted with the inexorable, inalterable certainty of *aeternum exsilium cumbae*, he turns at greater length to *modos leviore plectro* (2.1.40). For such is the world we enter in 2.4 and 2.5, Greek in its setting, artificial, sufficiently engrossed with its erotic obsessions to be totally isolated from the realities of contemporary Rome and effectively distanced even from the larger personal concerns of 2.2 and 2.3. 2.4–5 continue the progressive narrowing of focus that takes place within the opening poems of Book 2: from the vast scope of 2.1, its purview of a wide range of national and personal activities, Horace moves to the more personal but still broadly philosophical emphasis of 2.2 (including still a brief glance at public affairs—2.2.17 ff.), then to the far more private focus of 2.3, and finally to the severely restricted compass of 2.4–5.

The world of 2.4–5 is similar to that of 1.5 and 1.6, a world that in both books offers a haven from the harsh realities that are Horace's theme in the opening poems of the two books. Indeed, the thematic and tonal movement at the start of Books 1 and 2 proves strikingly parallel: poetic and national themes in the first poems (1.1 and 1.2, 2.1), philosophical themes, and especially an emphasis on death, in the succeeding poems (1.3 and 1.4, 2.2 and 2.3), followed by an abrupt shift to light erotic themes in the next pair (1.5 and 1.6, 2.4 and 2.5) and a return to a darker, more serious tone in the next poems (1.7, 2.6).[12]

The contrast between the dark resonances of *motum*, the first word of 2.1, and the narrowly erotic reference of *movit* in 2.4.4 and 5 vividly suggests how far 2.4 has moved from the scope and gravity with which Book 2 began—just as the contrast between the context and tone of the sea motif in 1.2 and 1.5 makes a similar point about the movement of Book 1. Again, as in 1.5, our subject is a flaxen-haired beauty, her doting but insecure lover, and a poet who in the final stanza gives assurance that he himself is no longer an interested party (1.5.13–16, 2.4.21–24). 2.4 gives us a heroine more responsible (though less dazzling) than Pyrrha, and the poem is not without its more serious touches—e.g., the *exempla* cited in 5–12, the *maeret* of line 16, the hint of moral considerations in 17–20, and the closing reference to time's passing, a theme picked up from 2.3 and poignantly applied here to Horace himself.[13] But the overall tone is of suave and sophisticated banter over topics that have an air of unreality, and the aura of human passivity and detachment is even more pronounced than at the end of 2.3: "Your love for a slave girl is just one of those things—it happens to the best of us (cf. lines 2–8). Not to worry—Phyllis is probably a slave only because of unfortunate circumstances beyond her control (cf. lines 15–16). Have faith, and let well enough alone; and, for goodness' sake, don't trouble yourself about me—I'm quite out of the picture."

This note of withdrawn passivity characterizes 2.5 also. Again the setting is Greek, again the protagonists are the stock

---

[12] The parallelism extends even to some particulars of the poems. 1.1 and 2.1: what others do, cf. what I do; both end with Muse(s). 1.2 and 2.1: civil war, need for expiation. 1.3 and 2.2: cf. *pennis non homini datis*, 1.3.35, *penna metuente solvi*, 2.2.7. 1.4 and 2.3: theme of death, and cf. *vitae summa brevis*, 1.4.15, *nimium brevis*, 2.3.13. 1.5 and 2.4: cf. Pyrrha's *flavam . . . comam*, 1.5.4, *Phyllidis flavae*, 2.4.14. 1.7 and 2.6: focus on Tibur as haven in both (1.7.12 ff., 2.6.5–8).

[13] *lucro aversam*, 2.4.19, also recalls the theme of 2.2 and especially its concluding stanza, the *integer* of line 22, the *integer* of another erotic poem, 1.22.1.

figures of the erotic universe—a lovely young girl and her eager but unhappy lover—and again the basic message, as in 2.4, is to let matters take their own course: "As surely as time passes, so surely will she eventually pursue you." This poem too has its darker undercurrents. The theme of time's passing sounds again, perhaps even more emphatically than in the previous poem (note the near-central position):[14]

> iam te sequetur: currit enim ferox
> aetas et illi quos tibi dempserit
>   apponet annos; iam proterva
>   fronte petit Lalage maritum . . .
>   (2.5.13–16)

Time's passage will affect both lover and beloved, and the swiftness of Lalage's transformation, emphasized as it is by the *iam . . . iam* of 13 and 15, carries a note of forced acceptance that ties in with the harsh animal imagery that describes Lalage early in the poem.

The poem's poignancy is the greater if we identify, as many do, its lover with Horace himself,[15] an identification that permits lines 13–15 to build on the reference to Horace's aging at the end of 2.4 and that encourages a comparison of the Horace and Lalage of 2.5 with the Horace and Lalage of 1.22. The lighthearted innocence of 1.22 is replaced here by an almost cynical realism. The exquisitely distant Lalage of 1.22 is soon to seek her lover *proterva fronte*, and Horace's single-minded concentration on his love in 1.22 yields here to his admission that Lalage will be just another in a long succession

---

[14] Reckford, *Horace*, 103–104, interprets *iam te sequetur*, 13, to mean that soon Lalage will follow Horace in growing older, a reading that lends even more melancholy to the poem and that looks ahead even more clearly to the emphasis on aging in 2.6. Note also how the *aetas* of 2.5.14 picks up the *aetas* of the two previous poems—2.3.15, 2.4.23. See also the perceptive comments on 2.5 in Boyle, *Ramus* 2 (1973): 178–180.

[15] On this possible identification, see Nisbet-Hubbard, *Commentary on Horace, Odes II*, 77 ff. Their commentary also documents the poem's roots in the erotic tradition.

of loves (17 ff.), an admission whose harshness the delicate beauty of the final six lines only heightens. These dark undercurrents of 2.5 lend the poem a certain emotional depth and effectively prepare for the melancholy of 2.6, but if anything they further reinforce its overriding sense of passivity, of humans manipulated by forces beyond their control. And despite its somewhat unexpected emotional depth, 2.5 remains solidly rooted in the artificialities of the erotic tradition and, within the design of Book 2, merely extends Horace's diversion from the more serious topics of 2.1–3.

2.6 returns us to the real world, but in terms of thematic movement it completes rather than controverts the thrust of the preceding poems. The sense of resignation and acceptance that has been growing since the second half of 2.3 finds its logical conclusion in 2.6 as Horace, weary of the sea and roads and military service (2.6.7–8), seeks a quiet haven for his old age and looks ahead to his own death. The acceptance of what the future will bring builds naturally upon the references to time's passing in the three preceding poems (2.3.13–16, 25–28, 2.4.21 ff., 2.5.13 ff.), but the calm resignation toward the future clashes sharply with the almost rebellious stance of 2.3.13–14 and indicates how far Horace has moved from the initiative and animation present early in the book. Pointing in the same direction is the contrast between the feverish activity of 2.1, a quality implicit in its very first word (*motum*) and heightened in the vivid vignettes that follow (note especially the sounds and sights of lines 17–24, the immediacy lent by the repeated *iam* in lines 17, 18, 19, and 21), and the pacific stillness of 2.6, with its quest for a secluded corner, its longing for mellow wines and mild winters, and its concluding vision of tears dampening warm ashes. Even within 2.6 itself there is a progression from the initiative, animation, and independence of the first stanza (*aditure, indoctum iuga ferre nostra,*[16] *aestuat unda*) to the utter stillness of the closing lines.

[16] Note the playful verbal join between *iuga ferre*, 2.6.2, and *ferre iugum*, 2.5.1.

Odes 2.1–12

Above all, the emphasis of the whole poem is again (as at the analogous point in Book 1) on escape, a natural conclusion to an impetus that is present at the close of 2.1, that is implicit in the *carpe diem* theme of 2.3.13–14, and that leads Horace in 2.4 and 2.5 to turn to a world largely sheltered from the troubling concerns of 2.1–3. It is fitting that in this world ruled by the *Parcae* (2.6.9) and by *Iuppiter* (18), the one first-person verb, *petam* (11), refers to Horace's search for a serene haven.

The final words, *vatis amici*, stand at the precise center of the collection—at the end of the forty-fourth poem in a collection of eighty-eight, words poised "at the still point of the turning world." But "at the still point, there the dance is," and behind the resignation and stillness of 2.6 are signs of new life.[17] *vatis amici* represents a point from which initiative and involvement will be reborn. For one thing, these very words suggest two themes that will become increasingly important, the themes of poetry and of human companionship. In addition, with this same last stanza of 2.6 Horace returns, after the digression of 2.4 and 2.5, to the theme of 2.3, the theme of death, which will become focal in the later portions of Book 2. The poem also returns from the artificial realms of 2.4–5 to the real world of Horace and his contemporaries—indeed, Horace's very use of the word *vates* at the end of 2.6 subtly foreshadows the more public character his poems will assume in the Roman Odes and even in some poems later in Book 2 itself (e.g., 2.15, 2.16, and 2.18).[18] Important also is the fact that 2.6 focuses squarely on Horace himself. For a significant aspect of the resurgence that will come in succeeding poems is the fact that in them Horace himself plays an increasingly active role. From this point of view, we may even see 2.6 as capping a subtle counter-movement in the

17 The passages are from T. S. Eliot, "Burnt Norton" II (*Four Quartets*).
18 Cf. Horace's use of *vates* at 2.20.3, in the poem that will lead directly into the Roman Odes. On the connotations of *vates* in these two poems and in the collection as a whole, see Newman, *Augustus and the New Poetry*, 130–135.

119

previous poems. Although the general progression within
these poems is clearly from action and initiative toward in-
activity and withdrawal, Horace's own role in them begins
to move in the opposite direction. The final thrust of 2.1 is
to isolate Horace from the serious concerns in which Pollio
is involved, to cast him as outside observer. Such is his stance
also in 2.2 and 2.3, in neither of which does Horace himself
appear except in the generalizing first-person plurals of 2.3,
and this role is explicitly articulated in the final stanza of 2.4.
2.5 brings Horace more into the picture insofar as we suspect
that *he* is the lover addressed, but only in 2.6 does he explicitly
come onto the stage. This gently rising counter-melody of
Horace's own involvement provides the basis for much of
what will develop in the next six poems (2.7–12) and fore-
shadows the central role he will play in most of the poems of
the second part of the book (2.13–20).[19]

In 2.7 the theme of escape remains strong—Horace's escape
from Philippi (13 ff.), the safe return of his friend (3 ff.), the
closing invitation to drink and forget (21, 26–28). The motif
of weariness sounds again in words closely reminiscent of 2.6
(cf. 2.7.18, 2.6.7–8), and the lines on Horace's flight at Philippi
(2.7.9–14) portray *virtus* as broken and a god as his only means
of escape:

> tecum Philippos et celerem fugam
> sensi relicta non bene parmula
>   cum fracta virtus, et minaces
>   turpe solum tetigere mento.

> sed me per hostis Mercurius celer
> denso paventem sustulit aere;
>   (2.7.9–14)

One must allow for the mock-epic exaggeration of the whole
passage, of course, but *fracta virtus, et minaces turpe solum tetigere*

---

[19] Cf. the way in which Horace's increased involvement in 1.13–19 fore-
shadows the more active role he will play in the second half of Book 1.

mento are strong words, and one suspects that the passage's irony hides a wound still raw, a *pudor* still alive.

On the other hand, 2.7 does herald the beginning of an upward movement that will continue virtually without break through the end of Book 2. The emphasis is no longer on death, as in 2.6, but on life. In contrast to 2.6's progression from activity to resignation, 2.7 both begins and ends in action. 2.6 finds sweetness in a quiet haven (*dulce pellitis ovibus Galaesi flumen . . . petam*, 2.6.10–11), 2.7 in wild celebration (*recepto dulce mihi furere est amico*, 2.7.27–28); 2.6 ends in the sprinkling of tears on ashes, 2.7 in the pouring of unguent, the preparation of moist garlands, and the drinking of wine at Venus's behest; the metonymic *Baccho* of 2.6.19 is replaced by Horace's own *bacchabor* of 2.7.27, the mellow Falernian of 2.6.19 by the powerful Massic of 2.7.21, the Septimius who will weep for his departed friend Horace (*vatis amici*, last words of 2.6) by the *amicus* whom Horace welcomes home (*recepto . . . amico*, last words of 2.7). Perhaps most significantly, the *tu* of 2.6.22 yields to the *ego* of 2.7.26 (at a precisely analogous place in the last stanza); the Horace who in 2.6.7–8 was weary, the passive recipient of his friend's attentions, now becomes a vigorous agent and initiator toward his weary friend (2.7.18). And where the movement of 2.6 was toward departure, whether to the distant parts mentioned in the opening stanzas or to death itself, the persistent impetus of 2.7 is toward return and restoration, a theme manifest both in Horace's recovery of his lost friend and in the *re-* compounds scattered through the poem—*redonavit* (3), *resorbens* (15), *redde* (17), *recepto* (27). The reflective *cancrizans* movement that will reverse the direction of 2.1–6 is clearly well on its way; even the passing of time, so negative a force in the previous poems, becomes in 2.7 an agent of reunion, bringing Pompeius home at long last to the friend who has been waiting for him and to the wine long since destined for their reunion (2.7.20).

In keeping with this movement toward restoration is the fact that in 2.7 Horace for the first time begins to face the traumas of his past. From the very start he alludes to his participation in Brutus's army, and if his irony toward the past seems too glib,[20] perhaps such glibness is the mask that alone enables him to confront the pain of that past. It is abundantly clear from all his mentions of the civil wars how deeply the general experience had scarred him—one thinks at once of *Epodes* 7 and 16, of *Odes* 1.2, 1.35, and 2.1. The very thought of those wars makes him ultimately turn away in 2.1, and it is scarcely surprising that throughout the first half of the collection he says nothing of his own painful involvement in those conflicts. Not until 2.7, the poem that opens the second half of Books 1–3, does he allude to Philippi directly. Lines 11–12 obviously refer to the shame and defeat of the whole republican army, but the surrounding verses, with the *sensi* of line 10 and the *me* of line 13, encourage the reader to apply this general picture to Horace himself. The very action of openly facing his *virtus fracta* represents an important step ahead, and appropriately he locates this mention in the poem that marks the reversal of momentum that will ultimately lead upward to the Roman Odes. When next he mentions Philippi (3.4.26), it is already in more balanced tones. In the same way, in 2.13, like 2.7 a significant starting point, he will first face another hitherto hidden trauma, the infamous falling tree incident.

With 2.7 the far marker has been rounded, and the next five poems work back toward where Horace was at the start of the book, in some respects falling short of this goal, in others surpassing it. The procedure, as we saw in Chapter I, involves a reversal, a retrograde version, of the movement of 2.1–6: first two lighter, erotic poems, 2.8–9, the counterparts of 2.4–5; then two more serious poems, 2.10–11, the second focusing on death (cf. 2.2–3); and a final poem, 2.12, which contrasts some imagined historical writings of Maecenas, in prose, with Horace's erotic poetry (cf. the contrast between

---

[20] On the seeming glibness of 2.7, see Nisbet-Hubbard, *Commentary to Horace, Odes II*, 109. On irony as Horace's mask in poems like 2.7, see W. R. Johnson, *The Idea of Lyric* (Berkeley, 1982), 135.

Pollio and Horace in 2.1). In the course of this progression
the artificial world of erotic lyric is slowly abandoned for the
real world of Rome, the human inefficacy that pervaded 2.3–
6 gradually replaced by a resurgent sense of initiative, in-
volvement, and freedom.

In keeping with the mirror symmetry of 2.1–12, Horace
must after 2.7 pass again through the artificial world of erotic
poetry before he again plunges into philosophical and political
subjects. 2.8–9 obviously revert to the erotic concerns of 2.4–
5, 2.8 with its delicious evocation of the devastating Barine,
a girl Pyrrha-like in both the brilliance of her glitter (cf. *eni-
tescis*, 2.8.6, *nites*, 1.5.13) and the fickleness of her breezes (cf.
tua ne retardet aura maritos, 2.8.23–24, *nescius aurae fallacis*,
1.5.11–12), 2.9 with its address to the bereaved Valgius, a
lover who, like the Tibullus of 1.33, seems perpetually mired
in elegiac complaint. The differences between the two pairs
of erotic poems are immediately apparent, however. 2.4–5
look forward in time, anticipate eventual harmony and hap-
piness in love, and draw us ever farther into their erotic
worlds. 2.8–9, in contrast, look back upon past erotic in-
volvements, view those involvements with considerable
irony, and increasingly distance the reader from their erotic
worlds, a movement that climaxes in the concluding words
of 2.9. And while 2.4–5 move from the disinterested Horace
of 2.4.21–24 to the involved Horace of 2.5, 2.8–9 reverse the
procedure, moving from the Horace who in 2.8 himself con-
fronts Barine to the Horace who in 2.9 observes Valgius's
erotic involvement from the outside. The progression both
between and within the two pairs thus creates a sense of en-
tering the erotic world in 2.4–5, of leaving it in 2.8–9.

The contents of the four poems complement and extend
this mirror-like movement. Whereas 2.4 and 2.5 emphasize
the passivity of the lover, the necessity of letting matters take
their own course, 2.8 and 2.9 increasingly stress human
agency. If the young men irresistibly drawn into Barine's
magnetic field are scarcely autonomous agents, Barine herself
certainly is—a human whose actions and intentions blithely

CHAPTER III

ignore divine sanctions and in the end win the laughter of the
goddess herself (2.8.13–16). More important, perhaps, is Hor-
ace's own stance toward Barine—amused, ironic, distanced,
a sane and positive attitude where about all he can control is
his own response!

This implicit stance of 2.8 becomes explicit in 2.9. Horace
does not make light of Valgius's loss—the *ademptum* of line
10 allows at least the possibility that Valgius is lamenting a
lover who is dead, not just one who is departed, and the
mythological *exempla* of 13–17, Antilochus and Troilus, both
support this possibility and lend depth to Valgius's feelings.
The thrust of the poem, however, is toward the cessation of
lament and the resumption of action. The sharp contrast be-
tween the *tu semper* of line 9 and the surrounding *non semper*
and *nec . . . semper* of lines 1 and 15–17 points Horace's mes-
sage plainly: there is a time to weep, to lament losses, a time
also to stop weeping, to return to living. The *desine mollium
tandem querelarum* of 17–18 openly expresses the undercurrent
of impatience implicit in the previous stanzas. With these
words Horace deftly bids farewell to the artificial world of
erotic poetry—he will not devote another full poem to it until
well into Book 3, though 2.12 will make a feint in that di-
rection. These same lines also introduce Horace's concluding
call to action (2.9.18–24), words that expressly lead back to
the real world of contemporary Rome in which the remainder
of Book 2 will largely be set:

> . . . et potius nova
> cantemus Augusti tropaea
>   Caesaris et rigidum Niphaten . . .
>   (2.9.18–20)

The three poems that immediately follow 2.9 sustain this
momentum, for 2.10 is addressed to a major public figure,
Licinius Murena, and both 2.11.1–3 and 2.12.9–12 explicitly
refer to current military concerns. 2.10 also further extends
the growing thrust toward initiative and action. As in the
preceding poems, there is no pretense that humans are in total

control—there are obviously powers loose in the world that no human can master (cf. 2.10.9–20). Humans can, however, control their own response to these superior powers, and the sense of proportion implicit in Horace's attitude toward Barine in 2.8 and toward Valgius in 2.9 becomes explicit in his advice to Murena in 2.10. To take a balanced stance toward both good fortune and bad is a choice humans can make, an action both possible and beneficial, and the emphasis throughout 2.10 is on making just such choices, taking just such action (note the emphatic futures of lines 1 and 23, the confident presents of lines 6, 7, and 13, the firm imperative of line 22). Just as 2.9 juxtaposes with inalterable loss the possibility of change (cf. 2.9.1–8, 13–18) and of action (2.9.18–24), so 2.10 recognizes the existence of superior forces but emphasizes the possibility of change (2.10.15–20) and urges positive human response within the context of these givens. Worth noting also is the fact that this response contains a moral dimension: *rectius vives*. *rectus* is a word that Horace uses repeatedly in the *Satires* and *Epistles*, rarely in the *Odes*. In the hexameter poems the word almost always carries moral connotations, and the *rectius* of 2.10.1 similarly suggests moral as well as physical uprightness. While the emphasis of the poem is clearly on survival, these opening words subtly reintroduce a moral dimension that was present in 2.10's counterpart, 2.2, but that has been lacking in the intervening poems.[21]

This moral emphasis implicit in 2.10 is suspended in 2.11, and the thrust of this poem is in one sense toward *carpe diem* escapism. In other respects, however, 2.11 marks another step forward. Like the poems that have immediately preceded, 2.11 juxtaposes aspects of life that we cannot control with ones that we can. The focus here, as in the balancing 2.3, is on the opposition between enjoyment of life and the certainty of its brevity. Again, though, as in the contrast between 2.4–5 and

---

[21] For representative instances of *rectus*, see *Satires* 1.1.107, 1.4.134, 2.1.21; *Epistles* 1.2.41, 1.6.29, 2.1.83. With *rectius vives*, 2.10.1. cf. *latius regnes*, 2.2.9, a similarity in line with 2.10's resumption of 2.2's moral emphasis. Both phrases also direct attention to aspects of life within human control.

2.8–9, there is a clear difference of emphasis, for while the stress in 2.3 is very much on the certainty of death, the impossibility of escape, that of 2.11 is instead on living life while one can. Due mention is made of the inalterable facts (2.11.5–12), but the balance of the poem emphasizes action, initiative, choice—note the emphatic imperatives with which the poem begins and ends (lines 3, 4, 22), the restless questions that start in line 11 and stretch through line 22.[22] Such questions appear also in 2.3.9–12, but whereas there they are followed by the bleak resignation of the poem's last four stanzas, in 2.11 they lead to the poem's climactic call to action (22–24).[23] The compass of 2.11 is less broad than that of 2.10—indeed, it begins with a specific renunciation of public affairs—but in restless energy and bold initiative it presses far beyond.

2.11 also marks a step ahead in terms of Horace's own involvement. We noted earlier that this involvement gradually increases through the early poems of the book (2.1–7), and this movement is sustained in 2.8–12. In 2.8 Horace is largely a bystander who watches Barine and laughs; in 2.9 and 2.10 he takes a more active role toward both Valgius and Murena; in 2.11 he again assumes the role of advisor, but this time he himself plays a prominent part in the action he recommends; and in 2.12 the central stanza of the poem abruptly zooms in on Horace himself, an appropriate conclusion to the movement of the preceding poems and an apt preparation for the central role he will play in 2.13–20.

2.12 also rounds out other progressions within 2.1–12. There is obvious irony in Horace's suggestion that Maecenas write of Caesar's victories (2.12.9–12)[24] rather than of recondite or mythological topics (1–8), but this advice nonetheless provides a deft conclusion to the movement back toward contemporary Roman concerns. Along the same lines, Horace

[22] Cf. the similarly agitated questions at 2.7.23–26.

[23] Cf. the strikingly different impact of the similarly placed *ocius* in 2.3.26 and 2.11.18.

[24] On the irony of this suggestion, see Fraenkel, *Horace*, 221, esp. note 2; Nisbet-Hubbard, *Commentary on Horace, Odes II*, 192–193.

will also direct his poetry toward what lies at hand—the charms and accomplishments of Licymnia. The progression back toward active initiative and involvement also peaks in 2.12, which not only emphasizes Maecenas's and Horace's literary activities but also creates by its mention of various topics, either those to be chosen or those to be avoided, a rich and varied pageant of human activity that ranges from Hannibal (2), Hercules (6), and Caesar (10) to the vigorous erotic by-play of the concluding stanzas. Even the unexpected change to an Asclepiad meter after the unvarying Alcaic-Sapphic alternation of the previous eleven poems embodies a theme prominent in 2.9 and 2.10 and implicit in 2.11—the possibility of change.

It is important also to recognize, however, the limitations of 2.12—not yet have we come the whole way. In magnitude and seriousness 2.12 still falls far short of 2.1. 2.12 may confront national issues, but it does so only briefly (9–12) and with little of the passion and sweep of 2.1. Moreover, its *recusatio* form is more clearly marked than is that of 2.1. Only at the end of 2.1 does Horace briefly and abruptly reject the topics he has associated with Pollio, while in 2.12 his demur on such topics is central (lines 13–16) and fully developed, and the overall tone of the poem, with its concluding description of Licymnia and her charms, is true to that demur.

At the same time, however, as these final stanzas draw the emphasis away from the more serious topics with which the poem began, they also recall several motifs from that opening section. Contrast, for instance, the gleaming (*fulgentis*, 15) eyes of Licymnia with the gleaming (*fulgens*, 8) house of Saturn, the flirtatious turn of Licymnia's neck (25–26) with the enslaved necks of enemy monarchs (12), her playful *saevitia* (26) with the savagery (*saevos*, 5) of the Lapiths, and perhaps even her dancing foot (*pedem*, 17) with the "pedestrian" (*pedestribus*, 9) histories in which Maecenas is to write of Caesar![25]

---

[25] On these and other verbal interconnections within 2.12, see G. I. Carlson, "From Numantia to Necking: Horace *Odes* 2.12," *CW* 71 (1978): 443 ff.

The verbal links between the two halves of the poem suggest a complementarity between Horace's lighter songs and Maecenas's weightier national themes, a complementarity that has important implications for Horace's verse and that leads directly into 2.13, where the love songs of Sappho and the more serious songs of Alcaeus are similarly placed side by side, their compatibility emphasized (2.13.24–32). Moreover, if the moral earnestness of 2.2 and 2.10, the national compass of 2.1, are lacking in 2.12, it is not insignificant that Horace includes in his description of Licymnia a passage that pays warm tribute to a moral quality (*et bene mutuis fidum pectus amoribus*, 15–16) and another that alludes to her participation in a national celebration (2.12.17–20). Neither passage in itself is especially impressive, but, like the implicit compatibility of Horace's verse with Maecenas's prose, they contain important hints of what is to come.

Foreshadowing is, in fact, a prime function not only of 2.12 but also of the whole group that this poem concludes. For if, as we have suggested, 2.13–20 is in several respects the "swing section" within the collection, 2.1–12 lays the groundwork for developments that will take place in this section. It draws attention to several themes that are central in 2.13–20—the themes of death and of friendship, for instance, and those of simplicity and restraint, of moderation and balance. Perhaps even more important is the fact that by the time he finishes 2.12, Horace has fully reestablished both the importance of human initiative and his own readiness to embrace such initiative, though 2.11 and 2.12 themselves do not fully exploit this potential. In 2.11 the vigorous impulse toward action remains directed toward escape more than toward confrontation, and in 2.12 Horace similarly directs his poetic energies not toward the real world but still toward the circumscribed world of erotic intrigue. 2.13–20 will more fully develop this sense of initiative and will focus it on broader, more serious issues; by the end of Book 2 the *vates* who in 2.6.22–24 is confronting his own death will literally be soaring to the skies, leaving an empty tomb behind.

Like 2.1–12, 2.13–20 opens with a dramatic forty-line Alcaic poem that recalls the first forty-line poem of the collection, 1.3. Like 1.3, 2.13 revolves around the themes of danger, death, and escape, like 1.3 it is addressed to an inanimate object (*arbos*, 2.13.3, cf. *navis*, 1.3.5) but really focuses on a poet to whom Horace feels close (Alcaeus in 2.13, Vergil in 1.3), and like 1.3 its almost stream-of-consciousness flow entails radical shifts of tone, theme, and focus. Underscoring 2.13's close affinity to 1.3 are a number of apparent Vergilian allusions, and this Vergil-imbued poem, like 1.3, follows closely upon a poem to Maecenas.[26]

As has so often been the case, however, the differences between the poems are as significant as their similarities and are directly related to the poems' differing positions in the collection. Both poems make thematic about-faces, but these reversals move in opposite directions. The flow of 1.3 is from its initial emphasis on departure, its initial admiration for human bravery, to its concluding emphasis on death, its depreciation of human initiative, a movement that coheres with and helps precipitate the downward thrust of the first half of Book 1. The thematic movement within 2.13, in contrast, is from the near-death of Horace to the continued life of poets in the underworld, from despair over death's inescapability to awe over the power of poetry to charm even the dead, a movement within 2.13 that builds upon the upward movement of 2.7–12 and that helps generate the dramatic upward thrust of 2.13–20. In 1.3 a somewhat conventional send-off to a friend turns

[26] Note especially the similarities between the underworld passage (2.13.21 ff.) and the underworld of *Georgics* 4 (perhaps also of *Aeneid* 6). Among specific links, cf. 2.13.23 with *Aeneid* 8.667 ff. (a resemblance that may point toward *discretas* in 2.13.23; one wonders, of course, which passage was chronologically prior!); and 2.13.33 ff. with *Georgics* 4.481 ff. With the Maecenas-Vergil sequence in 1.1–1.3, 2.12–2.13, cf. also the progression from 4.11 (Maecenas) to 4.12 (Vergil).

into a deeply pessimistic, almost paranoid excursus on the dangers of human enterprise and ends up with Horace shrinking from the impulse to such enterprise, while in 2.13 an initially lighthearted poem on his own narrow escape suddenly takes on darker colors only to end on a note of harmony, success, and new confidence. It is this unexpected discovery of life amidst death in 2.13 that provides the starting point both for Horace's head-on confrontation with death in 2.14 and for his subsequent affirmation of life in 2.19–20; in the same way, the note of despair on which 1.3 ends provides the backdrop both for the concluding focus on death in 1.4 and for the shift to lighter topics in 1.5 and 1.6.

Reminiscent also of 1.3 is the fact that 2.13 initially puzzles, even bewilders, by its abrupt shifts of moods, its seeming thematic and tonal incongruities, its mixture of obvious humor and exaggeration with deep feeling. But as with 1.3, this strange hybrid proves to be the vehicle for significant thematic developments, a not-atypical Horatian touch. One might compare, for instance, the puzzling Vergil poem, 4.12, the disturbing letter to Maecenas, *Epistles* 1.7, the striking but enigmatic *Epode* 16, all of which confront complex emotional situations with the tonal and thematic complexity they require and deserve, mixing humor with seriousness, irony with passion, indirection with candor.

Such is the case with 2.13, where the irony of the opening quickly leads to issues that are obviously of the greatest moment. Just as 2.7, the poem that marks the thematic turning point within 2.1–12, first confronts Horace's experience in the civil wars and at Philippi, so 2.13, the poem that introduces the crucial concluding section of this central book, first openly faces his escape from the tree. The irony and detachment that characterize the start of the poem point toward an effort to make light of the whole experience,[27] but the rapidity with which this initial humor leads into dark ruminations on death suggests that the falling tree has left its lasting emotional scars,

[27] Cf. the irony with which Horace mentions Philippi in 2.7.9–12.

an impression confirmed by the fact that the tree episode, once it is first mentioned here, persistently resurfaces in the poems that follow (in 2.17, 3.4, and 3.8). Horace's confrontation of this hitherto hidden trauma in 2.13 marks an important step forward, a significant index of a confidence and initiative that have moved well beyond the doubts and hesitations that marked 1.3 and 2.1.

Similarly indicative of this growing self-assurance is the way in which 2.13 deals with poetry and, in particular, with Alcaeus. For one thing, 2.13 affirms the power of poetry to survive death (21 ff.) and ends in an Orpheus-like portrayal of Alcaeus charming the savage and tormented creatures of the underworld. This association of Alcaeus with Orpheus in 2.13 represents, of course, yet one more link between 2.13 and Vergil, for the passage not only inevitably recalls the Orpheus scene of *Georgics* 4 but also looks back to Horace's own reference to Orpheus in 1.24.13 ff. Horace has, however, come a long way since 1.24. In that poem he reminds Vergil that not even Orpheus's music could restore Quintilius and advises Vergil to face the fact of his friend's death and to learn to live with it. In 2.13 he in effect acts upon his own advice, squarely confronting the tree incident and its intimations of his own mortality. In the very act of so doing, however, he finds in Alcaeus his own Orpheus, an apt image in that Alcaeus's example will indeed, especially in the poems that follow 2.13, point the way back toward new and expanded poetic life for Horace. The "Orphic" associations of Alcaeus also suggest a facet of 2.13 that we will only fully understand after we have reached the end of the collection—that 2.13 does indeed mark a turning point in the course of *Odes* 1–3, a point that here comes amidst the underworld scenes of 2.13 and 2.14 but that points ahead to the new life that will burgeon with 2.15–20 (cf. the repetition of the Orpheus theme in association with the pulsing vitality of Bacchus in 2.19.29–32).

In addition, Horace's portrayal of Alcaeus in 2.13 moves well beyond that of 1.32. The earlier poem emphasizes Alcaeus's ability to sing light songs even amidst his more serious

public pursuits (1.32.5–12), an obvious analogue to the focus
in the same poem on Horace's own lighter verse. 2.13, by
contrast, emphasizes the superiority of Alcaeus's serious songs
to the erotic songs of Sappho, and the shape of the poem
makes clear that it is Alcaeus whom Horace has now chosen
as his model. The shift of emphasis from 1.32 to 2.13 again
suggests Horace's growing willingness to tackle larger topics
and themes, a major step beyond the stance taken in 2.12.13–
28 and the start of a progression that leads through the serious
topics of 2.14–18 into the surging confidence of 2.19–20 and
hence to the Roman Odes at the start of Book 3. 2.13's treat-
ment of Alcaeus thus acts as catalyst for much of what follows,
and it is no accident that of the fourteen poems from 2.13
through 3.6 only two are not in the Alcaic meter.

Horace's growing confidence finds expression in other
forms also in 2.13. There is, for instance, the central position
he himself holds in the poem, a natural outgrowth of the
increasingly prominent role he has played in the poems leading
up to 2.13. There is also the ease with which he mingles serious
topics with light, personal with mythological, Roman with
Greek, a development beyond 2.12, where the complemen-
tarity of Maecenas's serious writings and Horace's light songs
is at most implicit, and a clear analogue to the picture 2.13
gives of Sappho and Alcaeus, where the erotic songs of the
one and the serious songs of the other fruitfully coexist:

utrumque sacro digna silentio
mirantur umbrae dicere;
                (2.13.29–30)

Above all there is the almost apocalyptic tone of the poem,
the sense of a poet for whom an accidental brush with death
has suddenly cast an entirely new perspective on life. Again
one is reminded of 1.3, where Horace's contemplation of a
simple event, Vergil's departure, suddenly leads him to look
at the whole of life from a new angle. Like the poems them-
selves, however, the two apocalypses lead in opposite direc-
tions. In 1.3 the vision of the turbulent sea (*qui vidit mare*

turbidum, 19) catapults Horace unexpectedly into the poem's pessimistic second half (21–40) and leads him to condemn human enterprise and audacity. In 2.13, on the other hand, Horace's near-death and his musings on death suddenly evoke the vision of the underworld (*quam paene furvae regna Proserpinae . . . vidimus*, 21–22) that fills the second half of the poem, a passage where Horace implicitly commits himself to a more daring conception of his own role. Whereas the vision of 1.3 suddenly highlights our fragility and our mortality, that of 2.13 as suddenly suggests our capacity to survive death. The *quam paene . . . vidimus* of 2.13.21–22 in turn leads directly to other visions in this same group—to the *visendus* of 2.14.17, the *vidi* of 2.19.2, and the *visam* of 2.20.14, all of them with similarly apocalyptic overtones.[28]

The dark tones of 2.14 contrast sharply with the note of affirmation on which 2.13 ends, and in terms of the overall movement of Book 2, 2.14 apparently marks a step backward from the confidence of 2.13, a slightly lower starting point from which to begin the upward surge of the remainder of the book. The very pessimism of 2.14 is directly related, however, to the resolute courage of 2.13. For just as in 2.13 Horace confronts his own near-death for the first time, so in 2.14, building on the reflections of 2.13.13–20, he confronts the fact of our mortality more directly than he has done before. Indeed, his very willingness to undertake the head-on confrontations of 2.13 and 2.14 is itself testimony to his rising tide of determination and courage. The Horace who in 2.13.26–28 praises Alcaeus as one who dares sing *dura navis, dura fugae mala*,[29] *dura belli* is the same Horace who in 2.14

---

[28] Note the near-central position of these words in 1.3, 2.13, 2.14, and 2.20 (cf. the outside positions of *vidi* and *vidit* in 2.19.2 and 29). The *visentur* of 2.15.3 may be part of the same network.

[29] The primary meaning of *fugae* in 2.13.28 may well be "exile," but in the context of other passages in the collection (e.g., *celerem fugam*, 2.7.9, *fugacem . . . virum*, 3.2.14) it carries at least connotations of "flight." That Alcaeus too had experienced *dura fugae mala* made him the more apt an exemplar for Horace. See Johnson, *The Idea of Lyric*, 136–137.

can face the harshness of death. The poems in a sense offer contrasting but complementary visions of the underworld, for it is the hope implicit in what follows the *quam paene . . . vidimus* of 2.13.21–22 that enables Horace in the underworld vision of 2.14 to contemplate death in all its horror.

Moreover, the grim message of 2.14 implicitly suggests two different stances toward death—either a resigned acceptance of the inevitable or a determined and vigorous use of the time one has. Within the previous group 2.3 and 2.11 point toward these alternative responses, with the resignation on which 2.3 ends carrying over to the mood of 2.6, the vigorous activity of 2.7 foreshadowing the energetic resistance on which 2.11 ends. 2.14 does not explicitly choose between these alternatives, but Horace's inclination is clear from the poems that immediately follow. For without exception 2.15–20 focus, albeit in different ways, on life and on living, on action and activity and initiative. In addition, these poems go far beyond the mere *carpe diem* stance with which 2.11 faces death. 2.15, 2.16, and 2.18 emphasize the moral choices and distinctions that enable one to live life well; 2.16, 2.17, and 2.18 all stress the warmth of human friendship, with 2.17 explicitly posing such companionship against a backdrop of death (*supremum carpere iter comites parati*, 11–12); and 2.16, 2.18, 2.19, and 2.20 all make Horace's poetry the focal point around which he builds his life. In terms of the larger movement of the book, 2.14 thus functions less as an end than as a beginning. For just as Horace's confrontation of his own near-death in 2.13 leads him to a new and broader vision of his poetic role in the second half of that poem, so 2.14's more general confrontation with our mortality serves as the springboard from which Horace develops in 2.15–20 a new and broader vision of how one should live life. In terms of the book as a whole, even the seemingly bitter final lines of 2.14 foreshadow the constructive thrust of 2.15–20. The *heres* of 2.14.25–28 may be a wastrel, but he is *dignior* (25) in that at least he chooses to live life while he can (cf. the similar suggestion at 2.11.4–5). And before one can consider *how* best to use life, the topic of 2.15–20 (and indeed of much of Book 3 as well), one must first confront both the fact of our frailty and also the fact of our capacity, both that we shall die and that "something ere the end, Some work of noble note, may yet be done."[30]

A new and broader focus is immediately apparent in 2.15. The poem is slight, and Horace's involvement is only peripheral—again, as in the progressions from 2.1 to 2.7, 2.8 to 2.13, there is a movement from poems in which Horace is primarily a bystander (2.14–15) to poems in which he holds center stage (2.19–20), with 2.16–18 here aptly representing the intermediate stages. The contribution of 2.15 is considerable, however, for here for the first time in the collection Horace devotes an entire poem to larger societal problems. As recently as 2.12 he was still suggesting that others must handle public issues; now, almost imperceptibly, he himself begins to deal with issues intimately related to Augustan programs.[31]

It is part of the larger design that only later in the collection will Horace develop these themes fully and associate them explicitly with Augustus, but the very act of focusing on peacetime domestic issues in 2.15 represents an important first step. The significance of this step is apparent when one thinks back to earlier national poems that, like 2.15, focus on contemporary issues, on the here and now. *Iam satis* begins 1.2, *Nunc est bibendum* 1.37; *iam . . . iam . . . iam . . . iam* sings 2.1.17 ff. But whereas the *iam* and *nunc* of these poems always refer to events associated with the civil wars, the *iam* with which 2.15 begins refers to a contemporary *social* issue. The continued impact of the wars is all Horace can think of in the early poems; virtually no attention is given to where society should move once these wars have become a thing of the past, and this lack of positive, practical suggestions for the future is a troubling aspect of both 1.2 and 1.12, one that remains

[30] Tennyson, *Ulysses* 51–52.
[31] Cf. Nisbet-Hubbard, *Commentary on Horace, Odes II*, 243, on the implicit connection between 2.15 and the programs of Augustus.

even in the otherwise more satisfying 1.35 and 1.37. 2.15 charts no dramatic course for the future, but it does move beyond total absorption in the civil wars: its *iam* looks to problems facing post-war Rome. It too turns to the past (10–20), but even here it looks beyond the civil wars—to an earlier, better time, one that may provide fruitful models for the Rome of the present (cf. the brief gesture in this direction in the catalogue of 1.12, the fuller exploitation of this pattern in the Roman Odes).

2.15 also marks a step beyond 2.2. For while the emphasis on positive moral choice in 2.2 provides the foundation on which 2.15 and subsequent poems build, the focus of 2.2 is on private morality while that of 2.15 is on issues that affect the whole society, a clear move toward the express consideration of larger, more public contemporary issues in 3.1–6.

Just as toward the end of Book 1 Horace moves from the brief 1.34 (sixteen lines) to the closely related but longer 1.35 (forty lines), so as he approaches the climax of Book 2 he builds the longer 2.16 (forty lines again) on the foundation laid by the briefer 2.15 (twenty lines). Again, as in 2.15, his focus is on life, not death; again he is concerned with moral choice—not just with living but with living well (cf. *vivitur . . . bene*, 2.16.13); and again his emphasis is on simplicity of life (2.16.13–16, 37–40, cf. 2.15.13–14). In other respects, however, 2.16 clearly outstrips 2.15—in magnitude, in scope, in degree of personal involvement, in sheer vigor and vividness of language. It is twice as long as 2.15, and it broadens the scope of 2.15 so as to deal not just with the public issues of 2.15 but also with individual morality, with poetry, with the tension between the cares and fears that hover about us and our longing for peace of mind. 2.16 thus retains the moral breadth of 2.15 but mingles with it a personal focus lacking in 2.15. For while 2.15 deals in broad generalities and does not bring Horace himself into the poem, 2.16, especially at the end, directly and poignantly relates its larger themes to the poet himself.

Three points about 2.16 are of particular importance. First, the effect of the poem is in many ways to answer the dilemma posed by 2.14. 2.16, like 2.14, emphasizes the inevitability of death (17 ff., 29 ff.), but to this fact of our existence it proposes a response that transcends the potential superficiality of *carpe diem*. For while the two central stanzas (lines 17–24) and the balancing third and eighth stanzas (lines 9–12, 29–32) emphasize our inability to escape death and anxiety, the two intervening (and again balancing) stanzas, lines 13–16 and 25–28, propose positive, specific, and related patterns of life that can minimize anxiety and make the most of what life we have:

vivitur parvo bene, cui paternum
splendet in mensa tenui salinum
nec levis somnos timor aut cupido
    sordidus aufert.
        (2.16.13–16)

laetus in praesens animus quod ultra est
oderit curare et amara lento
temperet risu; nihil est ab omni
    parte beatum.
        (2.16.25–28)

The emphasis of 2.14 is clearly on death, that of 2.16 as clearly on life, and the life it recommends is no mere negative escape. For while the poem begins with an *otium* that is largely negative in content, simply an antonym to *negotium*, the *otium* that it recommends in lines 13–16 and 25–28, like the *otium* with which it ends (37–40), is positive in content, the product of human initiative, involvement, and conscious choice, an *otium* that one may well describe by the *vivitur . . . bene* of line 13.

    Second, the poem clearly relates moral values to poetic values, Horace's life-style to his poetic style.[32] *vivitur parvo*

---

[32] See H. J. Mette, " 'genus tenue' und 'mensa tenuis' bei Horaz," *MH* 18 (1961): 136–139. Note also how 2.16.31–32 gives a positive twist to a phrase that in 2.5.14–15 had negative connotations.

bene (13) is clearly of a piece with the *parva rura* that Horace mentions in 37, these *parva rura* of a piece with the *spiritum . . . tenuem* of Horace's Muse (38), and this *spiritum . . . tenuem*, in turn, of a piece with the *mensa tenui* of 14. Only one previous poem in the collection has thus linked Horace's moral and his poetic values, 1.31. The relevant passage there, 1.31.15–20, points in the same direction as does 2.16, but it neither develops the implications of *frui paratis* (1.31.17), as do 2.16.13–16, 25–28, nor does it establish 2.16's close verbal link between a modest life-style and the choice to write poetry that is slender and refined.

The third point relates also to this very emphasis on the *parvum* and the *tenue* in 2.16. In several earlier poems—1.6, 2.1, 2.12, etc.—Horace either explicitly or implicitly builds an opposition between poetry that is *tenue* or *parvum* and that deals with trivial concerns and poetry that is *grande* and that deals with Important Matters. In 2.16, however, Horace implicitly bridges this opposition by writing a poem that is substantial both in bulk and in theme but that in both word and tone retains his allegiance to the *parvum* and the *tenue*. It is a step that obviously builds on, extends, and relates to Horace himself 2.13's implication that the serious poetry of Alcaeus and the lighter verse of Sappho can coexist. Moreover, whereas in earlier poems *tenue* and *parvum* suggest artificial realms into which to retreat, in 2.16 *vivitur parvo* and *mensa tenui* point toward ways of dealing with the world, and Horace's own *parva rura* and *tenuis spiritus Camenae* become the source of his strength and inner peace. Even the light touch inherent in the *tenue* mode takes on a positive, active role in the slow laugh that tempers life's bitterness:

> et amara lento
> temperet risu;
> (2.16.26–27)

The close of 2.16 suggests a poet at ease with life and sure both of his poetic gifts and of his ability to deal with life's dilemmas. The same confidence carries over to 2.17. Horace's assurance is now such that he can allude to the escape from the tree not as a reminder of mortal vulnerability but as evidence that should help dispel Maecenas's obsession with death (2.17.27–30). And while in 1.1 Horace calls Maecenas his *praesidium* and even in 2.17 itself addresses him as *columen . . . rerum* (4), 2.17 conveys the impression almost of a reversal of roles—that Horace is now a source of strength and protection for Maecenas.[33] There is a marked difference also between the stance of 2.17 and that of 2.12. In 2.12 Maecenas is to deal with larger issues, Horace merely with love poetry, but in 2.17 poet and patron are on an equal footing:

> ibimus, ibimus,
> utcumque praecedes, supremum
> carpere iter comites parati.
> (2.17.10–12)

These words not only breathe a new independence toward Maecenas but also express Horace's growing confidence toward the future, the unknown, and death itself. This Horace, like the Vergil of 1.3, is prepared to dare the journey, even under the threatening gaze of Capricorn, *tyrannus Hesperiae . . . undae*, 2.17.19–20 (cf. his awe of *arbiter Hadriae*, 1.3.15). The change that has taken place is underscored by the fact that Horace's *ibimus, ibimus . . . comites* (2.17.10–12) echoes the eminently Vergilian words of the sea-bound Teucer in 1.7.26: *ibimus, o socii comitesque*. The Horace who in 1.3 was a bystander to Vergil's departure, in 1.7 a mere reporter of Teucer's heroic words, in 2.17 himself leads the way, himself now voices encouragement for the journey.

Moreover, while 2.17 lacks the broad philosophical focus of 2.16, in other respects it clearly builds on 2.16. Its concluding contrast between Maecenas's grandiose offering and Horace's humble sacrifice (2.17.30–32) closely echoes the comparison between Grosphus and Horace on which 2.16 ends, with both passages growing out of the *vivitur parvo* of

---

[33] See Santirocco, *TAPA* 114 (1984): 246.

CHAPTER III

2.16.13. On a more general level, Horace's whole attitude toward Maecenas in 2.17 recalls 2.16.25–28 in that he counters Maecenas's irrational fears (cf. 2.16.9–12, 21–24) with the same emphasis on being *laetus in praesens*, the same reminder that *nihil est ab omni parte beatum*, the same inclination to temper harsh facts with gentle laughter. Like Horace's advice to Valgius in 2.9 (the fourth poem from the end of the first group in Book 2), his advice to Maecenas in 2.17 (the fourth poem from the end of the second group) urges a cessation of fruitless complaints (cf. *mollium . . . querelarum*, 2.9.17–18, *querelis*, 2.17.1)[34] in favor of a resolute stride into the future. In different form, it is the same emphasis on life and on living that was central to 2.16, and the humor and sense of perspective with which Horace approaches his patron puts into action the precept and spirit of that poem.

Horace does not name his addressee in 2.18, but the references to his *potentem amicum* (12) and to the Sabine farm (14) seem clearly to suggest Maecenas, the more so in that Maecenas is already in mind as the named addressee of 2.17.[35] Like 2.17, 2.18 directs toward Maecenas advice that builds upon 2.16. But whereas the thrust of 2.17 is practical, a putting into action of the precept of 2.16, that of 2.18 is philosophical, an analysis of Maecenas's life-style from a standpoint similar

[34] Cf. also the call to Tibullus to cease his *miserabilis . . . elegos* in 1.33.2–3, in a poem that occupies a position in Book 1 roughly analogous to that of 2.17 in Book 2.
[35] Note how *satis beatus unicis Sabinis*, 2.18.14, recalls *nihil est ab omni parte beatum*, 2.16.27–28, one more link between 2.18 and 2.16. The reminiscence suggests that while "beatitude" is by definition not fully attainable by humans, to the extent that is humanly possible Horace is *beatus* through Maecenas's generosity—a tactful touch in a poem some have judged tactless. Horace's stance toward Maecenas in 2.18 in fact shrewdly mixes tact with candor. He phrases those lines that compliment his patron (11–14) in such a way as unmistakably to suggest Maecenas, but he leaves the poem as a whole without a named addressee so as to allow for the possibility that the *tu* of line 17 refers not to Maecenas but to a generalized type of the rich man. For this interpretation of the poem, see Nisbet-Hubbard, *Commentary on Horace, Odes II*, 289 ff. On Maecenas as the unnamed addressee of 2.18, see also Kiessling-Heinze on 2.18.12–14; Santirocco, *TAPA* 114 (1984): 246–247.

to that adopted toward Grosphus in 2.16, a similarity under-
scored by the forty-line length common to 2.16 and 2.18 and
by their several shared thematic and verbal motifs.[36] We may
note especially how the contrast between rich and poor, a
contrast emphasized at the end of 2.16 (and reiterated at the
end of 2.17) receives a new twist at the end of 2.18: while for
the rich and powerful death brings confinement (*coercet*, 38),
for the *pauper* it brings release (38–40). This ending of 2.18 is
one of the many deft touches in this section by which Horace,
in response to 2.13 and 2.14, suggests a new and more positive
attitude toward death, and as such it neatly leads into 2.19,
where the emphasis is all on life.

Above all 2.18 builds a contrast between two life-styles—
Horace's simple, modest, and satisfying way of life (1–14),
and the extravagant, overreaching, and ultimately unsatisfying
life-style of his wealthy addressee. Like so much else in the
poem, this contrast grows out of motifs introduced in the
preceding poems—out of the contrast in 2.17 between Hor-
ace's humble lamb and Maecenas's grandiose temple, the con-
trast in 2.16 between Grosphus's and Horace's life-styles, even
the contrast in 2.15 between the extravagant private buildings
of the present and the simpler ones of the past. What seems
new in 2.18 is the blunt directness of the comparison, the
open condemnation of the wealthy landowner—qualities that
go far beyond even the ironic chiding of 2.17. Even here,
though, the way has been well prepared, for one can see the
extraordinary candor of 2.18 as the natural climax of a pro-
gression that has led from the generalized plain-speaking of
2.15 to the authoritative stance taken toward Grosphus in 2.16
and hence to the bold directness of 2.17. It is a progression
that has its clear complement in Horace's ever-increasing de-
gree of involvement in these poems—off-stage in 2.15, en-
tering quietly at the end of 2.16, a full participant in 2.17, at
center stage when 2.18 begins. The candor of both 2.17 and

[36] For thematic and verbal links between 2.18 and 2.16, see above,
p. 38.

2.18 also builds naturally on the *Parca non mendax* Horace mentions at the end of 2.16: no pulling of punches here, no glozing over the hard truth.

If the candor of 2.18 reveals a burgeoning self-confidence that will become even more marked in 2.19–20, it reveals also a friendship that has progressed far beyond the formality of 1.1, the studied informality of 1.20, or the subtle flattery of 2.12, beyond even the directness of 2.17. Even in 2.17 Maecenas is not only *meae . . . partem animae* (5) but also *grande decus columenque rerum* (4), a phrase clearly reminiscent of 1.1.2, while in 2.18 he is addressed without intervening epithets or titles. So blunt, in fact, are Horace's words at some points in 2.18 that one might think them potentially offensive and see their presence as one reason why Horace does not actually name Maecenas. One must also remember, however, Horace's predilection for plain-speaking among friends—cf. the description he gives of Vergil's and Varius's introduction of him to Maecenas (*Satires* 1.6.54–55) and of his own words on that occasion (ibid., 56–60), for instance, or his emphasis in the *Ars Poetica* on the importance of candid criticism among friends (*Epistles* 2.3.438 ff.), or the directness with which he speaks to Vergil in *Odes* 1.24 and to Maecenas in *Epistles* 1.7. In this context, the blunt candor of 2.18 is the mark not of tactlessness or disrespect but of true friendship, a friendship that now permits poet to address patron as equal to equal.[37] 2.16–18 all concern Horace's relationship with a person of superior means, and in all three he speaks with considerable candor, but only in 2.18 does the tone of his address embody the relationship described in 2.17.10–12. Horace's openness toward Maecenas in 2.18 provides the basis for his three very direct poems to Maecenas in Book 3 (3.8, 3.16, 3.29). It also

[37] Cf. H. Womble, "Repetition and Irony: Horace, *Odes* 2.18," *TAPA* 92 (1961): 540: ". . . but Maecenas is called not 'patron,' but 'friend.' The usual social stratigraphy was first reversed, now eliminated, and from it has come a relationship of friend to friend, a precious distinction the poet may well claim proudly, along with honesty and wit, among his valuable possessions." See also Santirocco, *TAPA* 114 (1984): 247.

serves as a model toward which he moves in Book 3 with respect to Augustus, for by the time he reaches 3.24 he can speak to the *princeps* with a candor that approaches that with which he addresses his patron in 2.18.

The independence of Horace's stance toward Maecenas in 2.18 provides an appropriate starting point for 2.19, where Horace's rising sense of achievement and initiative bursts fully into the open. The poet who in 1.3 warned against humans who strive too high now rejoices to find himself filled with the divine *afflatus*, and the poet who in 1.6 eschewed even singing of divine-human interaction now describes his own vision of Bacchus. His description, moreover, captures both the apocalyptic nature of the confrontation (1–8) and the awesome power of the god, a power that encompasses land and sea, war and peace, heaven and earth, animal and human. That Horace now associates his poetry with this fearsome, all-encompassing force dramatically reveals how far he has come from the careful circumspection of 1.6 and 2.1.37–40, from the resigned acceptance of the *vates*' death in 2.6, and even from the joyful but circumscribed poetic aspirations of 2.12.

The vision of 2.19 builds directly on the imagined vision of 2.13 (cf. *vidi*, 2.19.2, *quam paene . . . vidimus*, 2.13.21–22). In 2.13 Horace for the first time explores the full implications of his association with Alcaeus, for the first time emphasizes the larger themes of Alcaeus's poetry, while in 2.19 he explicitly associates his own verse with a similarly enlarged view of poetry. Verbal and thematic links between 2.19 and 1.32 and 2.13 further underscore the ties between the Bacchus of 2.19 and the Alcaeus of these poems. Both the Alcaeus of 2.13 and the Bacchus of 2.19 are Orpheus-like figures who enchant their audiences and soothe even Cerberus (audiences: 2.13.29 ff., 2.19.3–4; Cerberus: 2.13.33–35, 2.19.29–32). The Bacchus of 2.19.25–28 hovers between the light and the serious, between war and peace; so does the Alcaeus that emerges from 1.32 and 2.13. Alcaeus is a poet who in 2.13 outlives his physical death; Bacchus in 2.19 is an embodiment of life at every level of the universe. In associating himself with the powerful Bacchus of 2.19, a figure so reminiscent of his earlier pictures of Alcaeus, and especially of the Alcaeus of 2.13, Horace associates himself yet further with the larger Alcaean themes mentioned in 2.13 and clearly prepares for the series of Alcaic odes that begin Book 3, odes in which he, like Alcaeus in 2.13.26 ff., sings in fuller tones of captains and kings, of war and peace, and of attack and flight.[38]

One must not, of course, take 2.19 too seriously. Its surge of confidence is real, its enlarged vision of the power of poetry a natural development of the emphasis on poetry in 2.13, 2.16, and 2.18 and a perfect introduction to the soaring poetic claims of 2.20. But Horace can never take exaggerated claims too seriously, least of all his own, and just as Bacchus himself is as fit for jest and play as he is for weightier topics (cf. 2.19.25–28), so the piquant nymphs and satyrs with which 2.19 begins and the tail-wagging, foot-licking Cerberus with which it ends warn us not to take Horace's vision without at least a raised eyebrow. Moreover, if we miss the irony in 2.19, 2.20 obliges us to take notice, for who can read the details of Horace's "cygnification" in 2.20.9–12 without open laughter?[39]

This is not, of course, to say that 2.20 any more than 2.19 is merely to be laughed at. As 2.16.26–27 reminds us, Horace does not see laughter and seriousness as mutually exclusive, and not infrequently he calls forth a laugh, and especially a laugh at his own expense, in places where he is at his most

[38] Among the links, note *aureo . . . plectro*, 2.13.26–27 (of Alcaeus), *aureo cornu*, 2.19.29–30 (of Bacchus). Note how 2.19.21 ff. prepares for the references to the repulse of the Giants and Titans in the Roman Odes (3.1.7, 3.4.42 ff.). On the place of 2.19 in the overall movement of the collection, see Silk, *YCS* 21 (1969): 204 ff. On the structure of 2.19 and its relation to other poems in the collection, see esp. V. Pöschl, "Die Dionysosode des Horaz (c. 2, 19)," *Hermes* 101 (1973): 208–230.

[39] Not all critics take 2.20.9–12 as humorous: see, e.g., C. B. Pascal, "Another Look at the Swan Ode," *Latomus* 39 (1980): 101–105; K. Abel, "Hor. c. 2, 20," *RhM* 104 (1961): 81–94, esp. 91 ff. On the other side, see the penetrating comments of West, *Reading Horace*, 90–91.

serious (cf. his own comments at *Satires* 1.1.23 ff.). If Horace deliberately undercuts the bravado of 2.20 by this touch of the absurd, it is perhaps less to discount the bravado than to suggest his own amazement that he should be speaking in these terms! For the bravado of 2.20 is so far from Horace's earlier poetic stance that, on one level, he can only laugh at the incongruity. For here is the poet of the *tenue*, the poet who in 1.3 expressly condemns mortals who fly too high, who repeatedly stresses our mortal limitations, the certainty that we must confront the underworld waters (cf. 2.14.7 ff.), himself claiming that soon he will be borne aloft, Icarus-like, on a wing that is not *tenuis*, himself asserting his future freedom from the Stygian wave, his absolute escape from mortality, even the emptiness of his tomb.[40] Whether we think back to 1.3, to 1.6, to 2.6, or to 2.14, the distance we have come to the *vates* of 2.20 is remarkable.[41] Just as remarkable is the fact that the incredible upsurge of 2.20 is maintained in the poems that follow, for in every way the tone and character of the Roman Odes live up to the extravagant Alcaic prelude provided by 2.19 and 2.20. This fact alone must prevent us from merely laughing at 2.20.

So also must the fact that in every way it is an appropriate culmination to what has preceded. Horace's movement toward increased personal involvement, his ever-burgeoning sense of confidence and initiative, his rising impulse to trumpet the reality of life in response to 2.14's solemn sounding of the death dirge, his seemingly magnetic attraction toward poetry that dares high challenges—all these lead naturally up

---

[40] I side with those (e.g., Nisbet-Hubbard) who see in the *inani* of line 21 and perhaps even the *supervacuos* of 24 a reference to a cenotaph. For a different view, see, e.g., Kiessling-Heinze.

[41] Note in particular how the immortal *vates* of 2.20.3 responds to the dying *vates* of 2.6.24 and how the *absint . . . querimoniae* of 2.20.21–22 caps the "away with complaints" motif (cf. 1.33.1–3, 2.9.17–18, 2.17.1). On the movement from 2.13–14 to 2.19–20, see above, pp. 35–37. On the way 2.20 caps the upward surge of Book 2 and prepares for the Roman Odes, see E. T. Silk, "A Fresh Approach to Horace. II, 20," *AJP* 77 (1956): 255–263.

to 2.20. Its role is real and important, whether as necessary culmination of Book 2 or as obvious prelude to the Roman Odes.

What, then, is one to make of its occasional absurdities, of the grotesque transformation of lines 9–12, the empty tomb of the final stanza, the troubling comparison of the poet to Icarus (13)? The last detail may be the best clue, for whereas in 1.3.34–35 Horace condemns even the flight of Daedalus, here he explicitly associates himself with the overreaching flight of *Icarus*. This detail, along with the other obviously ironic touches, can only suggest Horace's own uncertainty as to the course he is on. He has arrived there by a natural progression, and he is going to stay on that course in the poems which follow, but the wings on which he will fly are not familiar (cf. 2.20.1), and the direct thematic and motivic oppositions between this poem and earlier poems in the collection underscore the strangeness of the flight (cf. the opposition between 1.2/1.12 and 1.6). The flight will, moreover, like Icarus's, come to an abrupt end. From the lofty tone, the national theme, of the Roman Odes Horace will plummet in 3.7 to more personal topics, a more *tenue* style (and, perhaps incidentally, to the decisive, dividing presence of the sea above which he so easily soars in 2.20: cf. 3.7.1 ff.); the sounding Alcaics of 2.19–20, 3.1–6 will not be heard again until the second half of Book 3, and not until the penultimate 3.29 will they again be used for a large poem. The undercurrent of irony in 2.20 is Horace's way of suggesting how dangerously far he is here departing from his usual role, his association of himself with Icarus a foreshadowing of the fact that the flight he now begins may soar too high and end in an abrupt descent.[42] For the time, though, the *vates* is truly aloft, and we can only wonder somewhat incredulously at this Horatian swan, at the soaring presumption of its reckless surge, the

---

[42] Cf. Silk, *YCS* 21 (1969): 208–209, on the fall that will follow the surge of 2.19–20. Cf. 4.2.1–4, where Horace's reference to the story of Icarus again clearly suggests the dangers of poetry that, swan-like, soars too high.

total absence of those hesitations and inhibitions that so recently restricted its flight.

Conclusion

In retrospect we can see that the movement of Book 2 is in several respects similar to that of Book 1. The opening poems begin the book with grandeur of tone and magnitude of theme and conception, but this initial surge of energy and confidence fades toward despair at the end of 2.3 and is succeeded by the elegant but comparatively inconsequential erotic concerns of 2.4 and 2.5 and the total resignation of 2.6. The next six poems reverse the movement of the first six and move back toward the seriousness and the confidence with which the book began, but it is only with the final group of eight that the book really begins to soar, attaining in 2.13–14 a new boldness in confronting our mortality, in 2.15, 2.16, and 2.18 a new breadth of moral vision and seriousness, in 2.17–18 a previously unexampled directness in its manner of addressing Maecenas, and in 2.19–20 a degree of initiative and confidence unlike anything we have met before. In its larger outlines this three-part progression is not unlike the overall movement of Book 1: initial descent (2.1–6, cf. the two parallel descents of 1.1–12), a middle section that regains some ground but that does not yet attain the confidence that characterized the opening (2.7–12, cf. 1.13–26), and a concluding ascent (2.13–20, cf. the two parallel ascents of 1.27–38). The fact that the opening poems of Book 2 in a number of respects run parallel to the opening poems of Book 1 underscores this overall parallelism of the two books.

There are, however, important differences. Most important is the fact that the overall movement of Book 2 is decidedly upward, with the end of the book attaining heights far above the beginning, whereas at best the end of Book 1 moves toward the level at which the book began, in some respects falling short of that level. Again a survey of the average length of poems affords some confirmation of this general picture.

The average length of poems in Book 1 begins with a hefty 30.67 lines in 1.1–6, continually descends from there until "bottoming out" in the 16.57-line average of 1.20–26, then rises modestly to the twenty- and twenty-two-line averages of the final two groups of six (1.27–32, 1.33–38). Book 2 begins with an average of 27.33 lines in its first six poems (lower than the average of 1.1–6 but higher than that of 1.33–38), descends slightly to the 25.33 of 2.7–12, then rises to the highest level yet in the thirty-two-line average of 2.13–20.

Moreover, the construction of the two books, while somewhat analogous in the overall tripartite movement of each, is in other respects disparate. Book 1 exhibits an overall mirror symmetry in which the downward-moving 1.1–12 correspond closely to the upward-moving 1.27–38, the largely static 1.13–19 to the similarly static 1.20–26. In Book 2 the first twelve poems exhibit a mirror-like symmetry of the same sort, with 2.7–12 corresponding to and reversing the movement of 2.1–6, but the final eight-poem group contains an upward surge that has no downward counterpart in the book or the collection. This "swing section" of Book 2 is the only group within *Odes* 1–3 that does not fit into a rigidly concentric pattern. Its structurally anomalous character lends this section a special importance, and its strong upward movement is perhaps the most distinctive characteristic of Book 2, one that has no counterpart in either Book 1 or Book 3. Suggesting also the overall upward thrust of Book 2 is the fact that, as our analysis has shown, in some ways the upward movement of 2.7–12 continues through 2.13, with 2.14 marking a lower starting point for the surge that will climax in 2.19–20. Such an arrangement would balance against the opening six-poem descent of 2.1–6 two answering seven-poem ascending groups, 2.7–13 and 2.14–20, again a structural embodiment of the gathering momentum that will dramatically climax in the Roman Odes.[43]

[43] Such an arrangement merely recognizes the function of 2.7 and 2.13 as pivots: each simultaneously caps the progression of the previous group and

Conclusion

Thematically also there are significant differences between Books 1 and 2. Book 1 begins with national poems (1.2 and 1.12) and in its final group gathers courage to tackle such themes again (1.35 and 1.37), while Book 2 begins with a national poem (2.1) but never again focuses on national issues. On the other hand, Book 1 touches only lightly on questions of national and personal morality, on how to live well, whereas such questions are important in 2.2 and become focal in 2.15, 2.16, and 2.18. In the same way, the theme of death is important at selected points in Book 1, though with the exception of 1.24 these poems all fall into the first or last groups of the book. In Book 2, however, death is prominent throughout, being focal in 2.3, 2.11, 2.13–14, 2.17, and 2.20 and a major sub-theme in several other poems. One might perhaps typify the contrasting characters of the two books by saying that the achievement of Book 1 is to renew Horace's sense of courage and initiative, to restore his willingness to tackle great issues, while in Book 2 he actually directs this renewed confidence toward several such issues themselves. He dares to face his own involvement at Philippi and his own near-death in the tree incident, he tackles head-on the fact of our mortality, and, perhaps most important, he moves beyond this confrontation with death to the question of how individuals and societies can best live what life they have. He does not in Book 2 specifically confront national issues, but this confrontation will come at the start of Book 3, and Book 2 has established the necessary groundwork. The many thematic links between the Roman Odes and 2.15, 2.16, and 2.18, and the fact that implicitly these three poems of Book 2 are already dealing with issues related to national programs and concerns, underline the complementary relationship of these sections. Without the thematic, motivic, and tonal preparation of 2.13–20, neither Horace nor the reader would be ready for the Roman Odes.

---

sets in motion a new progression. 3.16 and 3.25 serve analogous functions in Book 3: see below, pp. 186 ff., 197 ff., 211 ff.

Book 2 also goes beyond Book 1 in its treatment of the theme of poetry. Book 1 early on (1.6) restricts Horace's poetry to the narrowest of scopes, and his poem on Alcaeus near the end of the book (1.32) only implicitly suggests the possibility of expanding that scope. Book 2 also early on limits the scope of Horace's verse (2.1.37–40), and the last poem of the first section (2.12) reaffirms that stance. The poem that opens the next group (2.13), however, specifically uses the model of Alcaeus to point toward larger themes, and subsequent poems build on that suggestion and lead up to 2.19–20, where Horace seems ready and able to take on virtually anything—again, obvious preparation for what is to follow.

One can, finally, catch the distinctive differences between Books 1 and 2 by simply comparing the poems with which they end—the confident, serene, elegant, and self-contained 1.38 on the one hand, an embodiment of the *tenue*, the statement of a poet content to put aside his yearning for the *rosa sera*; and, on the other, the overstated, restless, slightly inelegant, and ambitious braggadocio of 2.20, a poem that bids farewell to the *tenue*, the statement of a poet who is both amused and exhilarated to find himself soaring so high, and who is all too aware that his wings are bonded but with wax.

BOOK 3: ROME, AUGUSTUS, AND HORACE

mea virtute me involvo

Introduction

In every respect the end of Book 2 has prepared for what comes at the start of Book 3. The growing magnitude of the poems within 2.13–20 leads directly into the unprecedented size of 3.1–6, the predominance of the Alcaic in these same eight poems to the sole presence of this meter in the Roman Odes, the soaring confidence of the *vates* in 2.20 to the hieratic tones with which the *Musarum sacerdos* begins Book 3. 2.13–20 also point the way for the Roman Odes in their density, their concentrated energy, and their moral urgency. Purely erotic poems and casual drinking songs (cf. 1.6.17–20) find no place either in 2.13–20 or in 3.1–6; both groups resolutely focus on the real world, real issues, real problems, and although both take full account of the ultimate fact of death, both suggest that the best response to death is to live life wisely and well. If 2.13–20 do not themselves explicitly deal with national themes, do not attain quite the grandeur and gravity of the Roman Odes, that is only because Horace is reserving these attainments for the Roman Odes themselves and wishes to end Book 2 still on a note of unfulfilled expectation.

In the onward flow of the collection Book 3 thus grows directly out of Book 2. In its structure, however, Book 3 is more akin to Book 1, which, of course, it balances in the overall symmetry of the collection. Like Book 1 it consists of four concentrically arranged groups, 3.1–6, 3.7–15, 3.16–24, and 3.25–30, and we have seen that various similarities between analogous sections of the two books reinforce their parallelism. In their movement too the books are closely related, for both begin with sections that, after a brave start, descend into despair; both have at their center balancing sections that, despite their essentially static quality, begin to regain lost ground; and both end with sections whose affirmative thrust counters the despair of the opening groups that they balance. In Book 3 both the initial descent and the concluding resurgence are more marked than in Book 1, and while in some significant respects the concluding six poems of Book 3 return to the model established by 1.1–6, in other equally significant respects they break entirely new ground and, in 3.29–30, project a secure sense of arrival found neither in 2.20 nor in the Roman Odes themselves, let alone in Book 1.

Odes 3.1–6

From its very inception 3.1 announces its close kinship to the odes that close Book 2. Its Alcaic meter, its serious and elevated tone, the public nature of its themes all argue a continuity with what has preceded, and numerous verbal connections underscore the relationship. The *Musarum sacerdos* of 3.1.3 parallels the *vates* of 2.20.3 (same line, same stanza), the *odi profanum vulgus* with which 3.1 opens echoes the *malignum spernere vulgus* with which 2.16 ends, and the *carmina non prius audita* (3.1.2–3) recalls the unfamiliar wing on which Horace is borne aloft in 2.20.1. The reference to the Gigantomachy in 3.1.7 both recalls the similar reference in 2.19.21 ff. and also looks ahead to the fuller treatment of this theme in 3.4.42 ff., just as the thematically and structurally central *desiderantem quod satis est* of 3.1.25 both recalls 2.18.14 and also looks ahead to the *quod satis est* of 3.16.44. 3.1.37–40 echoes 2.16.21–24 so closely that some have thought the latter to be an interpolation,[1] but the many other links between 3.1 and other poems late in Book 2 suggest rather that the similarity between the passages is no accident of the text but rather part of a large network of verbal and thematic relationships. The thematic ties between 3.1.33 ff. on the one hand, 2.15.1 ff. and 2.18.18 ff. on the other, are part of the same network, as are those between 3.1.21–23 and 2.16.13–16.

The thematic and verbal affinities of 3.1 to what has preceded are so marked that in a continuous reading of *Odes* 1–3 the initial effect of 3.1 is not to introduce a new set of odes but to continue along lines well established in the final odes of Book 2. The poem has a new grandeur about it, to be sure, and in retrospect we see that it introduces 3.1–6, but the philosophical thrust of 3.1, its focus both on personal and social morality, the active role it assigns to Horace and his poetry, even its closing reference to Horace's own farm (3.1.47–48, cf. 2.16.37, 2.18.14) all seem rather to sustain the thematic upswing of 2.16 and 2.18 rather than to introduce a new section. In magnitude, degree of personal involvement, and focus on contemporary issues the difference between 3.1 and these earlier poems is one of degree rather than of kind; only when 3.3 and 3.4 introduce a specifically national focus do we fully realize where the *carmina non prius audita* of 3.1. 2–3 was leading, and only when we have read the whole set of Roman Odes do we understand the degree to which 3.1.5–8 looks ahead to all the Roman Odes and not just back to 2.19.21 ff.

Indeed, the continuity of 3.1 with what has preceded is so strong that it is easy to overlook the dramatic advances it marks. It is the first poem of more than forty lines since 1.2 and 1.12 (a natural next step after the three forty-line poems within 2.13–20) and as such represents a clear repudiation of

---

[1] See, e.g., the editions of Klingner (Q. *Horati Flacci Opera* [Leipzig, 1950]) and Kiessling-Heinze. For an exhaustive discussion of the problem, and a defense of the lines in question, see Pöschl, *Horazische Lyrik*, 122–142. On the Roman Odes in general, see esp. Witke, *Horace's Roman Odes*, a sequential reading from which I have profited at every point.

the stance taken in 1.6, a clear fulfillment of the *non usitata nec tenui ferar penna* of 2.20.1–2. Moreover, where Book 2 opens with a serious, substantial, Alcaic poem in which Horace emphasizes that its large themes are for Pollio, not himself, to handle, Book 3 opens with an even more substantial Alcaic poem in which from the start Horace emphasizes that he himself will now deal with such themes. The lofty tone of the opening stanza, the reference to *carmina non prius audita*, the authoritative stance taken toward the *virginibus puerisque* of line 4 all suggest a new magnitude of theme and tone, and the second stanza with its vast purview—Jupiter's power over kings, kings' power over their people—and its epic themes and manner—the Gigantomachy, the echo in line 8 of *Iliad* 1.530—more than fulfills the high promises of the first.

In breadth, philosophic penetration, and assurance, 3.1 also far outstrips the poem that opens Book 1. Like 1.1, 3.1 surveys a panorama of human types, human aspirations, then at the end locates Horace against that background. But the review of 3.1.9–14 has a terse forcefulness lacking in the rather leisurely survey of 1.1.3–28, and the reminder of *Necessitas* to which it leads locates human aspirations within a philosophical context of which 1.1 contains no hint (a context that, of course, owes much to the exploration of human mortality that in Book 2 has led up to 3.1). Similarly, while in the concluding eight lines of both poems Horace locates himself within his pageant of humanity, in 3.1.41–48 he does this from the stance of one who has already found his place, thought through his values, whereas in 1.1.29–36 he merely voices hopes for an as-yet-unrealized future—hopes that, moreover, carry none of the ethical and philosophical considerations that inform the close of 3.1.

3.1 contrasts sharply not only with the opening poems of Books 1 and 2 but also with previous national poems in the collection. Unlike 1.2 and 1.12, it is concerned throughout with substantive ethical and religious issues—our relation to the gods, our mortality, our search for a manner of living that will enable us best to live the life we have. The whole poem operates from the premise that we ourselves determine the character of our life. We can choose the apparent security of wealth, power, influence, along with the anxiety that so often attends them, or we can choose a simpler, more self-contained way of life that offers a true inner peace and security. There is no recourse here to the divine and heroic catalogues of 1.2 and 1.12, no skirting of contemporary human agents and activities, no suggestion that defeating the Parthians will solve Rome's problems at home. For the hollow chauvinism and divine apparatus of 1.2 and 1.12, 3.1 offers solid substance, honest confrontation of everyday realities, a focus on mortals living human lives. Moreover, while the theme of *Necessitas* in 3.1.14 ff. obviously recalls 1.35.17 ff., 3.1's stance toward this force is positive, an active exploration of ways in which humans can live well in spite of this looming threat, while 1.35 focuses primarily on the threat itself with only a passing glance at more positive ways of dealing with it (in the puzzling 1.35.21 ff.). Positive also is the fact that while earlier national poems focus on the civil wars (1.2, 1.35.33–38, 1.37, 2.1) or on subsequent military undertakings (1.2.49 ff., 1.12.53 ff., 1.21.13 ff., 1.35.29 ff., 2.9.18 ff., 2.12.9 ff., etc.), 3.1 moves beyond this obsession with military concerns to a focus on current peacetime needs.

Perhaps the most positive step forward in 3.1 is the fact that Horace, building on themes of 2.16, now casts his *tenue* life-style not as an artificial retreat from the world but as a means of dealing with the world's concerns. He chooses his Sabine vale at the end of the poem (3.1.47–48) not because in singing with Tyndaris or of Lalage he will escape the world's care (as in 1.17 and 1.22) but because the simple life-style associated with his Sabine farm is the best means of confronting the anxieties inherent in the human condition. The central section of the poem (lines 21–32) makes the same point, that simplicity of life and an attenuated life-style, far from being a flight from the world, are, in fact, the only way to deal with the world. Horace does not expressly identify himself with the *agrestium . . . virorum* of 21–24 or with the *desiderantem quod satis est* of 25 ff., but the kinship of these figures to the Horace of 41–48 is obvious, the more so in that the references to shady banks and to the vale of Tempe in 23–24 immediately suggest the traditional *locus amoenus* of Horace and other poets. But whether or not we refer these lines to Horace, their basic thrust, their emphasis on the positive, active value of that which is self-contained (cf. the *mensa tenui* and the *parva rura* of 2.16.14 and 37), remain: whereas in 1.6 Horace's inclination toward the *tenue* brands him as unfit to deal with larger themes, by the time he reaches 3.1 a similar inclination provides the foundation and focus for his exploration of just such themes.

Although the emphases of 3.2 move rather closer to specific Augustan programs,[2] this poem too avoids any specific mention of Augustus, and it too contains numerous links to poems in the final section of Book 2. The heavenward course of *virtus* in 3.2.21–22 and the wing image of 3.2.24 strongly recall 2.20, the *coetus . . . vulgaris . . . spernit* of the same lines again recalls 2.16.39–40 (as well as 3.1.1), and the opening emphasis on *pauperies* picks up the importance of this theme in 2.18 (see lines 10, 33, 39).[3]

This second poem of Book 3 also looks back to the second poem of Book 2. Its reference to the wings by which *virtus* soars to immortality (3.2.23–24) recalls 2.2.7, and one suspects that the reminiscence is more than accidental when one realizes that *virtus* is central to both poems. The word first appears in 2.2, a major step toward the ethical thrust that will emerge later in Book 2, and in 3.2 *virtus* receives unusual emphasis through its repetition at the start of the fifth and sixth stanzas. Both poems circle around to this key word in their second halves, and both stress the fact that *virtus* is frequently at odds with public opinion (2.2.17 ff., 3.2.17 ff.).

The prominence of *virtus* in 3.2 also points ahead—to 3.5,

[2] See Williams, *Third Book of Horace's Odes*, 35 n. 2.
[3] Cf. also the *pauperum* of 2.20.5 and the thematic thrust of 2.16.13–16. One might also compare the brave *iter* of 3.2.22–24 with that of 2.17.10–12.

3.24, and 3.29; we shall have more to say about *virtus* when we come to those poems. Two points must be made about its appearance in 3.2, however. In the first place, it is important to recognize the ambivalence of the passage that leads up to *virtus* in 3.2.17 and 21. The poem begins with a straightforward (if not very attractive) portrayal of the Spartan-type training that is needed to foster military courage in the young Roman. It is with the second stanza that the ambiguities begin to flood in:

> illum ex moenibus hosticis
>   matrona bellantis tyranni
>   prospiciens et adulta virgo
>
> suspiret, eheu, ne rudis agminum
> sponsus lacessat regius asperum
>   tactu leonem, quem cruenta
>   per medias rapit ira caedis.
>   (3.2.6–12)

From line 6 on everything seems calculated to shift the reader's sympathy away from the young Roman—the specific mention of the mother and fiancée of the young *sponsus regius*, a passage alive with tragic resonances of *Iliad* 22, where Hector's mother and wife look out from the towers of Troy to see him dead; the pathetic *eheu* of line 9, a word Horace uses only in contexts of genuine feeling;[4] the extraordinary bloodthirstiness present in the description of the young Roman—*asperum tactu leonem, quem cruenta per medias rapit ira caedis.* This passage describing the death of the young enemy at the hands of the Roman youth provides the backdrop to the famous line 13:

> dulce et decorum est pro patria mori:

To whom does this line refer? Presumably to the brave young Roman. But neither the context nor the emotional thrust of

---

[4] Cf., for instance, 1.24.11, 1.35.33, 2.14.1, 3.11.42, 3.24.30, 4.1.33, 4.10.6, 4.13.17.

lines 6–12 prevents us from referring it also to the young enemy who bravely loses his life. Moreover, the three lines that follow and that extend the thrust of line 13 also fail to solve the riddle. For these lines too, with their emphasis on the fact that death comes to all, to the coward who flees as well as to the brave warrior who holds his ground, can refer as aptly to the courageous youth of lines 9–11 as they can to his Roman conqueror.

Such is the extraordinary ambivalence of the passage that precedes the mention of *virtus* in lines 17 and 21, and the *virtus* described in the second half of the poem sustains this ambivalence. For while the *virtus* of lines 17 and 21 immediately suggests military excellence, especially in the context of lines 1–16, what Horace says about *virtus* makes clear that here, as elsewhere in the collection, he is using the word in a far broader sense. The *virtus* of 17–24 is a quality as relevant to losers as to victors, to political courage as to martial courage, a function of inner excellence rather than merely a mark of external success. The final stanzas of the poem (lines 25–32) move on to qualities even less dependent on martial excellence and achievement. This central ambivalence in the *virtus* of 3.2 both undercuts the triumphant praise with which the poem begins and also foreshadows the connotations *virtus* will take on later in Book 3.

There are also deeply personal undercurrents in 3.2 that further complicate the poem, further color its depiction of *virtus*. The last appearance of *virtus* was in 2.7.11, where it was associated with Horace's flight at Philippi. Here again it appears in a context of flight from battle (3.2.14–16), albeit without overt reference to Horace's own flight. Moreover, the adjective *imbellis* by which Horace describes the coward who flees (3.2.15) is one that in 1.6.10 he uses of his own lyre (*imbellisque lyrae Musa potens*), in 1.15.15 of the lyre with which the cowardly Paris accompanies his songs to Helen (*imbelli cithara carmina divides*; cf. also *imbellis* of Horace himself at *Epode* 1.16). These verbal ties suggest that the central lines of 3.2, from the famous *dulce et decorum est pro patria mori* of 13 through the description of *virtus* in 17–24, have a special relevance to Horace himself, a man who had known what it means to flee from battle and who had felt the shame of *virtus fracta*. The central ambivalence of *virtus* in 3.2, and the question of whether *virtus* transcends military excellence, thus point not only toward Horace's exploration of what Roman *virtus* should be but also toward his concern to recover his own *virtus*, to move beyond the limits imposed by *pudor imbellisque lyrae Musa potens*.

Despite its ambiguities, 3.2 sustains throughout an emphasis on human initiative. Whether in the military scenes of the first half of the poem, the political overtones of *virtus* in 17–24, or the more private focus of the final two stanzas, the stress is on humans shaping their own destiny. It is an emphasis that sustains the positive thrust of 3.1, with its focus on the deliberate choices by which humans shape (or misshape) their lives, and one that also carries over into the opening stanzas of 3.3, with even the references to Jupiter at the end of 3.2 and the beginning of 3.3 pointing in this direction: mortals *can* so shape their lives as to avoid the wrath of Jupiter (3.2.25–32), can even have the courage to hold fast against the Thunderer himself (3.3.6). And the emphasis of 3.3.9–16 is explicitly on humans who attain the heavens through their own great deeds, a wider application of the theme of 2.20 and again a dramatic repudiation of 1.3's concluding admonition against flying too high. Whereas in 1.3 mortal ambition is branded as *scelus* and *stultitia* and blamed for bringing upon us the punishing bolts of Jupiter, in 3.3.1–16 similar ambition lifts men to divine estate and enables them to stand up to Jupiter's fulminations.[5]

The positive character of 3.3's opening is in many ways sustained in the Juno myth that follows. Most obviously, Juno's acceptance of Romulus's accession to Olympus further develops the theme of lines 9–16, with Romulus's draught of

---

[5] Note the different tone attached to Hercules' winning of immortality in 1.3.36 and 3.3.9–10.

nectar (34–35) recalling Augustus's (11–12), his *lucidas . . . sedes* (33–34) echoing the *arces . . . igneas* (10) attained by Pollux and Hercules. Positive also is the emphasis on reconciliation, on hostilities at last set aside, a worthy and productive peace begun. For the Rome that is to rise from the ashes of Troy is to have not only the military powers extolled at the start of 3.2 but also the moral qualities extolled in 3.1 and the second half of 3.2. She is indeed to be *bellicosa* (3.3.57, cf. the *robustus acri militia puer*, 3.2.2) and *horrenda* (3.3.45, cf. *metuendus*, 3.2.4), but her bravery is to show itself also in her justice and tenacity of purpose in political affairs (3.3.1–2, cf. 3.2.17–20) and in her rejection of wealth and avarice (*spernere fortior*, 3.3.50, cf. 3.1.25 ff., 45 ff.).

The national character of 3.3 is far clearer than is that of 3.2, where the reference to the Parthians (3.2.3) is the only explicit indication of the national character of the poem, and 3.3 is the first of the Roman Odes specifically to mention Augustus (11). More important, in 3.3 Horace explicitly associates Augustan Rome with human initiative and attainment, with reconciliation and renewal, with moral as well as military achievement, all positive themes with substantive, productive content. He has clearly moved a long way beyond 1.2 and 1.12, where he says little of Augustus beside voicing the hope that he may smash foreign enemies, beyond 1.35 and 1.37 as well, where the simple safety of the *princeps* and Rome, and again military success, remain central. That Horace has now reached the point at which he can explore Augustus and his regime in more depth, looking not just at external achievements but also at inner character, is clear not only from 3.3 itself but also from the way it associates Augustus, through its verbal and thematic links to 3.1 and 3.2, with the moral and philosophical explorations of the first two Romans Odes.

At the same time, however, the broadened scope of Horace's consideration entails that he must now begin also to deal with aspects of Augustus that trouble him as well as with those which please him. We saw that 3.2, for instance, which from the vantage point of 3.3 is firmly associated with Augustan Rome, introduced a significant measure of ambivalence into its exhortation to Roman military excellence. Hints of this same ambivalence appear at the very start of 3.3 as well, where the opening stanzas exalt not the valor of the winner but the courage of the individual who holds fast, even, if need be, in the face of the on-pressing tyrant. What follows clearly associates Augustus with the qualities praised in these opening lines, but the lines themselves precede any mention of Augustus, and they at once establish a broader ethical framework in which military achievement and loyalty to one's ruler take second place to ethical obligations.

3.3 also makes clear the high cost at which reconciliation has at long last been won. Juno's prohibition about rebuilding Troy seems deliberately vague in its reference, and as in all such situations, it is best not to force an unambiguous interpretation upon materials that Horace seems intentionally to have rendered ambiguous. What *is* certain, however, is that Juno's speech specifies the death of the old as requisite to the birth of the new: Troy must die if Rome is to be born. In the context of the death of the republic and the birth of the principate the larger thrust of the myth is quite clear, and the poignant reference to long-drawn-out civil wars (*nostrisque ductum seditionibus bellum resedit*, 29–30), a phrase that evokes the horrors of Rome's recent past all too vividly, underlines the point: Rome cannot return to, or resurrect, the past. The poem welcomes the cessation of civil war, celebrates the achievements of Romulus-Augustus, and expressly posits the surrender of the past as the necessary condition for the birth of the new. In the very act of establishing this condition, however, the poem recalls what has been lost, and significantly Juno's speech ends on a note of lamentation (61–68, esp. 67–68).[6]

---

[6] The weeping *uxor* of 3.3.67–68 recalls 3.2.6 ff. but brings the motif, with its echo of *Iliad* 22, closer to Rome and the Romans. On the significance of Juno's speech, see Witke, *Horace's Roman Odes*, 43.

Not only does Juno's speech implicitly lament the losses entailed in the winning of the new order, but also it clearly suggests another harsh corollary of this new order—a loss of human autonomy. The emphasis at the start of 3.3 is wholly on such autonomy—what humans can do for themselves, even in the face of gods who may oppose them, an emphasis that builds thematically on 3.1 and 3.2, both of which are also concerned with the capacity of humans to shape their own lives. With Juno's speech, however, all this changes dramatically. Instead of mortals attaining the citadels of heaven through their own efforts (1–16), now Romulus is to be allowed (*patiar*, 36) by Juno to enter the abode of light, a significant shift of emphasis and one that in fact coheres with what was historically happening in Rome at the time. The establishment of the principate and the cessation of the civil wars owed much to the determination and initiative of Augustus, and 3.3 openly celebrates Augustus's accomplishment. The establishment of the principate also, however, entailed for Rome's citizens some loss of initiative and control, and though 3.3 does not explicitly make this point, in form it moves from human initiative to divine, from human aspirations to directives from above, and the circumscribing of human autonomy is the note on which Juno's speech ends:

> sed bellicosis fata Quiritibus
> hac lege dico, ne nimium pii
>   rebusque fidentes avitae
>   tecta velint reparare Troiae . . .
>   (3.3.57–60)

New life is possible, for Romulus, for Rome; but let not the citizens of Rome try to shape their new world according to *their* wishes, for the power lies in the hands of the gods.

Such are the darker implications of Juno's speech—the necessity of accepting the loss of the past, of recognizing the new constraints on human freedom, as corollaries of the winning of peace, the establishment of a new order. And it is the presence of these tragic undercurrents that makes the seemingly abrupt shift at 3.3.69–72 comprehensible. For just as in 2.1 the confrontation of the cumulative horrors of the civil wars proves too much for Horace and leads him to turn aside to lighter topics (2.1.37–40), so here the confrontation of the full implications of the new order again tempts him, in a passage strikingly similar to 2.1.37–40, to leave this harsh world of contemporary realities for the artificial world of poetry, as in 1.6 to desert large issues for small:

> non hoc iocosae conveniet lyrae:
> quo, Musa, tendis? desine pervicax
>   referre sermones deorum et
>   magna modis tenuare parvis.
>   (3.3.69–72)

Appropriately, 3.4 immediately plunges us into the artificial world of poetry, replete with the usual groves, waters, and breezes (lines 5–8), to say nothing of the doves of fable (9 ff.) and the miraculous protection of the Muses (17 ff.). But the very first stanza, with its invitation to Calliope to sing a *longum melos*, makes clear that despite the conclusion of the previous poem Horace is not yet abandoning great themes for small, not yet ceasing to report the speeches of gods. And if the opening of 3.4 does indeed show signs of the *iocosae . . . lyrae* of 3.3.69—surely we believe in the doves and snakes of 3.4.9–20 scarcely more than we do in the swan of 2.20.9–12!—from line 37 on the poem eschews these lighter touches and turns very much to the real world and to serious concerns.

The opening of 3.4, with its slightly overdone emphasis on the inviolability of the poet, recalls both the theme and the manner of 2.20, and the immediate effect of 3.4 is to counter the downward pull implicit in Juno's speech in 3.3 and to reestablish the upward momentum of 2.20. 3.4 accomplishes this most obviously by building on the very theme of rebirth, of starting afresh, that is implicit in Juno's speech and that, indeed, has been gathering strength ever since 2.19. The freshness of the Bacchic experience in 2.19.1–8, the newness of flight in 2.20.1 ff., the *carmina non prius audita* of 3.1.2–3, even

the young Roman learning new ways in 3.2.1–6—all of these
lead into the emphasis on new beginnings in 3.3 and into the
birth and rebirth motifs of 3.4: the entry into sacred groves
(lines 5–8), the miraculous birth of Horace (9–20), the "re-
creation" of Augustus after his labors (37–40), Apollo washing
his hair in the pure dew of Castalia (61–64). But whereas 3.3
projects the new world as a tentative possibility contingent
upon rigid adherence to stiff conditions, 3.4 presents it as
something already won. The wars are over, and Augustus
now seeks to end his labors. Moreover, Horace himself can
now look back with a measure of calm on his own past ag-
onies—Philippi, the tree, the sea itself (26–28). Indeed, the
mysterious *Sicula Palinurus unda* (28) seems designed less to
recall an actual (otherwise unknown) incident in Horace's life
than to express via the familiar sea imagery his confidence
that he can now survive anything, a theme given explicit
expression in the two stanzas that immediately follow (29–
36).[7]

3.4 thus suggests more strongly than did 3.3 Horace's con-
fidence both in himself and in Augustus. It is in many ways
a poem about human accomplishments, about humans who
are willing to take the initiative. On the other hand, like 3.3
it contains also its disturbing cross-currents. There is again a
suggestion, stronger here even than in 3.2, of the negative
side of force. This theme, implicit in the centrally located *lene
consilium* of line 41, provides the apparent focus for the myth
of Jupiter and the Titans and receives explicit and rather om-
inous emphasis at 3.4.65–68:

> vis consili expers mole ruit sua:
> vim temperatam di quoque provehunt
>   in maius; idem odere viris
>   omne nefas animo moventis.

With this passage Horace clearly moves well beyond the em-
phasis on military success in earlier poems. His stance toward

[7] For a different view on line 28, see M. W. Thomson, "The Date of
Horace's First Epode," *CQ* 20 (1970): 30–31.

Augustus is now such that he can, albeit indirectly, speak of the negative implications of Augustus's power as well as of the positive; he can even suggest the divine displeasure that would attend misuse of Augustan might. The crucial word in his advice is the same one used in Book 2 as a keystone of the personal morality explored there—*temperatam* (cf. 2.2.3, 2.3.3, also the *temperet* of 2.16.27). The *temperatam* of line 66 also picks up the *temperat* used of Jupiter in line 45, as if to suggest that by its very nature to rule is to rule temperately, that governance without moderation is scarcely worthy of the name.[8] Like 3.3, 3.4 thus celebrates the birth of the Augustan peace but emphasizes the conditions on which its continuance depends. 3.4 in a sense plays a variation on the central theme of 3.3—the need to move beyond the past. A focus on military might may have been necessary in the past, but now is the time to resettle the war-weary soldiers, to court a rebirth of *lene consilium* (cf. the Pierian setting of lines 39–40), and to reject all but *vis temperata*. The very fact that Horace makes his point so strongly, and in so many different ways, suggests that he felt the potential for *vis consili expers* to be all too real.

Another disturbing undercurrent in 3.4 is that again, like 3.3, it strongly suggests the presence of forces that limit human autonomy. The power of the Muses over the young Horace may be too patent (and too benign!) a poetic fiction to be worth considering in this respect (9–28), and certainly by the time one reaches the *temptabo* of 31 and the repeated *visam* of 33 and 35, one has a strong sense of the autonomy and initiative of Horace. Some of this carries over to Augustus in 37–42, though these lines have retreated considerably from the opening of 3.3 with respect to human autonomy. In the final half of the poem, however, as in the final portions of 3.3, all is the gods. Moreover, if the thrust of 3.3 is to praise those who strive ever higher, that of 3.4 is decidedly opposed to such upward mobility. True, the Titans and Giants of 3.4 are scarcely in the same class as the heroic figures mentioned

---

[8] Cf. *qui . . . temperat* of Jupiter in 1.12.15–16, one more instance of a passage in 1.12 that foreshadows later developments: cf. above, pp. 74 ff.

in 3.3.9–16, but the fact remains that 3.3 praises the effort to scale the heights while 3.4 depreciates it. And while at the start of 3.3 humans win heaven by their own merits—even, indeed, by resistance to authority—in the remainder of 3.3 and in most of 3.4 the initiative has passed to the gods, who of their lofty grace confer rewards on mortals below. The somewhat surprising tone of the end of 3.4 perhaps reflects this movement away from human initiative and freedom. For while the passage deals with individuals who have deserved their punishment, the dominant motifs sounded are those of immobility, impotence, bondage—and, as at the end of 3.3, of sorrow: *dolet . . . maeretque* (73–74—cf. the *ploret*, 3.3.68, on which Juno's speech ends).[9]

As if to repair this lapse from human initiative, this increasing concentration on divine power, on forces beyond human control, Horace, following the lead of 3.1.5–8, begins 3.5 by recognizing the place of the gods and then for the remainder of the poem focuses on the human realm. Jupiter may rule in heaven (lines 1–2), but Augustus's status on earth is the product of human deeds (2–4), and other humans also make conscious choices and live with the consequences (5 ff.). Moreover, from its early emphasis on the disgrace that Crassus's soldiers have brought upon themselves the poem rises to a noble conclusion in the courage of Regulus, a hero who truly lives up to the model established in 3.3. Indeed, the *iustum et tenacem propositi virum* of 3.3.1 ff., with his fearless resistance to all pressures, in retrospect seems to foreshadow the Regulus of 3.5.[10] In place of the Olympian myths that end 3.3 and 3.4, with their correlative suspension of human initiative and independence, we have in Regulus a figure of the same type as the Cleopatra of 1.37—self-contained, courageous, an autonomous victor even in defeat.

[9] Cf. Witke, *Horace's Roman Odes*, 47, on the close of 3.4: "its mournful aftermath."

[10] Note resistance to public pressure as a motif common to both (3.3.2, 3.5.45 ff.). The motif is present also in 3.2.19–20, and it is perhaps already implicit in the *odi profanum vulgus* of 3.1.1.

The problem, however, is that Regulus in 3.5 is introduced not as a model for current Romans to emulate but as a contrast to what current Romans have become. The whole point of Regulus's story in 3.5 is that *virtus* of the sort he embodies is a quality that, once lost, can never be regained (cf. 29–36). In the scheme of 3.5 Regulus represents an exemplar as unattainable as it is magnificent, and the poem suggests not that the Romans of Horace's time can strive upward toward noble goals, like the humans praised at the start of 3.3, but that they are fallen creatures for whom such upward strivings are now impossible. The poem thus implicitly pulls against 3.2, which urges that contemporary Romans be schooled in the rugged *virtus* of their ancestors, and against 3.4, which emphasizes the possibility of rebirth and renewal. It pulls also against 3.3, but in a more complex fashion. Like 3.3 it suggests that the past is irretrievable, but whereas 3.3 sets the unredeemable loss of Troy as the price for the glorious birth of Rome, 3.5 grimly contrasts the lost moral stature of the past with the irremediable degeneracy of the present.

Even Augustus himself, the one hope held out for the present, is here associated not with *lene consilium, vis temperata*, as in 3.4 (and, by implication, in 3.3), but once again only with military force—the chauvinistic cry to destroy the Britons and the Parthians, a course of action quite irrelevant to the regaining of *virtus*. For *virtus* in 3.5, as in 2.2 and 3.2, is something that fundamentally transcends mere might and courage in battle. The *virtus* of Regulus has, of course, a military side and is related to the qualities that make for a successful fighter (cf. 3.5.29–36), but the evidence of this quality in Regulus is not that he fights well, still less that he wins, but that his inner greatness, like Cleopatra's, remains untouched and untainted by external disaster.

As in 3.2, the mention of *virtus* in 3.5 implicitly recalls Horace's own experience in war, his flight at Philippi and his own sense of *virtus fracta*. The reminiscence is underscored by the fact that Regulus's words on *virtus*, like the famous lines 13–16 of 3.2, closely fit Horace's own experience:

neque amissos colores
lana refert medicata fuco,

nec vera virtus, cum semel excidit,
curat reponi deterioribus.

(3.5.27–30)

Again 3.5 seems to pull against the previous poem. For while
3.4 places Horace's escape from Philippi in a context that
emphasizes new life and renewed courage (3.4.25–36), 3.5
suggests that merely to save one's life is scarcely to live and
explicitly denies the possibility of recovering *virtus* once it is
lost. The point is allied to the general theme that 3.5 develops
against the backdrop of 3.2–4. For while these poems suggest
new patterns, fresh beginnings, the possibility of rebirth, 3.5
argues that greatness once gone is gone forever. An eventual
victory over the Parthians may avenge a past defeat, but such
a victory can no more restore the inner quality of *virtus* than
can Horace's mere survival of Philippi repair his nagging sense
that his own *virtus* is somehow broken.

Despite 3.5's confident start and its noble picture of Re-
gulus, the thrust of the poem is thus toward despair. In it
Horace's attempt bravely to eschew the previous poems' em-
phasis on divine initiative and to focus instead on contem-
porary Rome and the possibility of human-initiated regen-
eration leads instead to recognition of the vast obstacles to
such regeneration, of the yawning gulf that must be bridged
before a true rebirth can occur, the discouraging limitations
inherent in mortal initiative and aspiration. 3.6 moves in very
much the same directions, first emphasizing the need for hu-
man initiative, then confronting in despair the problems that
must be solved, and finally juxtaposing with these contem-
porary realities the vision of a past that was better but that is
now hopelessly gone.

The parallel between the two poems is, in fact, very close.
Both begin with the need for human action, setting such
action both against a context of our place in the hierarchy of
the universe (3.5.1–4, 3.6.1–8) and against the backdrop of

recent Roman military losses (3.5.5 ff., 3.6.9 ff.). Mention of these debacles leads not, however, to a return to the specific initiatives mentioned at the start of the poems—the need for foreign campaigns in 3.5, the need to repair the temples in 3.6—but rather to a fuller consideration of the moral decline that lies behind them—the lack of *virtus* in Crassus's men in 3.5.5 ff., the degenerate morals of contemporary Rome in 3.6.17 ff. And it is from this dismal portrait of the present that in each instance Horace turns to the memory of the bygone age of the Punic Wars—to the courage of a Regulus (3.5.13 ff.) and the simple virtues of the early Romans (3.6.33 ff.)

Despite this parallelism of theme and movement, there are important differences of emphasis between 3.5 and 3.6, and these differences effectively underscore the black despair of 3.6. For one thing, the theme of contemporary degeneracy in 3.5 is treated relatively briefly (5–12) and with reference only to Crassus's troops; moreover, the possibility of such cowardice in the troops of Regulus's own time is openly acknowledged (13 ff.). In 3.6, however, the degeneracy of contemporary Rome comes across as a characteristic of Roman society in general, is treated at length (17–32), and stands in stark contrast to the moral fiber of early Roman society. Moreover, 3.5 suggests the impossibility of recovery only indirectly, through the words of Regulus, and ends on the positive note of Regulus's greatness, while 3.6 introduces contemporary moral degeneracy as almost a fact of nature (3.6.17–20) and ends by focusing expressly on the continuous and irreversible process of decline:

> damnosa quid non imminuit dies?
> aetas parentum peior avis tulit
>   nos nequiores, mox daturos
>   progeniem vitiosiorem.
>   (3.6.45–48)

Despite 3.5's implicit reminder of the gulf between past and present, between *virtus* that is *integra* and *virtus* that is *fracta*, what one takes away from the poem is above all its noble recreation of the *virtus* of Regulus. From 3.6, in contrast, one retains above all a sense of the moral pollution of the present, a theme merely rendered the more bleak by the brief evocation of a past as irretrievable as it was lustrous.

The overall movement of the Roman Odes is toward ever closer concern with Augustus and his programs. The broad ethical theme of 3.1 yields to the narrower focus on military issues in 3.2, with the Parthian reference of 3.2.3 suggesting a more specifically national character than did anything in 3.1. Augustus himself comes on the scene in a passing role in 3.3, a central position in 3.4. And 3.5 and 3.6 deal with specific Augustan projects—the foreign campaigns, especially that to retrieve the Parthian disgrace, in 3.5, and the program to rebuild the temples and to restore Roman morality in 3.6. The fact that increasingly in these poems Horace deals directly with Augustus and his programs represents a major advance over his approach in Book 1. There he dealt with Augustus himself only in passing, and with almost no reference to substantive issues beyond those of the "Get the Parthians" ilk. Here, in contrast, he probes in some detail and at some depth into Augustus's accomplishments and programs, into the qualities he will need to cultivate, and into the societal problems he must face. What lends to the group as a whole a note of considerable pessimism, however, is the fact that the closer Horace comes to Augustus, the more deeply he probes into Augustan programs and into contemporary realities, the more despairing the poems become. The overall positive thrust of 3.1 yields to the central ambiguities of 3.2; the emphasis on human initiative in 3.1 and 3.2 and the start of 3.3 is replaced by the emphasis on divine control in the remainder of 3.3 and most of 3.4; the emphasis on rebirth in 3.2–4 yields to the suggestion, implicit in 3.5 and explicit in 3.6, that rebirth is impossible. And the close focus in the final two poems on specific Augustan initiatives ends up implying that these initiatives are irrelevant to the problems they must meet: neither can defeating the Parthians restore lost *virtus* nor can rebuild-

ing temples restore lost morality—indeed, the particular ini-
tiatives with which 3.5 and 3.6 begin are forgotten by the
time the poems end. 3.3's seemingly hopeful advice to forget
the past so as to build the future is replaced in 3.5 and 3.6 by
a suggestion that if the past cannot be retrieved there is no
hope for the present; and even the glow of nobility that shines
with Regulus at the end of 3.5 yields to the dark death-knell
at the close of 3.6. The rising momentum of 2.20, which
introduced the Roman Odes and which is still very much
present at the start of 3.3 and 3.4, leads into the fallen Giants
of 3.4, the focus on fallen *virtus* in 3.5, and the express em-
phasis on ubiquitous and irreversible decline on which 3.6
ends. And the general tonal movement of the set finds re-
flection in the relative magnitude of the poems, which rises
from forty-eight and thirty-two lines in 3.1 and 3.2 to a peak
of seventy-two and eighty lines in 3.3 and 3.4, only to fall at
the end to fifty-six lines in 3.5 and forty-eight in 3.6.

Odes 3.7–15

The ultimate sense of decline in 3.1–6, the movement from
confident initiative in 3.1–4 to hopeless despair in 3.6, from
visions of renewal in 3.1–4 to recognition of immutable de-
cline in 3.6, closely parallel the movements of the first groups
of Books 1 and 2, in each of which high hopes yield to loss
of confidence. And just as in both previous books an initial
concern with large issues is replaced by a concentration on
more circumscribed topics, so in Book 3 the bold grandeur
of the Roman Odes yields to the more personal, less grand
mode of the two groups that follow, 3.7–15 and 3.16–24. In
these two groups most poems are short, many are artificial
in setting and erotic or sympotic in theme, and national con-
cerns, initially at least, are either absent or touched on only
in passing. The majestic Alcaic, increasingly dominant toward
the end of Book 2 and the sole meter of 3.1–6, disappears
completely in 3.7–15.
The parallel between Book 3 and Book 1 is especially close,

with each following its initial group with two analogous groups of largely personal poems and a final group that balances the opening section but reverses its movement. And just as the two central groups of Book 1 gradually work back toward themes abandoned after 1.1–12 and thus prepare the way for the final upward thrust of 1.27–38, so the two central groups of Book 3 steadily move back toward the magnitude and seriousness of the Roman Odes and lead directly into the final surge that comes with 3.25–30.

Moreover, at the same time as the two central groups of Book 3 retreat from the lofty grandeur of the Roman Odes, they constantly recall the thematic foci of these odes, often through seemingly playful variations. One such focus is the tension between unbridled *vis* on the one hand, *vis temperata* and *lene consilium* on the other.[11] This tension is, of course, central to 3.4, but in various forms it figures also in several other Roman Odes. It plays a part in 3.2, which implicitly questions the nature of *virtus*: Is it the sheer military excellence praised at the start of the poem, or is it rather a larger quality that includes the inner courage of lines 13–16, the public *virtus* of lines 17–24, and the private virtues of lines 25–32?[12] The Regulus ode points in the same direction, for the *virtus* that distinguishes Regulus from Crassus's soldiers, or from Regulus's own fellow soldiers, is something more inner, more intangible, and more invulnerable than mere bravery in battle. The same tension is implicit also in Juno's praise of Rome, which emphasizes both military might (3.3.45–48, 53–56) and moral strength (49–52), and one might even see this tension reflected in the contrasting central themes of 3.1 and 3.2, 3.5 and 3.6, with larger moral concerns being uppermost in 3.1 and 3.6, a more military focus central to 3.2 and 3.5. The general question of whether the Augustan regime will focus on *lene consilium* or on sheer *vis*, a question that in effect hinges

[11] One of the themes foreshadowed in 1.12: cf. above, p. 74.

[12] Note how 3.2 steadily moves from external to internal qualities, from physical to spiritual excellence, a movement that reflects the overall movement of the collection.

on the very definition of *virtus*, thus radiates out from its explicit statement in 3.4 to become a recurrent focus of all the Roman Odes, and there are many echoes of this thematic tension in the shorter, more personal poems that follow.

A second tension central to the Roman Odes concerns the relationship of past to present and focuses on a contradiction implicit in the Augustan regime and its programs. On the one hand the Augustan principate was necessarily a new departure, an abandonment of old patterns that had led to a century of civil war, and both Augustus and Horace saw the need for welcoming this fresh start and for consciously rejecting any attempt to go back to the republic. On the other hand, Augustus's own programs explicitly emphasized restoring the simple family-oriented virtues of the republican past, reviving the inner qualities that had made early Rome strong, and maintaining political patterns and institutions from the republic. What was involved was a delicate balancing act that simultaneously stressed giving up a disastrous past so as to build a better future and renewing the present by restoring the best in the past. At their best these contrasting approaches were complementary, not contradictory, but we have seen that at a number of points the Roman Odes suggest their potential incompatibility. Of this thematic tension too there are many echoes in the shorter poems that follow.

The implicit presence of these thematic tensions in 3.7–24 provides a counterpoint to the apparent thrust of these poems, which is to turn away from the larger concerns of 3.1–6 and to focus on more private and personal issues. This echoing of the thematic tensions of the Roman Odes is a feature that renders the two central groups of Book 3 different from the corresponding central groups of Book 1. The books differ also in that whereas a prevailing emphasis of 1.13–26 is on escape from involvement, in 3.7–24 a frequent emphasis is on action, initiative, how to live. The large concerns of the preceding poems—the preoccupation with death in 2.13–20, with political themes in 3.1–6—indeed disappear for a time, and in 3.7–15 there is slight reference even to the ethical concerns of

2.15, 2.16, 2.18, and 3.1–6. There remains, however, a persistent emphasis on facing real problems and real situations. The situations and problems dealt with at times seem insignificant, even artificial, but more often than not they play delicate variations on themes given larger treatment in these earlier groups. The poems of 3.7–15, despite their predominantly Greek settings and artificial character (cf. the similar qualities of the analogous 1.13–19), frequently hint at themes of renewal, rebirth, return; and the long central poem of this group, 3.11, plays a poignant variation on the theme of *vis* and *vis temperata*. 3.16–24, which are more Roman in character (cf. 1.20–26), constantly deal with questions of how to live life here and now, and the large opening poem, 3.16, brings this practical orientation to bear on some of the personal and ethical questions raised in the Roman Odes. As this happens the Alcaic meter begins to return, the length of poems to grow, and by the time we reach 3.24 Horace is again dealing with large national issues on the scale (though not in the meter) of the Roman Odes.

The essence of 3.7–24 is that human problems, be they national or personal, require human answers, and despite the fact that most of these poems abandon the magnitude and the seriousness of the Roman Odes, there remain a prevailing openness and honesty, a flexibility toward necessary compromise, and above all an emphasis on human initiative, which mark major steps ahead from the position taken in the parallel odes of Book 1. And if the bitter despair at the end of the Roman Odes breathes a pessimism darker perhaps than that even at the nadirs of Books 1 and 2, Horace does not in the poems that follow abandon his determination to confront real issues honestly. Indeed, the darkest of the Roman Odes, 3.6, itself points the way ahead in that it resolutely faces Rome's true moral degradation—not just the fact of fallen temples but the reality of fallen character—and bluntly places the burden of regeneration on the Romans themselves (note the balancing *Romane*, 3.6.2, and *nos*, 3.6.47).[13] And such is the prevailing

[13] The balancing positions of these two words are probably not accidental:

emphasis of the two groups that follow, on the need for the individual, be it Asterie (3.7), Lydia and her lover (3.9), Hypermnestra (3.11), Chloris (3.15), or Phidyle (3.23), to discover human answers to human problems. Moral regeneration must begin with such individual agents, and the despairing *nos* of 3.6.47 leads directly to the active *nos* of 3.24.45 and 47: *we* ourselves are the ones who must face facts, bring about revival. Even national issues, when they arise in these poems, are set in a similar personal context, with the climax coming in Horace's blunt words about Augustus at 3.24.25 ff. If an element of diminishment and despair is undeniable in 3.7–24, especially in contrast with the grandiose Roman Odes, these groups eventually move toward a conclusion that is more satisfying than the Roman Odes—more satisfying because more human, more personal, and more real.

3.7 immediately establishes the mode for the new group. Its erotic theme, Greek addressee, bantering tone, and gentle Asclepiads all mark the departure from the Roman Odes. But if its setting is somewhat artificial, its situation and advice are not. The poem deals with a real and specific problem, a husband's extended absence from his wife and the attendant temptations to dalliance upon both of them, and the *adhuc* ("up to now") of 22 and the *difficilis* ("hard-to-get"?) of 32 seem not to rule out entirely the possibility of passing flirtations. Horace's advice to Asterie, however, though spoken with a smile, is direct and to the point: "Gyges has tried his best to remain true. You do the same." The realistic approach to a real problem is implicit from the opening *Quid fles*: what is needed is not tears but patience and fidelity.[14] This candid facing of facts is of a piece with 3.6, as indeed is the theme of temptation and adultery, but 3.7 touches also upon 3.3's and 3.4's themes

---

cf. the balance of poems that stand in comparable positions—second from beginning and second from end: 1.2 and 3.29, 1.2 and 1.37, *Epodes* 2 and 16. On the call to action implicit in 3.6, see Witke, *Horace's Roman Odes*, 74 ff.

[14] Cf. the theme of banishing needless complaints in 1.33, 2.9, and 2.17. On the tone and theme of 3.7 and its function in the collection as a whole, see Mutschler, *SO* 53 (1978): 111–131.

of restoration and new life. For whereas Horace's facing of facts in 3.6 leads only to despair, to a sense of the impossibility of regeneration, Asterie's confrontation of the truth about herself and her temptations holds the possibility that she as well as Gyges will remain *integer* (cf. 3.7.22) for the restoration and return that will come with the spring. The poem offers no sweeping answers to the problems faced in 3.6, but its tactful urging of individual morality in the face of individual temptation may be an answer more to the point than the most sweeping of national programs—the only way, perhaps, toward genuine moral rebirth. The delicacy, grace, and humor in which Horace cloaks this inherently serious theme themselves contribute to the poem's more positive thrust. With 3.7 we leave behind the heavy despair of 3.6 and begin the long ascent toward the heights of 3.30.

3.8 ends on an escapist note with its deliberate renouncing of the serious public issues that were central in the Roman Odes (3.8.17–28).[15] In other respects, however, the poem deals very much with the real world and, as with 3.7, does so in a down-to-earth manner. Horace's escape from the tree, here mentioned for the last time, is handled with gruff humor (*prope funeratus*, 7) and with none of the histrionics of 2.12. The same sense of balance and perspective is present throughout the poem, whether in the ease of address toward Maecenas, the decorum that is to characterize the party (cf. lines 15–16), or the avoidance of the darker *carpe diem* themes that the poem could so easily have fallen into with the *dona praesentis cape laetus horae* of line 27. This poem too, like 3.7, celebrates recovery and restoration (cf. lines 13–14), relating present joy to past memories by its reference to wine bottled in the year before Horace's birth. Thus out of past and present, escape and danger, themes prominent in the Roman Odes on a vastly larger scale, 3.8 creates a harmonious counterpoint,

[15] On the tone of this passage, see Williams, *Third Book of Horace's Odes*, 73–74.

and in its limited compass even the troubled affairs of the state seem for the time to fall into place (18 ff.).

The exquisite, lilting 3.9 is even farther from the real world of Rome than is 3.7, but again it deals with themes central to the Roman Odes and to the book—with reconciliation and renewal, with transcending a troubled past and building a harmonious future. And if in tone and theme it retreats from contemporary Rome, in its emphasis on human initiative, on the capacity to change and the will to make things work, it points, despite its piquant, ironic manner, in directions as applicable to societies as they are to individuals.

Just as 3.7 and 3.9, two poems that deal with male-female separations and reunions, enclose Horace's bachelor party (3.8), so, by a thematic inversion of sorts, the next trio contains balancing poems on unrequited love (3.10 and 3.12; cf. the eventual reunions of 3.7 and 3.9) which enclose the longer and fuller 3.11, with its focus on Hypermnestra's love for Lynceus, a love that she expresses by sending him away (cf. Horace's invitation to Maecenas in 3.8). 3.10 and 3.12 both deal with doors closed to love, 3.10 literally through the medium of the *paraklausithuron* (cf. the similar motifs in 3.7.29 ff., 3.9.20), 3.12 thematically through its depiction of the young Neobule, whose love for Hebrus is denied an outlet. The main function of these two poems is to set off 3.11, but even they touch upon important themes. Both, like 3.7, are poems that bluntly face facts—the reality both of Lyce's character and of Horace's plight in 3.10, the anguish of Neobule's feelings and her plight in 3.12. Both also present the negative alternative to the theme of 3.9. For while Lydia and her lover take action, bring about change, Neobule is but a passive victim unable either to take the initiative or to give play to her feelings, and Lyce's lover is scarcely less a prisoner, though the last two lines at least hint at the possibility of his abandoning his folly.

The start of 3.11 suggests once again a small poem on a light topic, something in the vein of the short erotic poems elsewhere in this group. In fact, however, this central poem of 3.7–15 transforms its erotic subject into a major personal statement, and by the end both Lyde and Hermes, the figures with whom it begins, have been virtually forgotten. Moreover, while 3.10 and 3.12 focus on immobility, the incapacity to change oneself or one's situation, 3.11 from the start emphasizes flexibility, motion, the potential for change, whether in Amphion's power to move the stones (1–2), Mercury's ability to coax the lyre into music (3–6), or Lyde's implied capacity to grow beyond her present skittishness (7–12). The theme becomes still more marked in the Orpheus-like powers of Mercury (13–24—note especially his ability to open doors, 15–16) and climaxes in the story of Hypermnestra, a woman who, like Cleopatra in 1.37, is able to move beyond the role others have slated for her, to deal with a situation that others would find unmanageable.[16] Like the Mercury to whom Horace directs his appeal, and in contrast to the helpless lovers of 3.10 and 3.12, Hypermnestra is an opener of doors: *neque intra claustra tenebo* (43–44). Her words represent a powerful reversal of the door motif introduced in 3.7.29, for while hitherto the closed door has separated the eager lover outside from his beloved within, here Hypermnestra opens the door from within and sends forth her lover to his freedom, a powerful index of her love and a significant shift of direction in the book. Both 3.7 and 3.9 deal on a small scale with the capacity of human action to work productive change, but neither has the stature really to controvert the despair and frustration on which 3.6 ends. In Hypermnestra such capacity approaches heroic proportions, the scale of a Cleopatra or a Regulus, however, and 3.11 marks a major step away from the despairing impotence of 3.6.45–48 and toward the confident sense of power on which Book 3 will end.

Hypermnestra's act also picks up from 3.1–6 the central tension between *vis* and *lene consilium*. The *virtus* (such is not

---

[16] Note how Horace's admiration for Hypermnestra calls forth a verbal complexity and density comparable to that evoked by Cleopatra: cf., e.g., 3.11.34–36, 1.37.31–32. With Mercury's Orpheus-like qualities (3.11.13 ff.), cf. the similar qualities of Alcaeus in 2.13.33 ff. and Dionysus in 2.19.29 ff.

too strong a word) of Hypermnestra lies in her opposition to
blind violence, her innate certainty that humans can and must
transcend the savagery of beasts (cf. lines 41 ff.), her exercise
of loving *clementia* (cf. line 46). Her *virtus* rises above the
accepted commonplaces of morality into a world where dis-
obedience is noble and lying splendid, where courage is a
woman's part and consists of something more internal than
brute force. This *virtus* remains untainted by the *scelus* and
culpa (25, 29) that surround her, and in the inner qualities of
such individuals perhaps more than in any political program
lies Horace's deepest hope for a regeneration of Rome from
her miasma of *culpa* (3.6.17–20) and her heritage of *scelus*.[17]

In the final triptych of this section the lighter 3.13 and 3.15
surround the weightier 3.14 much as 3.7 and 3.9 enclose 3.8,
with 3.13 and 3.15, like 3.7 and 3.9, belonging more to the
artificial world of poetry, 3.14, like 3.8, more to the real world
of Rome. But in 3.13, as in 3.11, this artificial world becomes
the stage for profound variations on the central themes of the
book and the collection. The poem plays off the hot vigor of
the young kid against the cold clarity of Bandusia, the bloody
violence of his sacrifice against the spring's glassy calm, the
death of the victim against the renewal the spring offers to
the flocks, and the lasting music of poetry against the fluid
chatter of the spring. The starting point for the poem is the
same as for 3.11, the transforming power of poetry, and just
as in 3.11 Mercury's lyre can charm the tormented dead and
Hypermnestra's virtue rescue life from death, so in 3.13 Hor-
ace himself evokes from the cold spring and the sacrifice that
stains it an image not of a world defiled but of life reborn.

---

[17] The thematic contrasts between 3.10 and 3.11 are emphasized by the fact
that numerous motifs are common to the poems: cf. *extremum Tanain*, 3.10.1,
extremos . . . agros, 3.11.47; *saevo nupta viro*, 3.10.2, *viro clemens misero*, 3.11.46
(cf. *saevis*, 45); *ingratam*, 3.10.9, *neque grata, grato*, 3.11.5, 23; *parens*, 3.10.12,
parentem, 3.11.34; *parcas*, 3.10.17, *peperci*, 3.11.46; *mollior*, 3.10.17, *mollior*,
3.11.43; *anguibus*, 3.10.18, *angues*, 3.11.18 (same line); and the whole contrast
between the outstretched, wakeful lover of 3.10 and the sleeping lover of 3.11
to whom Hypermnestra says *surge . . . surge* (3.11.37, 38).

As with other poems of the group, the poetic setting is far from Rome, but the themes—violence, sacrifice, renewal, rebirth, the transitory present transmuted into the eternal future—all have their echoes of the Roman Odes, and the very brilliance with which Horace rings their changes is itself an affirmation of the same human capacity to transform that crowned the *virtus* of Hypermnestra.

3.14 also carries a sense of affirmation that transcends its relatively short compass and its sympotic genre. Its opening praises of Augustus seem hollow and overblown, but the reference to him in the central stanza (lines 13–16) is heartfelt; and the deeply personal character of the final stanzas (lines 17–28) both cuts through the bombast of the poem's opening and underscores the sincerity of its central core.[18] The safe return of Augustus in 3.14 balances Horace's own escape in 3.8,[19] and the closeness of poet to *princeps* is further suggested by the fact that Horace here approaches Augustus not through the grandiose forms of a national ode like 1.2, 1.12, or the Roman Odes, but through the personal medium of a drinking song, the same form that he uses for his invitation to Maecenas in the balancing 3.8.

In keeping with its more personal flavor is the fact that 3.14's praise of Augustus focuses on what Horace himself feels to be important: Augustus's safe return from the war (1–4)[20] and the role Augustus must play in preventing a renewal of civil strife (13–16). There is no chauvinistic trumpeting of great victories, only the *Hispana . . . victor ab ora* of 3–4, no extravagant claims of deification, only the opening reference to Hercules, which here points not to Augustus's divine status

---

[18] Note that 3.14's movement from public themes to private reverses the movement of its counterpart, 3.8, which moves from private concerns (lines 1–16) to public (lines 17–24).

[19] A point emphasized by the link between *sospitis*, 3.8.14, and *sospitum*, 3.14.10, with the word coming at the same place in the two stanzas.

[20] Cf. the prayer for Augustus's safety as he departs for battle in 1.35.29 ff., with *iuvenumque nuper sospitum*, 3.14.9–10, perhaps recalling *iuvenum recens examen*, 1.35.30–31.

but to his mortal ability to overcome great obstacles (1–2).[21] Even lines 5–10, despite their slightly cloying hyperbole, deal with quintessentially human qualities and emotions, and the overall context of the poem places Horace's praise of Augustus into an eminently human setting.

Horace further extends the poem's aura of affirmation by juxtaposing the security of the present (13–16) with the insecurity of the past (17–20), his current willingness to accept compromise and rebuff (21–26—the door motif once more!) with the hot temper of his youth (27—cf. also the immobilized lover of 3.10). It is into this context of bittersweet contentment that Horace weaves his closing reference to the critical year 42 B.C., the consulship of Plancus, that year in which he had opposed Augustus at Philippi. The poem, which in its first half hails Augustus's recent return and which at its center stresses Rome's current need of Augustan leadership, thus ends with Horace both subtly recalling the divisions of the past and simultaneously emphasizing his own capacity to transcend them.

In sum, 3.14 is a deeply personal confrontation of issues basic to the collection. Its very limitations of compass are significant in that here for the first time Horace deals directly with Augustus in a personal rather than a ceremonial fashion, an important step toward the bold candor of 3.24. The poem also moves forward with respect to the basic tensions of the Roman Odes. It complements its early reference to Augustan military *vis* with its more emphatic central suggestion of Augustus's role in tempering *vis* (note the negative force of *vim* in 15), and the context in which Horace mentions Plancus's fateful consulship suggests the possibility of reconciling the broken dreams of the past with bright hopes for the future.[22]

---

[21] The reference to Hercules builds, of course, on the references to him in 1.3.36, 1.12.25, and 3.3.9. On the significance of Hercules in 3.14, and on the overall thrust of the poem, see the fine analysis of U. W. Scholz, "Herculis ritu—Augustus—consule Planco (Horaz c. 3, 14)," *WS* 84 (1971): 123–137.

[22] With the mention of Plancus in 3.14 in a poem that expressly celebrates Augustus's role and that stresses making necessary compromises, cf. 1.7,

CHAPTER IV

The end of 3.14, which finds Horace accepting the changes, even the losses, time has brought, leads directly into 3.15, where Horace urges the aging Chloris to do the same.[23] This poem is an apt counterpart to 3.7 in that Horace's advice to Chloris, like his advice to Asterie, is realistic and practical: face facts, look clearly at yourself, and do what is both right and sensible. This theme of adjusting to the inevitable changes wrought by time is subtly heightened in 3.15 by the fact that its Chloris *is* older than when we last met her as the radiant young woman of 2.5.18. She shares this feature with other figures in this section of Book 3. The Gyges of 3.7 is no longer the young man he was in 2.5.20–24, the Chloe of 3.7.10 ff. and 3.9.6 and 9 ff. has obviously become *tempestiva sequi viro* (cf. 1.23.12), and Horace himself is fully aware of the passing of his own youth (3.14.25–28, cf. 3.8.9–10).[24]

Indeed, the passing of time plays a significant role not only in 3.14 and 3.15 but in most of the poems of this section. It brings Gyges home to Asterie in 3.7 (cf. 1 ff.), provides the occasion for Horace's invitation to Maecenas in 3.8 (cf. 9), reconciles Lydia and her lover in 3.9 (cf. 17 ff.), offers the possibility of relief to the rejected lover of 3.10 (cf. 19–20)— and will bring immortality to Bandusia in 3.13 (cf. 13 ff.). Most applications of this theme are personal, but given the place of this theme in the public 3.14, it is not far-fetched to

where Plancus appears in a poem that makes no mention of Augustus, that specifically mentions intra-family strife (21–22), and that ends with a departure into the unknown that verbally and tonally recalls the despairing departure of *Epode* 16. On the tone of the concluding lines of 3.14, see M. Dyson, "Horace, *Odes* iii.14," *G & R* 20 (1973): 177–179.

[23] Is there perhaps even a link between the labor-finishing Hercules of 3.14.1 ff. and Horace's admonition to Chloris, *tandem . . . fige modum . . . famosisque laboribus*, 3.15.2–3? Note also yet another hint of the door motif: 3.15.9. On the door motif throughout this section, see W. L. Henderson, "The Paraklausithyron Motif in Horace's *Odes*," *AC* 16 (1973): 60–67.

[24] The Lydia of 3.9 also seems to have moved beyond the Lydia of 1.8 and 1.13 (though scarcely beyond the Lydia of 1.25!). On the possible continuity of figures such as Lydia and Chloe throughout *Odes* 1–3, see Henderson, *AC* 16 (1973): 59; Dettmer, *Horace: A Study in Structure*, 198–199, 433–445.

see its prominence throughout 3.7–15 as a personal variation on a theme that carried public connotations in the Roman Odes. And whereas the Roman Odes end with deep pessimism toward the flow of time and the deleterious decline it brings, the odes that follow, while recognizing the losses that accompany this flow, stress rather its positive benefits and the possibility of adjusting oneself to its relentless progression. Old memories can make way for new departures, new initiatives find their way back to old patterns. The emphasis on dealing positively with time's inevitable movement is especially prominent in the final poems of 3.7–15, an effective entrée to 3.16–24's prevailing focus on positive, practical action.

Before we move on to this next section, however, it is worthwhile briefly to contrast the group we have just considered with its counterpart in Book 1. For while in many respects 3.7–15 is parallel to 1.13–19, in other respects it moves well beyond that earlier group. In place of the emphasis in 1.13, 1.16, and 1.19 on escape from passion, abatement of its impact, 3.7, 3.9, and 3.15 face the ups and downs of actual relationships with a certain equanimity. In place of the voyages that bode danger and destruction in 1.14 and 1.15, the desperate hope of rescue in 1.14 and the certainty that there can be no escape in 1.15, 3.8 and 3.14 celebrate Horace's escape from the tree, Augustus's safe return, the abatement of foreign threats to Roman safety, and the cessation of tumult and violence in Rome itself. In place of the poetic vale that Horace offers Tyndaris in 1.17, a vale isolated from the violence, passion, and brawling of the real world, Horace offers Bandusia, a spring whose talking waters absorb the blood of the young goat, transmuting into immortal verse that very vigor which once boded passion and fighting. And for 1.18's possibility of drowning cares in wine, a possibility as uncertain as it is temporary, 3.8 and 3.14 offer real wine, real escape, and a deliberate avoidance of the excesses and violence to which wine can lead (3.8.15–16, cf. 1.18.7 ff.).

CHAPTER IV

Odes 3.16–24

The poems of 3.16–24 return toward the magnitude of the
Roman Odes after the relative shortness of the poems in 3.7–
15, a movement heralded by the forty-four-line 3.16 and cli-
maxing in the sixty-four-line 3.24. The Alcaic meter, absent
in 3.7–15, also returns (3.17, 3.21, 3.23), though not until
3.29 will it again be used for a longer ode. And whereas six
of the nine addressees of 3.7–15 are Greek, six of the nine
poems erotic in theme, only two of the poems in 3.16–24
have Greek addressees, and the brief 3.20 is the only erotic
poem. The large framing poems set the tone of the group
with their hard-eyed practical look at the realities of contem-
porary Roman society. The express topicality of these two
long poems contrasts with the distanced setting of the only
long poem of the previous group, 3.11, a poem whose con-
siderable relevance to contemporary Rome remains at most
indirect, and the contrast is characteristic of the significant
differences between the two groups.

Most of the other poems of 3.16–24 also have their setting
in the world of contemporary Rome, though the practical
realities they face are scarcely of the magnitude of those faced
in 3.16 and 3.24. 3.19 and 3.21 are balancing drinking songs
to important Roman friends. Both poems present a no-non-
sense view of the drinking party—its pleasures, its hazards
(cf. *rixarum*, 3.19.16, *rixam*, 3.21.3), and its association with
love—and both remain remarkably free of *carpe diem* melan-
choly despite the fact that both openly refer to the passage of
time. 3.17, a poem bidding Aelius Lamia to prepare for a
festival on the morrow, is similarly lacking in any such
touches, though the *dum potes* of line 13 would seem an ob-
vious invitation to such. The balancing poem to Phidyle, 3.23,
offers similarly down-to-earth assurance that her humble of-
ferings are as welcome to the gods, and as effective, as are
the more munificent offerings of the rich. 3.18 and 3.22, two
short poems to Faunus and to Diana, both promise a sacrifice

in return for protection, and both evoke a Breughel-like rus-
ticity far more realistic in tone than are the settings of the
Faunus and Diana poems of Book 1 (1.17 and 1.21).

Against this backdrop of the practical, the everyday, and
the real, 3.20, the centerpiece of the group, stands out as
boldly as did the centerpiece of the previous group, 3.11. But
whereas 3.11 owes its preeminence to its magnitude and the
seriousness of the issues with which it deals, 3.20, despite its
motivic ties to 3.11, stands out by virtue of its reversion to
the ideal world of poetic play. Addressed to Pyrrhus and warn-
ing of danger courted unaware, the poem in tone, theme, and
addressee recalls the Pyrrha ode of Book 1, also sixteen lines
long. Like 1.5, 3.20 ends with a third party who is free of the
turmoil to which others are subject. Here, though, the indi-
vidual untouched by danger is not the former lover, as in 1.5,
but the object of the others' affections, another *puer* marble-
like in his repose, with his own perfumed hair (cf. the per-
fumes with which the *puer* of 1.5 presses his attentions on
Pyrrha).

This abrupt reversion to the escape poetry of Book 1 has
two effects. In the first place, it reminds us of how far Horace
has come in Book 3—that he is now dealing primarily with
the real world, a world in which 3.20 seems even more out
of place than did the diminutive 3.12, with its unique and
lovely Ionics, in the previous group. In 3.16–24 Horace has
left behind the escapist world of Book 1; aside from 3.20,
about all that here remains of that world is the brief idyll of
3.18.9–14, and even that is rudely dispelled by the realistic
note on which the poem ends (15–16).

But 3.20 works also in the opposite direction, suggesting
not just what Horace has gained by this immersion in the
realistic but also what he has lost. There is a certain similarity
between what happens in 3.16–24 and what happens in 3.1–
6. The Roman Odes mark an advance in that in them Horace
at last looks at Rome realistically, assessing weaknesses as well
as strengths, putting what has been gained against what has
been lost. On the other side, this overview becomes despairing

in proportion to its realism: the closer Horace looks at the realities of contemporary Rome, the more despairing he becomes, a movement that peaks in the thoroughgoing pessimism of 3.6. In the same way, 3.16–24 mark an advance over 3.7–15 in that increasingly they focus on the real rather than the imaginary world. At the same time, though, the very flight from the world of poetic fancy, from the ideal realm of Lydia and Bandusia, and the very focusing on reality, entail a tendency to the prosaic, a tendency that peaks in the down-to-earth advice to Phidyle in 3.23 and in 3.24's harsh realism. Indeed, the words with which 3.24 ends are applicable to this group itself: *tamen curtae nescio quid semper abest rei* (3.24.63–64). Despite their undeniable merits as the destination of Horace's voyage from escape to reality, these poems lack something—they tend to saunter rather than to soar. Aside from the fleeting 3.20, there is little here of the poetic glitter of Bandusia, the passion of 3.11, the charm of 3.9: that world seems now gone. That this apparent deficiency of 3.16–24 is again part of Horace's design is suggested by the fact that he places 3.20 at the center of the group, a reminder of what is elsewhere missing in 3.16–24, and by the fact that he does not end his collection with 3.24. The final group, 3.25–30, both recoups the imaginative properties that are wanting in much of 3.16–24 and also provides a climax that does soar, though this time Horace's course is more sober, less Icarean, than that of 2.20—a course that has its own clear-headed realism.

Before we turn to this last group, however, we need to consider the individual poems of 3.16–24. The Maecenas poem, 3.16, like the Maecenas ode that begins the second half of Book 1, both marks a new beginning and establishes the tone of the group to follow. True to its solid, practical tone, its focus is specifically on greed and the power of money rather than on the sexual mores and the *vis–lene consilium* themes that have hitherto been dominant in the book. Its emphasis on trimming sails, limiting wants, living within the boundaries of what is possible, transmutes Horace's advice to Chloris (3.15) from the erotic to the economic sphere and foreshadows the two final poems of the group, 3.23 and 3.24.[25] The concluding *quod satis est* (44) clearly echoes the central *quod satis est* of 3.1, the poem that opened the first half of Book 3, while the general tone and thematic thrust, and in particular Horace's almost crass bluntness toward Maecenas, take us back to 2.18. This same directness toward his patron foreshadows Horace's comparable directness toward Augustus in the balancing 3.24, while the central lines, 3.16.21–24, significantly point the way toward Horace's stance in his final poem to Maecenas, 3.29 (cf. 32 ff.).

The door motif, so common in 3.7–15, makes its final and dramatic appearance at the start of 3.16—appropriately, for 3.16 serves as threshold to a new and different world. The poem, with its transformation of Danae's shower of gold into the lure of lucre (1–8), is not especially attractive, but for that very reason it marks an apt entry into 3.16–24.[26] And its verbal and tonal links back to 2.18 and 3.1, and ahead to 3.24 and 3.29, enable it to serve as pivot point between what has preceded and what is to follow, a role not unlike that played by 1.20 in Book 1.

Of particular importance in 3.16, again as a link between what has preceded and what is to come, is the following passage from the central stanza:

> nil cupientium
> nudus castra peto et transfuga divitum
> partis linquere gestio . . .
> (3.16.22–24)

---

[25] Note in particular how the *uxor pauperis Ibyci* of 3.15.1 leads into the emphasis on poverty in 3.16.37 and 3.24.42 (cf. also 3.21.18). The motif sounds also in 3.2.1 and 1.12.43 (again a foreshadowing of later developments), and it climaxes in 3.29.14 and 56. Cf. above, Chapter I, note 41, for a related motivic link.

[26] See Fraenkel, *Horace*, 229–230, both on 3.16's placement at the start of a new section and on the tone of the poem: " . . . it has no wings." The final line of 3.15 prepares for the sordid start of 3.16: . . . *nec poti vetulam faece tenus cadi.*

Here for the first time the motif of flight from battle, a motif that in 3.2.14–16 had negative associations and that in 2.7.9–10 was explicitly associated with the flight at Philippi, takes on a clearly positive coloration. That this tonal shift comes in the opening poem of a new section is also significant (cf. the first mention of Philippi in 2.7, of the tree in 2.13), for it is a change that clears the way for Horace to move beyond the memory of *virtus fracta* in 2.7.11 (cf. also 3.5.27–30) and to advance toward the broader, more ethical, and more positive connotations *virtus* will carry in 3.24 and 3.29.

Although 3.17 begins with Lamia's lofty ancestry, it abruptly and amusingly descends from there to the rustic accents of the final two stanzas, where the strewn seaweed and the aged crow set the tone, where the nobly-descended Lamia will celebrate a simple feast along with his slaves (16), and where the potentially ominous *dum potes* of line 13 leads to nothing more than laying up dry wood and looking forward to pork and wine on the morrow.

This resolute focus on the realities of rustic life carries over to 3.18. In keeping with the poem's robust humor is the fact that Horace's prayer has much the tone of a business arrangement in which Horace's sacrifice is the condition for Faunus's good behavior.[27] Again the down-to-earth atmosphere is that of a rural feast day, and the passing idyll of lines 9–14, with the cattle cavorting in the field, man and beast at ease together, wolf consorting with lamb, is enclosed by delightfully realistic touches—the old altar smoking under its excess of incense (7–8) and the ditch-digger pounding the hated earth in vindictive three-step (15–16). Whereas elsewhere the sacrifice of a *haedus* calls forth a wealth of descriptive detail and the passing of time evokes dark philosophic reflections, in 3.18.5 both are treated as facts of life and quickly passed over, the potential melancholy sounded only in the passing *tener*.

---

[27] A not-unusual feature in ancient prayers, but more marked here than in most of Horace's other such poems. Note esp. the pointed *abeasque* (3), on which see Williams, *Third Book of Horace's Odes*, 106. On the differences between 3.18 and 1.17, see Fraenkel, *Horace*, 205 n. 2.

The opening of 3.19 sustains the realistic cast of 3.16–18 in its protest against irrelevant mythological talk (1–4) and its call to deal with the present needs of the party (5–8). Indeed, it is typical of the practical character of this whole section that the first question raised in lines 5–8 concerns the cost of the wine (*quo Chium pretio cadum mercemur*). Although the poem mentions the occasion for the party, the inception of Murena's augurship, it does not explore the broader ramifications of this new beginning. Nor does it explore the possible connotations of the chill outside (8) and the scattering of roses (22), though elsewhere these same motifs call forth reflection and melancholy. A sense of satisfaction with the here and now, not unlike that which Horace expresses in 3.14 and urges upon Chloris in 3.15, here characterizes the preparations both for carousing and for love. At this party each will drink in accordance with his own needs and wishes, be they for strong or weak wine (11–17), and here (in contrast to the situation of the neighboring Lycus) love will match like with like to the satisfaction of all. Telephus, no longer Horace's rival (cf. 1.13), will have a ready lover in Rhode (*tempestiva*, 27, cf. the not-yet-*tempestiva* Chloe of 1.23), and Horace himself will glow in lingering dalliance with the hitherto-elusive Glycera (cf. 1.19, 1.30, 1.33). The contrast with the mismatches of 1.27 and 1.33 could scarcely be more striking.

The erotic emphasis at the end of 3.19 leads directly into 3.20, with the evening-star luster of Telephus and his gleaming hair specifically foreshadowing the youthful beauty and the flowing hair of the *arbiter pugnae* at the end of 3.20. In other respects, though, the relationship of the poems is that of opposites, with the here-and-now details of 3.19 highlighting the distant artificiality of 3.20, 3.19's picture of lovers united setting off the harsh oppositions of 3.20's savage triangle. As we have already mentioned, the opposition functions in both directions, for just as the placement of 3.20 in the center of the realistic 3.16–24 underscores its artificial unreality, so in turn the ethereal, other-world elegance of 3.20

points up the resolute and at times hard-edged realism of the poems that surround it.

Such is certainly the effect of the abrupt shift from the transcendent calm and clarity of 3.20's last stanza to the genial *bonhomie* with which Horace opens 3.21, a poem addressed to a wine jar! The poem immediately recaptures the realistic tenor of 3.19, the more so because of its many links to that poem, and like 3.19 it avoids any temptation to soar high or probe deep. Like 3.8, 3.14, 3.17, and 3.19, it places an important figure in an everyday context, and this leveling of distinctions finds reinforcement in the emphasis placed on the universal appeal of wine (9–20). Even *virtus*, elsewhere always a key word, here appears in the centrally located line 12 without eliciting philosophical reflection or advice, nor does the fact that the wine comes from the year of Horace's own birth evoke personal revelation. The wine in the bottle may bring quarrels or jests, brawls or loves or sleep (1–4), and life itself represents a similar unknown, capable of bringing riches or poverty, hope or despair, love or war (cf. 17 ff.). The poem accepts whatever the bottle may hold and breathes acceptance also of life's unknowns; it is a warm, relaxed, satisfied poem, mellow like the wine, and somewhat languid (cf. line 8).[28]

3.21's closing mention of Phoebus eases the transition to one of Horace's gems, his exquisite poem to Diana, 3.22. The delicacy and refinement of this minute piece set off the prosaic quality of the two poems that surround it, but even it belongs to the real world where childbirth brings pain and even death (cf. lines 2–3) and where the goddess's favor must be insured by a sacrifice. The poem belongs to Horace's own world and is infused with his own happiness (6), a happiness that can again look forward with pleasure to the passing of time (cf. *per exactos ego laetus annos*, 6), and that can now see a tree as a symbol of safety! Even Horace's address of Diana as *diva*

---

[28] Note that just as in 3.14, the second of the two drinking poems within 3.7–15, Horace mentions Plancus, consul in the year of Philippi, so in 3.21, the second of the two drinking poems within 3.16–24, he speaks of Messalla, like Horace a partisan of Brutus in 42 B.C. The poem in some ways recalls 2.7, another ode to a fellow veteran of Brutus's campaigns.

triformis (4)—maiden, wife, crone—carries implicitly the recognition that change and transformation are simple facts of life.

3.23 too presupposes the acceptance of life as it is and the possibility of finding satisfaction in the passing years. It does not mask the differences between rich and poor, and it does not romanticize *rustica Phidyle*, but it finds both charm and dignity in the simple offerings that she can bring to the gods, and it assures her of their efficacy. As with most poems in the group, 3.23 addresses the question of how to deal with a particular situation and proposes down-to-earth advice. Human-divine relations are seen from a practical rather than a philosophical perspective, and the stance taken toward life stresses not the ultimate fact of death but the unfolding realities of life, not a *carpe diem* enjoyment of the brief present but a tempered savoring of the passing years. The focus is very much on the deliberate and thoughtful management of those aspects of life which humans can control.

3.24 represents in every sense the destination toward which this whole section has been moving.[29] It is by far the longest poem in the group, by far the largest also in theme and conception, and it imbues its prevailingly practical and realistic themes with genuine feeling. As 3.14 places Augustus in a setting similar to that of the balancing Maecenas poem, 3.8, so 3.24 takes its cue from the balancing 3.16 and approaches Augustus with a hardheaded realism reminiscent of the tone adopted in 3.16 toward Maecenas:

> o quisquis volet impias
> caedis et rabiem tollere civicam,
> si quaeret PATER URBIUM
> subscribi statuis, indomitam audeat
> refrenare licentiam,
> clarus postgenitis:
> (3.24.25–30)

[29] On the relationship of 3.24 to the Roman Odes, see F. Solmsen, "Horace's First Roman Ode," *AJP* 68 (1947): 343 ff.

As elsewhere in this section the focus is on facing facts, on action rather than on words,[30] on daring to do what one can do. The focus is also unrelentingly on what *humans* can do, be they the citizens subsumed in the emphatic *nos* of 45 and 47 or Augustus himself, and it is scarcely accidental that these two relevant agents are mentioned at roughly balancing places in the poem.[31]

It is in such a context that Horace returns to *virtus*. The word has been used sparingly early in the collection—introduced in 2.2 and 2.7, explored in some depth in 3.2 and 3.5, glossed over in 3.21; its final, highly personal appearance will be in 3.29, but 3.24, in which it appears three times (lines 22, 31, 44), represents Horace's fullest exploration of its public implications. Two aspects of this exploration are especially important. First, *virtus* here again is a quality that clearly transcends military might. The poem does mention the sort of Spartan hardiness that leads up to 3.2's mention of *virtus* (3.24.52 ff., cf. 3.2.1 ff.), but the contexts in which *virtus* itself appears, and the thrust of the entire poem, suggest a larger, more inner quality. In lines 22 and 31 *virtus* is closely associated with one focus of the poem, the need to foster sexual morality and restrain license, in line 44 with the other focus, the need to check avarice and profligacy and to foster a simpler lifestyle. It is with reference to this latter type of *virtus* that the poem at lines 52–54 speaks, in tones reminiscent of 3.2.1 ff., of fostering a new hardiness in the young. The military focus of 3.2.1 ff. is, however, completely absent in 3.24, both in lines 52–54 and in what follows, where, in a passage that neatly sums up the poem's twin thrusts, Horace speaks first of personal morality (56–60, cf. 17–30), then of greed (61–64, cf. 36–52).

[30] Note the application to the public realm of the "complaint" motif: for Rome, as for Tibullus (1.33.1 ff.), Valgius (2.9.17 ff.), Maecenas (2.17.1 ff.), and Asterie (3.7.1 ff.), the need is for action, not complaints and tears: *quid tristes querimoniae . . .* (3.24.33 ff.).

[31] Cf. the balancing *Romane* and *nos* in 3.6.2 and 47, on which see note 13 above.

Second, the poem's exclusively human context[32] establishes the proper provenance of *virtus*, the fact that *virtus* entails the application of human capacities to human problems. This emphasis on human action and initiative is the goal toward which the practical thrust of the preceding poems has been moving, and it is with this emphasis on human capacity that Horace now returns to the broad scope of the Roman Odes.

3.24 is the last large poem in Books 1–3 to deal primarily with national and public themes, and in it for the first time Horace both approaches Augustus with complete openness and sets the needs of Rome in an exclusively human context. Gone are 1.2's and 1.12's lengthy catalogues of assisting divinities, gone 3.3's and 3.4's recourse to divine myth, gone the association of Augustus with divine status, that theme which is so marked in 1.2 and 1.12 and which still seems just around the corner in the otherwise straightforward 3.14. In 3.24 Augustus himself is a human, and Horace speaks to him as man to man, calling for human action that will reap a human reward—the title *pater urbium*. Nor does Horace stop with Augustus. The rest of the Romans—and the *nos* of 45 and 47 makes clear that Horace includes himself among this number—are also to join in this human enterprise in which, as in previous poems of this group, humans great and small, rich and poor, will participate in common endeavor.[33] Such shared human action is Horace's final answer to the *culpa* (cf. line 34) and *scelus* (cf. line 50) that in earlier poems he saw as plaguing Rome (cf. 1.2.29, 1.35.33, 3.6.17). It is an answer that both in its focus on inner morality and restraint and in its demand for clear vision and courageous action recalls the response Hypermnestra makes to her situation in 3.11.

The *virtus* called for in 3.24 resembles Hypermnestra's also in that it relies not on might and power but on *lene consilium*. For noticeably absent from 3.24 is any reference to restoring

---

[32] The personified *Necessitas* of 6 and the metonymic *Cererem* of 13 are the closest 3.24 comes to mentioning the gods.

[33] Cf. variations on the leveling of distinctions in 3.17.14–16, 3.18.11 ff., 3.21.17 ff., 3.23.

the state by defeating the barbarians, that sort of chauvinistic cliché which was so common in earlier poems. Indeed, 3.24 goes so far as to suggest that the Romans might well take the Scythians or the Getae (9 ff., cf. the anti-Scythian thrust of 1.35.9, 3.8.23) as their models toward regaining a lost simplicity of life, a lost purity of family life, a lost *virtus* (cf. line 22).

3.24, like other members of this group, is a poem that tends not to soar, that from start to finish concentrates on the real world and its knotty problems. But this very quality is its triumph. The poem dares to look at human agents, not divine, for the initiative that will save the state; it dares to concentrate on real problems at home, not the distant Parthian disgrace, as the proper concern of Romans interested in fostering new life, a new sense of *virtus*; and it dares to speak bluntly and directly both to Rome and to Augustus about what needs to be done. It is the very realism of these qualities that enables 3.24 to rise above both the empty optimism of 1.2 and 1.12 and the despairing pessimism of 3.6. It makes no pretense that the way to rebirth is easy: like the course Hypermnestra must follow (or, for that matter, Asterie, Chloris, Phidyle), Rome's course will be marked by tough choices, by acceptance of compromise, and by hardships unassuaged by any magical divine assistance. But inasmuch as the course is that of autonomous agents who can see what must be done and take steps to do it, the way is open for humans to reverse the downward curve charted in 3.6.45–48. *virtutis . . . viam . . . arduae* (3.24.44): virtue's path is steep, but it is upward.

It is also steadily forward, for a notable feature of 3.24, one shared with many poems within 3.16–24, is that it resolutely faces the present and the immediate future, eschewing alike nostalgia for Rome's bygone past and visionary dreams of a golden future, horror over her recent past and grave prognostications of her imminent decline. Thus 3.24's early vignette of a better and simpler life, a more disciplined private morality (3.24.9–24), is set not in the lost republican past (as in 3.5 and 3.6) but among the Getae and the Scythians, and the concluding call to abolish the wealth that fosters greed and to inculcate hardiness in the young similarly makes no mention of Rome's republican past (cf. 2.15.10 ff.). In the same way, the poem offers no future visions of Rome Ruling the World (as in 3.3.38 ff.), of Augustus sipping nectar (cf. 3.3.11–12) or being hailed as a Present Divinity (cf. 3.5.2–4), but concentrates instead on what Augustus and his people can and must do now. Moreover, the poem makes no reference to the recent civil wars, and if the vision it projects of the future is scarcely rosy, neither is it, in the manner of 3.6, totally despairing.

Such is Horace's final response to the future-past tension in the Roman Odes. In 3.1–6 he draws attention to a contradiction implicit in the Augustan program—that it seems to insist both upon abandoning the past so as to build the future, and upon recovering the past so as to build the future. In 3.24, in contrast, he draws attention away from this potential contradiction by focusing squarely on the present—its problems, needs, possibilities. This stance toward past and future both reflects the solid realism of 3.24 itself and also grows out of the preceding poems of this group. For these too, as we have seen, eschew excursions into the distant past or visions of the far-flung future to focus on the here and now. Thus 3.17 treats Lamia's noble ancestry with open irony and 3.19 urges the irrelevance of ancient genealogies and wars; and the future glimpsed in 3.18.5 and 3.22.6 is that of the passing years, not the distant immortality of Bandusia or the Horatian swan.

3.24, with its steep road of *virtus*, restores something of the upward thrust of 2.20 and 3.3, though for their heady surge it substitutes the rugged path up the mountain. The words *virtutis . . . viam . . . arduae* also recall the *nil mortalibus ardui est* of 1.3.37. The reminiscence is appropriate, for the road Horace lays out for Rome in 3.24, like that of Vergil and the other human strivers of 1.3, is not the god-attended jaunt of 1.2 or 1.12 but a lonely and often dangerous ascent on which mortals may often feel themselves pitted against the "gods."

In 3.24 Horace himself also takes to that same tough climb,

for not only does he expressly associate himself with the task he therein lays upon the Romans, but his very act of writing the poem itself represents the sort of Vergilian daring from which he stands apart in 1.3 and which he explicitly rejects in 1.6. For like Vergil in the *Aeneid*, Horace in 3.24 dares to deal openly, honestly, and even bluntly with basic public issues, to confront real needs at home rather than to escape them in dreams of foreign conquest, and to focus solely on what humans, without recourse to a *deus ex machina*, can do for themselves. The poem itself marks a goal toward which Horace's political poetry has been climbing throughout the collection. It also marks an important step along the steep road by which Horace will at the end of the collection at last come to terms with his own *virtus*.

3.24 is thus a major point of arrival in *Odes* 1–3, a poem that pulls together and builds on numerous important motifs from earlier in the collection. The hard-hitting realism that is its special virtue, however, a quality emphasized by its tonal and thematic affinity to the *Satires*, itself makes it too earthbound to serve as conclusion to the collection. 3.24 also seems, unlike the *Satires*, to contain too little of Horace himself to be an adequate conclusion. Again, though, these very defects play their part in the overall design. The poem leaves us with a slight sense of incompleteness, a sense underscored by the ode's concluding words (*tamen curtae nescio quid semper abest rei*), and our longing for a conclusion that attains greater heights and contains more of Horace himself is amply satisfied in the six poems that follow.

Odes 3.25–30

3.25 both celebrates the goals attained in 3.24 and introduces the final section of the collection. Its joyous words on Augustus, the most extravagant we have heard since early in Book 3, look back to Horace's significant advances in his treatment of Augustus and his programs in 3.24:

> quibus
> antris egregii Caesaris audiar
> aeternum meditans decus
> stellis inserere et consilio Iovis?
> (3.25.3–6)

The tenor of these lines builds on the undercurrent of cautious optimism in 3.24, as if to say, "If Augustus really moves in the directions charted in 3.24, *then* there will be reason to praise him to the stars, to name him among the gods." These same lines of 3.25 also, however, underscore the fact that the hopes of 3.24 are as yet unfulfilled, and significantly none of the remaining five poems of Book 3 focuses on national issues or praises Augustus. 3.24 represents an identification of what desperately needs to be done, and the interrogatives with which 3.25 opens (*quo me . . . , quae nemora . . . , quos agor . . . , quibus antris . . .*), the futures with which it continues (*audiar, dicam, loquar*), look to action whose accomplishment remains still uncertain, still in the future. Like the bacchante of his poem (3.25.8 ff.), Horace at this point is still but surveying the vista, looking into an empty grove. In Book 4 Horace does confer on Augustus praise of just the sort he describes in 3.25, and he does so in words that recall what he recommends in 3.24:

indomitam audeat	et ordinem
refrenare licentiam . . .	rectum evaganti *frena licentiae*
(3.24.28–29)	iniecit (4.15.9–11)

| si non supplicio *culpa* reciditur | emovitque *culpas*[34] |
| (3.24.34) | (4.15.11) |

As if to emphasize further this close relationship between the hopes of 3.24–25 and the realities attained by the time of Book 4, Horace also echoes in the central poem of Book 4 the final line of 3.25:

---

[34] Cf. also *culpari* and *culpam* in 4.5.20 and 24.

cingentem *viridi tempora pampino*
(3.25.20)
ornatus *viridi tempora pampino*[35]
(4.8.33)

Apparently Horace felt that Augustus had responded to the hopes voiced in 3.24 and 3.25, and the echoes of these poems in Book 4 graciously if subtly acknowledge that response.

Within Books 1–3, however, 3.25 marks that point after which Horace unexpectedly abandons his national themes. This surprise is only one of several that Horace concocts in this brilliant concluding section, and 3.25 is an apt entrée into this land of *paraprosdokia*. This sudden Dionysiac incursion, so unexpected after the low-lying 3.23–24, immediately raises the question of where it will lead: like 2.19, which it so resembles, into another Icarean flight (cf. 2.20)—exciting, dramatic, overstated? Like 2.19–20 into another set of national poems (cf. 3.1–6)? Or perhaps back into the world of poetic escape? All of these alternatives are possible sequels to 3.25, all in tune with the *exsomnis . . . Euhias* who dominates its central lines.

In the long run, however, none of these proves the correct answer. Lines 3–6 and 14–20 lead us strongly to expect another set of national odes, especially after the sequence that led from 2.19 into the Roman Odes, but we get no more national odes. Moreover, 3.26 at once undercuts any thought that 3.25 will lead to another 2.20, for clearly 3.26, with its tonal and the-

---

[35] This nexus of Book 4 echoes of 3.24 and 3.25 may be one good reason for retaining the suspected 4.8.33. For other arguments in its favor, see H. C. Toll, "Unity in the *Odes* of Horace," *Phoenix* 9 (1955): 161–162, and D. H. Porter, "A Note on the Text of Horace, C. 4.8," *AJP* 107 (1986): 416–421. For the arguments in favor of deleting the line (along with others in the poem), see esp. C. Becker, "Donarem pateras," *Hermes* 87 (1959): 212–222. On the place of 3.25 in the movement of the collection, see Silk, *YCS* 21 (1969): 209 ff.; on the way it mingles affirmation with uncertainty, even doubt, see P. J. Connor, "Enthusiasm, Poetry, and Politics: A Consideration of Horace, *Odes*, III, 25," *AJP* 92 (1971): 266–274.

matic similarities to 1.5, its battles of love so reminiscent of 1.6.17–20, returns us to the very realm of the *tenue* which 2.20.1 left behind. Like 2.20, 3.25 seems to point in precisely the opposite direction from 1.6, the poem it balances in the collection, but 3.26 makes us ask, "Can *this* delicate poem be what Horace meant when he promised *dicam insigne recens adhuc indictum ore alio; nil parvum aut humili modo, nil mortale loquar* (3.25.7–8, 17–18)? Is *this* cautious piece the creation of the poet filled with the Bacchic spirit, the poet to whom danger is sweet (cf. 3.25.1–3, 18–20)?"

3.26 exists partly to puncture, by a typical Horatian surprise, the high promises of 3.25, but we should not fail to notice that despite its clear links to 1.5 it also differs from that ode significantly. While the Horace of 1.5 has hung up his wet clothes in gratitude for his escape from Pyrrha and has apparently no intention of plunging into those waters again, the poet of 3.26, who also has hung up the accoutrements of love on the sacred wall (lines 1–8), is, in yet another surprise, already asking Venus to lead him back into the fray (lines 9–12). The change of direction is important, for where the characteristic movement at the start of Book 1 is away from action and involvement, that at the close of Book 3 is toward new adventure, a movement clearly introduced in 3.25 and, in the end, sustained in 3.26. Moreover, the poems that immediately follow, 3.27 and 3.28, do indeed take us once more to the realm of *Venus marina* (3.26.5, cf. 3.28.13–16, the sea setting of 3.27.26–66), and 3.29 climaxes in Horace himself bravely taking to the sea. Thus while at the time 3.26 seems merely a stumbling block to the bold projections of 3.25, in retrospect it turns out to be a not-inappropriate introduction to the poems that follow, poems in which, in fact, Horace will sing something *insigne recens adhuc indictum ore alio*. Even the jauntily retrospective *vixi* with which 3.26 begins turns out to foreshadow the proud *vixi* of 3.29.43.

If 3.26 initially appears to contradict the promises of 3.25, 3.27 at first seems in many ways to fulfill them. Horace has

CHAPTER IV

given us other mythological excursions—1.15, 3.11, the myths of 3.3 and 3.4; but what we have here is in scope, tone, and development of central character quite unique. This *is* the work of a poet *velox mente nova* (3.25.3), one who, like the bacchante of 3.25 8 ff., is surveying a new and uncharted land. Even its central figure, Europa, fits this theme, for she too is entering a new and frightening world, she too encountering a *periculum* that, in the end, proves to be *dulce*. Like the lover who looks to a new love at the end of 3.26,[36] the poet who ponders an uncharted future in 3.25.1 ff., Europa finds herself swept on toward destinations as yet unknown. Both in substance and manner 3.27 thus seems to fulfill expectations raised by 3.25.

The poem also responds, as we saw in Chapter I, to 1.3, but as with the balance of 1.5 and 3.26, the relationship of the two poems is in several respects one of opposition. 1.3 moves toward pessimistic conclusions about the folly of humans who dare great voyages and ends by suggesting that such humans bring upon themselves the thunderbolts of Jupiter. 3.27 moves toward Venus's laughter over mortal fears and ends with the revelation that Jupiter himself is the agent who brought Europa on the hazardous voyage. Moreover, if in 1.3 Horace seems at least implicitly to recoil from the dangerous epic voyage on which Vergil was currently embarked, in 3.27 he himself unexpectedly, and with dapper aplomb, plunges into epic waters such as hitherto he has avoided.

3.28, with its light tone and its concluding erotic touch that recalls 3.26, neatly rounds out this trio of love poems in which the slight 3.26 and 3.28 enclose the lengthy 3.27.[37] All three

---

[36] It is in keeping with the pervading emphasis on newness and freshness in 3.25–30 that the Chloe of 3.26 regains the bright freshness of the Chloe of 1.23 (cf. the Chloe of 3.7 and 3.9). For a different interpretation of 3.26 (one that also emphasizes the balance of 3.26 and 1.5), see C. P. Jones, "*Tange Chloen semel arrogantem*," *HSCP* 75 (1971): 81–83.

[37] On this trio of love poems, see Kiessling-Heinze, Introduction to 3.26. The construction of 3.26–28 recalls that of 3.10–12: in each instance two

of these poems, with their Greek addressees and artificial settings, seem deliberately to pull away from the realism of 3.16–24 and to retreat into an escapist realm reminiscent of 1.5 and 1.6. This tendency is highlighted in 3.28 in that while the dating of the wine by reference to the consulship of Bibulus recalls similar motifs in 3.8, 3.14, and 3.21, this poem totally lacks both the important public figures—Maecenas, Augustus, Messalla—central to those three poems and those poems' allusions to contemporary Roman events. In addition, 3.28.5–8 contains the first clear hint of the *carpe diem* motif that we have met in Book 3, another apparent reversion to the mode and model of Book 1 and the first twelve poems of Book 2.

Despite the magnitude of 3.27 and the new avenues it explores, the overall effect of 3.26–28 is thus to counter the thrust of 3.25, to move away from its announced national themes, and to lead the reader to expect a falling, escapist close to the collection. Indeed, a prime function of the gentle and diminutive 3.28 is to set up yet one more surprise, for what follows is one of Horace's grandest and most daring odes, the large, serious, highly personal 3.29. At the same time, however, 3.28's focus on Neptune and the sea provides a neat motivic bridge between the depiction of Europa's sea journey in 3.27 and Horace's envisioned voyage at the end of 3.29. It is typical of Horace's art that this brief poem can both create sharp contrasts with the large poems that surround it and also by its imagery serve as the connecting link between them.[38]

Not only is 3.29 the last thing we would expect after 3.28, but also it obliges us to revise our estimate of 3.27. For whereas 3.27 seems initially to fulfill the promises of 3.25, with 3.29 we suddenly see that it, not 3.27, is the goal toward which 3.25 was directing us, and we begin for the first time

---

shorter love poems (3.10 and 3.12, 3.26 and 3.28) surround a longer love poem that focuses on a mythological heroine (3.11, 3.27). On the way in which 3.26 leads into 3.27, see T. Berres, "Zur Europaode des Horaz (c. 3.27)," *Hermes* 102 (1974): 85.

[38] Cf. the binding effect of the recurrent sea imagery in the poems at the start of the collection.

to see 3.27 for the lovely but lightweight froth that it is. 3.29 is the first large Alcaic poem since the Roman Odes, and as such it both stands out in itself and also suggests a return to the vigor and the confidence that found expression in the great Alcaic outburst of 2.19–3.6. It is also a poem that skillfully weaves together numerous themes and motifs from the rest of the collection: *virtus*, rivers in flood, *pauperies*, rich and poor contrasts, escape from care, sea-voyaging, the folly of mere complaints, human-divine opposition—all these and more find their place in this ode. And at its precise center, here clearly sounded for the first time in Book 3, but set in a new and larger context, is the *carpe diem* motif:

> quod adest memento

> componere aequus;
>   (3.29.32–33)

3.29 stands out also because of its intensely personal focus, a focus highlighted by the movement of the poem, which begins with wide-angle glimpses at a variety of subjects—Maecenas and his home, the bustle of Rome, astrological indications, country scenes, public affairs, the Tiber—but concludes with a close-up shot of Horace himself, alone upon the Aegean. It is the absence of this personal element in 3.24 which above all leaves that poem feeling incomplete, and to a lesser degree the same is true of 3.27, where the movement is precisely the opposite of 3.29—from Horace's initial involvement to his virtual disappearance as we become caught up in the tale of Europa. It is this intensely personal thrust of 3.29 that, even more than its sheer size, its Alcaic meter, and its position of importance, renders it such an appropriate climax to the collection.

Here Horace dares to stand alone, exemplar of the courage, independence, and initiative that have been his themes throughout, dares even, if necessary, to stand up to the dread *Pater* himself (43 ff.). Even the *carpe diem* stance struck in the central lines points not toward escape but toward involvement.

It is a stance that presupposes Book 3's frequent emphasis on living life, making the necessary adjustments, accepting the good with the bad, but that also dares to confront the ultimate realities—death, the unpredictability of the gods—with a directness not found in 3.7–24. The *vixi* of line 43 has none of the blithe insouciance of 3.26.1; instead it is more akin to the wonderful passage near the end of *Satires* 1.1:

> inde fit ut raro qui se vixisse beatum
> dicat, et exacto contentus tempore vita
> cedat uti conviva satur, reperire queamus
> (*Sat.* 1.1.117–119)

For not unlike the Satire from which this passage comes, 3.29 sets its *carpe diem* in a context not of wine, women, and song but of *virtus, proba pauperies*, the conscious choice as to how one should respond to forces beyond one's control (cf. 53 ff.).

Like 3.24, 3.29 picks up and responds to specific motifs from a number of earlier poems. Its links to the poems at the very start of the collection are especially close, and these links establish it both as a thematic goal within the collection and also as a crucial point of arrival in Horace's personal journey of the spirit. Thus Horace opens 1.1, the collection's first poem to Maecenas, by addressing his patron as *praesidium* (1.1.2), but he closes 3.29, the last poem to Maecenas, by speaking of his confidence in the *praesidium* of his own small boat (3.29.62).[39] At the start of 1.3 he shrinks from the voyage Vergil is about to make and speaks of the *aes triplex* that must gird the hearts of those who brave the deep; in 3.29, however, he boldly professes his own readiness to take to the sea, wrapped only in the armor of his own virtue. In 1.3 he calls on *diva potens Cypri* and the Dioscuri to help Vergil, but in

[39] On these relationships, see Santirocco, *TAPA* 114 (1984): 252. 2.17 strikes a stance midway between that of 1.1 and that of 3.29, still recognizing Maecenas's protective role (2.17.4) but at the same time adopting a protective posture toward Maecenas (*passim*, and esp. 10–12). On the tone and character of 3.29, see esp. V. Pöschl, "Die grosse Maecenasode des Horaz (c. 3, 29)," *SHAW* 1961, 1, *passim*.

3.29.41 he is *potens sui*, and his certainty of the Dioscuri's assistance expresses not his belief in the gods but his faith in himself. This new self-reliance in 3.29 enables Horace also to attain a different and deeper understanding even of the gods' wisdom. In 1.3.21–24, at the start of the second half of his poem to Vergil, he writes:

> nequiquam *deus* abscidit
> *prudens* Oceano dissociabili
> terras, si tamen impiae
> non tangenda rates transiliunt vada.

In 3.29.29–32, at the end of the first half of his poem to Maecenas, he responds:

> *prudens* futuri temporis exitum
> caliginosa nocte premit *deus*,
> ridetque si mortalis ultra
> fas trepidat.

Both passages speak of limits set by the gods, limits within which humans must learn to live. But whereas 1.3's understanding of divine wisdom leads Horace to recommend human caution and to denigrate human daring and enterprise, 3.29's deepened perception of the divine purpose is the basis for the courageous stance he recommends in the lines that immediately follow and the backdrop to his celebration of his own daring enterprise in 3.30. Moreover, whereas in 1.2 Horace appeals to the gods for aid against the violent Tiber flood, in 3.29 he finds in humans themselves the resources to stand up to a similarly awesome Tiber flood. And while 1.2 hopes for divine release from the Sky Father (1–4) and turns at the end to the winged Mercury for assistance (cf. 42), 3.29 declares Horace's readiness to stand up to the fickle Father himself (43–48) and not to be shaken if Fortune rustles her threatening wings (53 ff.).[40]

---

[40] Cf. also the *ludus* of Mars in 1.2.37, of fortune in 3.29.50. In 3.29 Horace himself can stand up to divine *ludus*, while in 1.2 humans must look to divine

The intensely personal character of 3.29 renders it unique among the larger Alcaic poems of the collection, but it is important to recognize also the poem's public implications. It is Horace's mention of Maecenas's public concerns (25–28) that leads into the long passage which deals with the self-possession and courage of the individual, and it is clear that these comments on how individuals are to deal with uncertainty are relevant to the public realm as well. For Rome too, as 3.24 makes very plain, the way to deal with the uncertainties of the future is to consolidate what it has (cf. 3.29.32–33), to pursue *proba pauperies* (cf. 3.29.55–56), and to wrap herself in *virtus* (cf. 3.29.55). That the flooding Tiber of 3.29 balances and recalls the flooding Tiber of 1.2, the *Pater* of 3.29.44 the *Pater* of 1.2.2, further suggests the public relevance of what Horace says in 3.29 about how to withstand the ravages of the flood, the blows of the *Pater*. Whether for states or for individuals, the crucial point is to recognize that while powers do exist beyond human ken and control, the best response to these powers is for humans to take every initiative toward those aspects of life they can control and to accept with dignity those they cannot. Whether it be the mast of Horace's *scapha* that groans (3.29.57–58) or that of the ship of state (cf. 1.14.5), it is such a stance, not pathetic complaints (cf. *miseras preces*, 3.29.58, *tristes querimoniae*, 3.24.33), that can withstand the tumult of sea and storm, of civil uprising, and of inner anxiety and care.[41]

Perhaps the most significant cross-reference between 3.29 and an earlier poem involves *mea virtute me involvo* (3.29.54–55). This phrase recalls most immediately the repeated mentions of *virtus* in 3.24, a reminiscence that further suggests the

---

mandate for an end to the cruel *ludus* of war. Cf. also the *ludum . . . Fortunae* of 2.1.3.

[41] With the *Aegaeos tumultus* of 3.29.63, cf. the *tumultus* of inner care in 2.16.10, of civil uprising in 3.14.14, of Orion's descent in 3.27.17; also the *tumultuosum . . . mare* of 3.1.26. Note also the clear parallel between Horace's self-sufficiency in 3.29, the penultimate poem of Book 3, and Cleopatra's in 1.37, the penultimate poem of Book 1: cf. above, p. 52.

public dimension implicit in 3.29. 3.29.55 recalls also, however, Horace's crucial reference to *virtus* in 2.7.11, and the contrast between these two passages is one of the more striking indices of the thematic movement of the collection. The very fact that Horace can in 3.29 express total confidence in his own *virtus* indicates how far he has risen above the sense of *virtus fracta* in 2.7. Even in 3.2 and 3.5 the very mention of *virtus* seemed to evoke, almost as if by conditioned response, thoughts of Horace's own flight. Here in 3.29, however, Horace's *virtus* is so fully restored that he can don it as the armor in which he will now face whatever may come.

Horace does not expressly define the *virtus* of 3.29.55, but clearly it again is a quality that transcends mere military bravery. That courage is part of this *virtus* is obvious, but it is a courage which, like the *virtus* of 3.24,[42] above all is inner, the product not of physical strength but of spiritual fiber. One can perhaps not find a better statement of its full connotations in 3.29 than in Reinhold Niebuhr's famous words: ". . . serenity to accept what cannot be changed, courage to change what should be changed, and wisdom to distinguish the one from the other."[43] It is precisely because the collection has moved toward a *virtus* that is spiritual rather than physical, that deals with a range of human situations rather than just with martial concerns, and that is a matter of one's ongoing response to the challenge of life rather than of one's actions on a particular battlefield, that Horace can now see that, in any significant sense, his own *virtus*, far from being fractured, is a source of strength, not weakness, a cause for pride, not shame.

We are now in a position to discuss the significant differences between 3.27 and 3.29. For while numerous motivic

[42] Note the association of *virtus* with a simple life-style in both 3.24 and 3.29: see 3.24.45 ff., immediately following the mention of *virtus* in line 44; 3.29.55–56, *probam . . . pauperiem quaero*, immediately following the mention of *virtus* in line 55.

[43] From a prayer composed by Niebuhr in 1934. See the opening page (unnumbered) of J. Bingham, *Courage to Change. An Introduction to the Life and Thought of Reinhold Niebuhr* (New York, 1961).

links mark the complementary relationship of these two large poems in the last section,[44] these same links also emphasize the vast gulf between them. The sea in 3.27 is a source of terror for humans, while 3.29 ends with a human fearless before the sea. Europa's salvation comes from the gods—from the Venus who consoles her and the Jupiter who will render her famous; the *potens sui* of 3.29.41 finds salvation in his own resources and can stand up even to Jupiter. Europa's sole recourse is to prayers and complaints (cf. *querenti*, 3.27.66); Horace rejects the flight *ad miseras preces* (3.29.58–59). All of these contrasts point in the same direction: while 3.27 focuses on a human wholly dependent on the gods, the emphasis of 3.29 is entirely on human initiative. Europa does nothing to help herself, the *potens sui* of 3.29 everything.

In addition, 3.29 has a moral urgency, a philosophical seriousness, lacking in 3.27. 3.27 places Europa in a totally amoral universe, one where her *virtus*, or lack of it, is unrelated to what happens to her, while 3.29 posits rational moral choice as the necessary basis for dealing with the world: what you are, and how you act, *do* matter. Both the terrors of 3.29 and the human responses to those terrors are real, while in 3.27 the terrors are exaggerated and the response to them childish, almost frivolous. 3.27 merely laughs, charmingly but meaninglessly, at the folly of both gods and men, while 3.29 dares to confront the absurdity of the universe and to posit a human response that is profoundly serious—although not without its concluding touch of irony, its hint of the *lentus risus* of 2.16.26–27.

It is in these ways that 3.29 reveals by contrast the shallowness of 3.27, and in retrospect we see that the high promises of 3.25 point not to 3.27 but to 3.29. Two of the great thematic movements of the collection have been its thrust toward human initiative and autonomy and its ever-increasing emphasis on ethical distinctions, on *virtus*. 3.27, with its amoral tone and its pawn of a heroine, moves counter to these two pre-

---

[44] For links between 3.27 and 3.29, see above, pp. 48–49.

vailing thrusts, while 3.29, with its seriousness of tone and its emphasis on human autonomy, lends impetus to both.

Book 3 holds one more poem, and one more surprise. We have seen that in many ways 3.29 functions as a point of arrival, a goal toward which the whole collection has been moving, and in magnitude of conception and execution it is indeed the climax of *Odes* 1–3. But if we are expecting a falling close such as that provided by *Persicos odi* in Book 1, 3.30 foils our expectations by moving yet one step higher. For the lofty dwelling (3.29.10) of Maecenas, *Tyrrhena regum progenies* (3.29.1), we now have Horace's own poetic monument, *regali . . . situ pyramidum altius* (3.30.2), a poetic edifice whose indestructibility contrasts sharply with the transience of all material entities in 3.29 (cf. esp. *lapides adesos*, 3.29.36, *quod non imber edax . . . possit diruere*, 3.30.3–4). The *potens sui* ready to say *vixi* in the face of an unknown future (3.29.41–43) yields to the *ex humili potens* (3.30.12) who begins 3.30 with the proud *exegi*, a proclamation that he has now completed what he set out to do and hence a reminder of his statement at 3.29.45–48:

> non tamen irritum,
> quodcumque retro est, efficiet neque
>   diffinget infectumque reddet
>   quod fugiens semel hora vexit.

A river in flood suggests human frailty at 3.29.36 ff. while the *violens . . . Aufidus* at 3.30.10 will participate in Horace's poetic immortality. Horace counts himself among the *pauperes* at 3.29.14 (cf. also 56) but does not hesitate to use the word *princeps* of his accomplishments at 3.30.13. And the Horace who begins 3.29 by promising roses for Maecenas's hair ends 3.30 by claiming the laurel for his own. Moreover, if 3.29 seemed *surely* to be the goal toward which 3.25 was looking, the numerous clear verbal ties between 3.25 and 3.30 make it clear that at least the motivic strands of 3.25 find full completion only in 3.30.[45]

[45] For links between 3.25 and 3.30, see above, pp. 47–48.

3.30, like other poems in this final group, also picks up strands from several earlier poems and especially from those at the opposite end of the collection, 1.1–3. Its relation to 1.1 is obvious and familiar. Above all it marks the achievement of the goals proposed in 1.1, with the proud perfect *exegi* on which it begins responding to the conditional futures with which 1.1 ends (*quodsi . . . inseres, . . . feriam*). 1.1 looks longingly toward the garlands of the Muses (29–30), 3.30 haughtily[46] claims them (3.30.14–16); 1.1.33–34 hopes the Muse will not refuse to tune the Lesbian lyre, 3.30.13–14 proclaims Horace's achievement of fitting Aeolic song to Italic measures. But while 1.1 proposes airy flight toward the stars, 3.30 roots Horace's accomplishment firmly in the earth, and this same difference distinguishes it also from the extravagant flight of 2.20. For where 2.20 soars with too-reckless abandon over the earth, 3.30 ties Horace's verse to Apulia, to Rome, to the lofty but solid pyramids. 2.20 claims immortality for Horace by referring rather absurdly to his empty tomb. 3.30, true to the tone of 3.29—and indeed to the realistic cast of much of Book 3—confronts the unavoidable fact of Horace's mortality but erects his verse as the monument that will transcend that mortality:

> exegi monumentum aere perennius . . .
>
> non omnis moriar, multaque pars mei
> vitabit Libitinam:
>
> (3.30.1, 6–7)

The indestructible *monumentum* of 3.30.1 recalls also the threatened *monumenta* of 1.2.15, its *violens Aufidus* (3.30.10) the violent Tiber of 1.2.13–15 (cf. *violenter*, 14). 1.2 sees Rome

---

[46] Note esp. the remarkable *superbiam* of 3.30.14. *superbus* and *superbia* are words Horace normally uses with strong derogatory connotations (e.g., of Rome's enemies at *Carmen Saeculare* 55 and 4.15.7; of haughty triumphs at 1.35.3, 1.37.31; of haughty lovers at 3.10.9 and 4.10.2; of Tantalus at 2.18.36; of a pushy social climber at *Epode* 4.5); in 3.30 he dares use it, with obviously positive connotations, of his own poetic accomplishment.

in danger, the Vestal Virgins ineffective (cf. 1.2.26 ff.), while
3.30 envisions Rome's eternal future mirrored in the silent
Vestal climbing the Capitol (3.30.8–9). 1.2 climaxes in Au-
gustus as *princeps* (1.2.50), 3.30 in Horace as *princeps Aeolium
carmen ad Italos deduxisse modos* (3.30.13–14).

3.30 responds also to 1.3. For the *aes triplex* that he admired
and half envied in 1.3.9 Horace now gives us his own creation,
aere perennius, a creation far less vulnerable to wind and water
than the fragile ship of 1.3 (cf. *Aquilonibus*, 1.3.13, *Aquilo*,
3.30.3). Where in 1.3.1 Horace prayed to *diva potens Cypri*
that Vergil, the half of his soul, might escape, in 3.30 his own
power (*ex humili potens*, 12)[47] assures that part of his own soul
(*multaque pars mei*, 6) will escape Libitina.

These numerous links to 1.2 and 1.3 emphasize 3.30's thrust
toward human accomplishment, its theme of indestructible
human creation. And whereas elsewhere in the collection the
escapes envisioned often involve closing one's eyes to reality
and provide at best a temporary respite, the escape envisioned
in 3.30 has its eyes open to the ultimate fact of death and will
be as lasting as the Eternal City herself.[48] 3.30 thus marks a

[47] *humilis* is a word Horace uses sparingly, and always with value-laden
connotations; he frequently associates it with himself. The following are its
only appearances: 1.37.32, 2.17.32, 3.1.22, 3.4.16, 3.25.17, 3.30.12, *Epistles*
2.2.50, 2.3.229. The link between *ex humili potens*, 3.30.12, and *non humilis
mulier*, 1.37.32, is just one of several between 1.37 and 3.30: cf. *Capitolio*,
1.37.6, *Capitolium*, 3.30.8 (the only other mentions are the significant 3.3.42
and 3.24.45); *impotens*, 1.37.10, *potens*, 3.30.12; *deduci*, 1.37.31, *deduxisse*,
3.30.14 (cf. *deducte* in 2.7.2, the only other appearance of the word in *Odes*
1–3); *superbo . . . triumpho*, 1.37.31–32, *superbiam*, 3.30.14. The verbal links
serve both to point the similarity of spirit between the Horace of 3.30 and the
Cleopatra of 1.37 and also to contrast their fates: the Capitol survived Cleo-
patra's assault and will attest to Horace's fame; Cleopatra escaped the disgrace
of being led in haughty triumph, while Horace's *superbia* springs from his
"having led" (*deduxisse*) Aeolic song to Italian measures; Cleopatra, *impotens
sperare*, saw her kingdom fall from grandeur to ruin (cf. *iacentem . . . regiam*,
1.37.25), while Horace, *ex humili potens*, has risen from humble origins to
grandeur and now surveys his creation, *regali . . . situ . . . altius* (3.30.2).

[48] Note in the *vitabit* of 3.30.7 a final appearance of the escape motif so
common early in Book 1: see 1.8.10, 1.14.20, 1.15.18, 1.17.18, 1.23.1. The

Conclusion

noble and appropriate conclusion to a collection in which
Horace's initial inclination to seek the easy way out, to avoid
danger and responsibility, gradually yields to a renewed con-
fidence that in 3.29 discovers in his own *virtus* an invulnerable
praesidium and in 3.30 finds in his own poetry a permanent
refuge.

Conclusion

The final group of Book 3, like the final groups of the two
previous books (1.27–38, 2.13–20), represents one more sharp
ascent, and again the ascent moves increasingly toward in-
volvement, intensity, self-confidence, and magnitude of con-
ception. This movement is apparent at several different levels
within 3.25–30. It is perhaps most easily seen in the progres-
sion from the trio of linked love poems, 3.26–28, to the con-
cluding pair, with the first three limiting their purview to the
artificial realms of poetry—the accepted commonplaces of the
love lyric (3.26) and the drinking song (3.28), the elegant,
ironic lightness of the Alexandrian epyllion (3.27)—while the
final two face the full range of human problems and concerns
and deal with these against the backdrop of Augustan Rome.
One can see a similarly clear ascent from 3.27 to 3.29, and
there is a hint of such movement even from 3.26 to 3.28, with
3.28 not only being slightly longer than 3.26 but also speaking
with somewhat more self-possession, somewhat more inde-
pendence toward the gods, somewhat more initiative toward
life itself. Of the climactic character of 3.30, the fact that in
tone it rises even higher than 3.29, we have spoken already.

What, however, is the role of 3.25 in this final group? It is,
like 2.13, a pivotal threshold poem that looks both back to the
poems which precede it and forward to those which follow.
Its tone of triumphant arrival obviously marks the fact that

---

only intervening appearance of *vito* is *quid quisque vitet numquam homini satis
cautum est*, 2.13.13–14, to which the *vitabit Libitinam* of 3.30 offers a trium-
phant response.

in 3.24 Horace has spoken with a new and constructive open-
ness both toward Augustus and about Rome, and from this
standpoint it stands to 3.24 as 2.13 does to 2.12 (where Horace
has attained a new openness toward Maecenas), or as 3.30
does to 3.29. But 3.25 also obviously looks ahead, and we
have seen how its bold promises lead apparently to 3.27 but
find their true goal only in 3.29 and 3.30.

3.25 also leads into the final ascent by subtly preparing for
the mode of 3.26–28. The great achievement of 3.24 has been
to deal with human problems exclusively on the human level,
but paradoxically the very way in which 3.25 celebrates that
achievement reintroduces two of the superhuman touches that
mark earlier national poems—the emphasis on Augustus's dei-
fication (cf. 3.25.5–6), and the emphasis on divine initiative
(1 ff.). We have seen that on one level these aspects of 3.25
look ahead to the future, to possibilities that indeed find ful-
fillment in Book 4. Within Book 3 itself, however, they lead
easily into the resumption in 3.26–28 of modes that 3.24 seems
to have surmounted. For both 3.26 and 3.27 stress divine
initiative more than human, and 3.27 even holds out to Europa
the ultimate promise of her Divine Connection (73–76)! In
contrast, the emphasis in 3.29–30 is again very much on human
initiative, human aspirations, set against a backdrop of human
limitations. 3.25 thus bridges the gulf between 3.24 and 3.26
and prepares for the final ascent; in the same way, 3.28, which
recommends human action but also stresses divine preemi-
nence, bridges the gulf between 3.27 and 3.29 and leads into
the final ascent of 3.29–30.

The overall structure of Book 3 thus proves closely parallel
to that of Book 1, with an initial descent (3.1–6, cf. 1.1–12),
a gradual recouping in its two balanced middle sections (3.7–
15, 3.16–24, cf. 1.13–19, 1.20–26), and a final triumphant
upward surge (3.25–30, cf. 1.27–38). In addition, the overall
shape recalls that of Book 2 as well, for that book also begins
with initial descent (2.1–6), continues with gradual ascent
(2.7–12), and climaxes in a great rush upward (2.13–20). At
every point, however, the movement of Book 3 marks an

Conclusion

advance over that of the two previous books. 3.1–6 consider national issues with a depth, range, and degree of personal involvement not approached in 1.2 and 1.12; in addition, while 3.3.69–72 suddenly reverts to the theme and tone of 1.6, and at a point within 3.1–6 closely analogous to that of 1.6 within 1.1–12, this regression is short-lived. For in 3.4 Horace at once returns to a *longum melos*, while 1.6 marks an abandonment of larger themes that, with only the exception of 1.12, will not be reversed until the final section of Book 1. In the same way, the central groups of Book 3 substitute a realistic confrontation of life, both public and private, for the frequently escapist orientation of the central poems of Book 1, and the sense of personal attainment and confidence at the end of Book 3 rises far above that expressed at the end of Book 1.

The progress of Book 3 beyond Book 2 is also clearly marked. The essentially personal emphasis of Book 2, an emphasis that in part represents a retreat from the fearsome national miasma evoked in 2.1.25–36, is replaced in Book 3 by a focus that comprehends both personal and public issues. The frankness Horace attains toward Maecenas in 2.12 and 2.17–18 comes now to characterize even what he has to say toward Augustus in 3.14 and 3.24, and the moral issues first explored in 2.15, 2.16, and 2.18 receive a broader treatment and a more clearly national focus in the Roman Odes and 3.24. In the same way, Book 2 mentions *virtus* in connection both with Philippi and with general moral concerns, but 3.2, 3.5, and 3.24 give additional focus and development to both the public and the private ramifications of *virtus*, and the motif does not reach its full climax until 3.29. Finally, just as the degree of confidence and of personal involvement expressed in 2.19–20 marks a significant advance over that expressed in 1.37–38, so the initiative and autonomy of 3.29–30 both rise higher than those of 2.19–20 and seem more solidly based, untainted as they are by the obvious exaggerations and absurdities that mark 2.19–20.

This overall sense of ascent in Book 3 is not, however,

without its limitations. While 3.29–30 represent a point of arrival to which the whole collection has been moving, the fact remains that neither the final group (3.25–30) nor anything else in the collection comes close to matching the Roman Odes in sheer grandeur of conception and execution. Again numerical indicators, imperfect though they be, suggest the larger outlines. From an average of 56 lines per poem in 3.1–6 Horace falls to 25.33 in 3.7–15, and the subsequent ascent leads to averages of only 26.22 lines in 3.16–24 and 34 in 3.25–30. This last average is the highest of any group save the Roman Odes, a huge advance over the 21-line average of 1.27–38 and a comfortable step beyond the 28.67-line average of 1.1–12 or the 32-line average of 2.13–20; but it falls far below the level of the Roman Odes. This is not to say that the end of the collection represents a letdown, only that Horace never again soars with the unconstricted bravado of the six poems that follow the flight of the swan in 2.20. Indeed, the very fact that the remainder of Book 3, even in its final and climactic poems, remains more restrained, more restricted in sheer bulk, than 3.1–6, results not from a loss of energy and initiative but rather, as we shall see, from the conscious choice of a middle course over the Icarean excesses of 2.20.

THEMES AND PATTERNS OF *ODES* 1–3: A RETROSPECTIVE LOOK

libera per vacuum posui vestigia princeps . . .

The Overall Movement of the Collection

If the pattern of each book consists of an initial decline and a concluding rise, that of the collection as a whole contains a long initial decline that extends through much of Book 1, a gradual rise that reaches an all-time peak at the end of Book 2 and the start of Book 3, a sharp fall following the Roman Odes, and a gradual rise toward the more modest heights of 3.25–30. As is so often the case, the relative lengths of poems throughout the collection suggest, albeit imperfectly, both the falling, then rising movement of each book and also the more complex shape of the whole collection. This larger pattern by which the insupportable height of the Roman Odes yields first to a sharp descent, then to a more restrained concluding surge, not only makes itself felt in such mechanical features as number of lines and choice of meter (with a prevalence of the Alcaic regularly marking the high points) but also shapes the movement of the several thematic foci of the collection. (See Diagram 9.)

Before we look at these various themes, however, let us briefly review the role each book plays in the overall pattern. Book 1 begins with three large poems dealing with serious issues—Horace's calling (1.1), the needs of the state (1.2), the glories and dangers attendant upon human daring (1.3)—then, after a shorter poem on mortality (1.4), moves consistently toward poems that deal on a smaller scale with smaller themes.

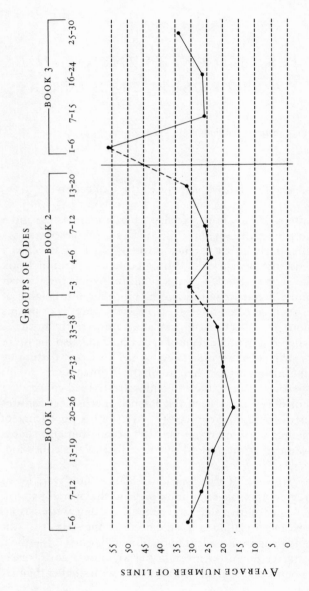

DIAGRAM 9. Graph of Average Length of Poems in Groups of *Odes* 1–3

The large 1.12 represents only an apparent brake to this progression, for in fact it too largely skirts the issues raised in 1.1–4. The central groups, 1.13–19 and 1.20–26, continue the descent in magnitude but also foreshadow the ascent to come, 1.13–19 by the simple fact that these poems signal an involvement on Horace's part, at times unwilling, that rises above the cavalier distance assumed in 1.5 and 1.6, 1.20–26 by the fact that these poems begin again to deal with real people, explicitly to mention public issues (cf. the allegorical indirections of 1.14–15), and to confront the issue of human mortality. The final twelve-poem group, in its two parallel movements, builds on these foundations, confronting human mortality and fragility head-on in several poems, expressly dealing with public issues in a similarly direct manner in 1.35 and 1.37, and throughout suggesting a degree of willing involvement on Horace's part that contrasts sharply with the escapist stance adopted earlier. Crucial features of this concluding surge are Horace's express identification of Alcaeus as his model, an identification complemented by his use of the Alcaic meter for six of these final twelve poems, and his emphasis in the Cleopatra ode on the capacity of inner *virtus* to survive and even surmount external catastrophe.

Book 2, riding on this concluding surge of Book 1, again begins with three poems on large issues—national concerns (2.1), ethical issues (2.2), and mortality (2.3). With 2.4 and 2.5, however, Horace turns away from such topics, and 2.6 gives us a Horace totally absorbed in the quest for a quiet haven in which to grow old and die. As in 1.13–26, 2.7–12 begin the movement back, alluding to national issues, albeit in passing, at several points, confronting in 2.10 and 2.11 ethical and philosophical issues of the sort raised in 2.2 and 2.3, and throughout suggesting the possibility of active human initiative and response, both in general and with particular reference to Horace himself. This second group ends, however, with Horace still relegating national themes to Maecenas's pen, and it is only in the concluding eight poems of the book that the real surge comes. Here, rising above the resignation of 2.6, Horace actively confronts death in several poems, here for the first time since 2.2 he considers ethical issues in depth (2.15, 2.16, 2.18), and here, building on the foundation laid in 1.32, he first fully explores the implications of his adoption of Alcaeus as his model. Again the explicit reference to Alcaeus unleashes a flood of Alcaic poems, and it is on this Alcaic surge that Horace rises to the extraordinary assurance of 2.20, where his human capacities emerge as capable of storming the skies and defeating death itself.

Book 3 opens with six large Alcaic poems that sustain this concluding upswing of Book 2. In their serious and large-scale confrontation of basic philosophical and national issues these poems build upon the thrust of 2.15, 2.16, and 2.18, while the central emphasis on Horace's poetic role (3.1.1 ff., 3.4.1 ff.) builds on 2.19 and 2.20. This initial surge too, however, is short-lived, with the ambivalent feelings implicit in several of the poems leading eventually to the total despair on which 3.6 ends. Again the two middle groups (3.7–15, 3.16–24) both mark a descent from the initial heights and also prepare for a subsequent resurgence, with the serious issues implicit in 3.7–15 becoming increasingly explicit in 3.16–24 and leading up to 3.24's stark honesty toward Augustus and Rome. It is on this more realistic foundation that the final upward surge of 3.25–30 builds, a surge that never attains the reckless assurance of 2.20 or the sustained magnitude of the Roman Odes but that also avoids both the Icarean excesses of 2.20 and the ultimate despair of the Roman Odes.

The falling-rising movement of each book thus creates both a basic parallelism of movement between the individual books and also the overall movement of the collection as a whole. In this way the effective but potentially static parallelism of the inner parts itself provides the basis for the larger dynamic movement to which these inner parts are subordinate, just as the potentially static concentric arrangement of the collection provides a complement to its evolving thematic and tonal patterns. The concentric framework with its in-built parallelism guarantees an architectural solidity that is necessary if so large and diverse a collection is to hold together, while the

ongoing thematic progressions assure that as the mirror sym-
metries unfold the reader or listener will feel not the frustra-
tion of a retreat to home base but rather the exhilaration of
"arriving where we started and knowing the place for the first
time."[1]

To oversimplify the larger structure slightly, one might say
that in Book 1 Horace raises great issues, then retreats from
them, but by the end reaches the point at which he is ready
truly to begin confronting them. Book 2, after its initial re-
treat, brings the head-on confrontation with several personal
and philosophical issues, foremost among them our mortality.
In facing these issues Horace also mentions for the first time
his own experiences in the civil wars and with the tree, and
it is only after these personal revelations of Book 2 that he is
ready to proceed to the larger national questions with which
Book 3 begins, questions raised but not really faced at the
start of both Book 1 and Book 2. The Roman Odes end in
despair over the degeneracy of contemporary Rome, but this
very focus on the realities of the present provides the keynote
for the varied poems that follow in the rest of the book, poems
in which the theme of how to live life is as consistently focal
as was the theme of how to face death in Book 2. In the
parallel stages of the larger structure, Book 1 thus moves from
the Horace who is put off by human daring to the Horace
who can admire Cleopatra's courage, Book 2 from the Horace
who turns away from the horrors of the civil wars to the
Horace who can confront his own place in those wars and can
face the horrors of death itself, Book 3 from the Horace who
despairs over Rome's future in 3.6 to the Horace who bravely
and realistically faces his own and his city's future in 3.24–
30. Each book is a necessary step to what follows, and only
at the end, as the final six poems both recall, in retrograde
succession, the first six, and provide the final critical steps in
Horace's journey, do both the concentric organization of the
whole and its linear progressions find their fitting conclusion.

We have seen that in the larger context of this overall pro-

---

[1] T. S. Eliot, "Little Gidding" V (*Four Quartets*).

gression the otherwise puzzling 2.20 makes sense. While its placement and the magnitude of its claims raise the expectation that the Roman Odes will be the climax and the goal of the collection, its overdone irony gives fair warning that, as indeed proves to be the case, this climax may prove anti-climactic. Following this false climax the collection eventually builds to a more earthbound but more satisfying conclusion, 3.29–30, with 3.30, a poem in placement and theme reminiscent of 2.20 but lacking the earlier poem's excesses, marking the true point of arrival.

In yet another way the apparently anomalous 2.20, when seen in this larger context, proves not a stumbling block but a key to understanding, for its very image of Icarean flight provides an important clue to the overall shape of the collection. That shape, as we have seen, is one that alternates between flying low and flying high, between excessive restraint and caution at some points, excessive confidence elsewhere, a shape that finds its conclusion in the more restrained confidence of 3.29–30. The whole collection might in this way be seen as Horace's quest for the *aurea mediocritas* he recommends to Murena in 2.10. It is a quality he approaches at several points in the collection—2.16 is perhaps his closest brush with it—but fully attains only in 3.29–30. In 3.29 the voyage on which Horace is prepared to set forth alone, that voyage which is the image of his new-found security, will contain the same blend of daring and good sense that Horace recommends to Murena, via similar nautical imagery, at the start and end of 2.10. Horace's confidence in 3.30 has a similarly solid basis and charts a similarly sensible course, recognizing as it does both his own mortality and his poetry's lasting merits, both his own humble origins and his soaring attainments.

In contrast to this solidly-based confidence of 3.29–30 stand the extremes Horace approaches elsewhere in the collection, and fittingly these extremes are related at two critical points to the story of Daedalus and Icarus. It is in 1.3 that Horace first, and perhaps most dramatically, reveals the excessive caution, the shrinking from daring, that will represent one of the

extremes between which he vacillates, and one of the myth-
ological exempla cited there is that of Daedalus:

> expertus vacuum Daedalus aera
> pennis non homini datis;
> (1.3.34–35)

But if in 1.3 Horace shrinks even from the example of Dae-
dalus, who after all not only flew a middle course but was an
examplar of the craftsman-creator, in 2.20 he goes to precisely
the opposite extreme by adopting for himself the model of
Icarus:

> iam Daedaleo notior Icaro
> visam gementis litora Bosphori . . .
> (2.20.13–14)

These two contrasting passages thus chart the extremes ex-
plored in Books 1–3, with the Daedalus image in the early
1.3 suggesting an excessive caution that will find explicit
expression in passages like 1.6.9–12 and 17–20, 2.1.37–40,
3.3.69–72, the Icarus image of 2.20, standing at the entrance
to the high-flying Roman Odes, suggesting the possibility of
overconfidence and presaging the swift descent that is to
come.[2] Thus the striking but puzzling Icarus image of 2.20
both prepares for what is to follow and also, by the larger
context of the myth, points toward the overall pattern of the
collection, that movement which after its giddy swoops and
surges at last finds its Daedalean middle course at the end of
Book 3.

---

[2] That Horace consciously associated this image with his own poetic course
is further suggested by the fact that only in 1.3, in a poem to Vergil, and in
2.20, in a poem on himself, does he in *Odes* 1–3 refer to the story of Icarus
and Daedalus. The one allusion to the story in *Odes* 4 is again associated with
poetic creation and with Horace's own poetic ideals (4.2.2–4). The *Icariis
fluctibus* of 1.1.15 and the *scopulis . . . Icari* of 3.7.21 do not seem to carry
any significant reference to the story of Daedalus and Icarus. On the other
hand, the *penna metuente solvi* of 2.2.7 and the *humum fugiente penna* of 3.2.24,
especially in association with the manifest references to Daedalus-Icarus in
the *pennis* of 1.3.35 and 4.2.3, the *penna* of 2.20.2, may well carry connotations
of the myth. Cf. also *decisis . . . pennis* in *Epistles* 2.2.50.

Something analogous to this same pattern is apparent also
in Horace's development of the different themes of the col-
lection. With respect to each theme, Book 1, especially in its
first twelve poems, introduces both the heights and the depths
associated with this theme—much as 1.3 suggests both the
heights to which humans can soar and the depths to which
they can fall. The center of the collection, 2.1–12, plumbs the
depths, the portion from 2.19 through the Roman Odes ex-
plores the heights, and the end of Book 3 arrives at a happier
medium. With reference to Horace's treatment of national
concerns, for instance, 1.2 and 1.12 suggest Horace's capacity
for the grand style, 1.6 his innate shrinking from that style.
Book 2, after its opening poem on national themes, subse-
quently avoids any focal treatment of national subjects. The
poems that follow 2.6, however, gradually prepare the way
for the Roman Odes by mentioning such themes in passing
and by beginning, in 2.15, 2.16, and 2.18, to deal with ethical
themes closely related to the subjects Horace will consider in
explicitly Augustan contexts in 3.1–6. The peak of Horace's
treatment of such themes comes in the Roman Odes, where
he sustains the grand style in a manner unparalleled elsewhere
in the collection, while the sharp descent from this style her-
alded by 3.7 leads eventually to two poems, 3.14 and 3.24, in
which he deals with Augustus on a more personal level and
approaches national problems in a manner less confident but
more realistic, less exuberant but more direct, than that of
the Roman Odes.

With reference to the theme of mortality, the ends of both
1.1 and 1.2 suggest humans' capacity to transcend their mor-
tality, to approach divine status, while the next two poems,
1.3 and 1.4, stress the inevitability of death, a message un-
derscored by 1.9 and 1.11. A series of poems at the center of
the collection focus on this fact of our mortality—2.3, 2.11,
2.13, 2.14, with the nadir coming in 2.6 as Horace with res-
ignation anticipates his own death. By the time we reach 2.19
and 2.20, however, Horace is asserting the capacity of humans
to find union with the divine, fully to escape their mortality.
These unreasonable heights are maintained in the overdone

assertion of Augustus's future immortality in 3.3.11–12 and
3.5.2–4 and in the extravagant excesses with which Horace in
3.4 trumpets his own divine associations and his consequent
invulnerability. The darker themes of 3.5 and 3.6 brutally
remind us of mortal limitations, however, and the poems of
the next groups, 3.7–15 and 3.16–24, deal in various ways with
humans who live within these limitations. By the end of the
collection, in 3.29 and 3.30, Horace has found a middle course
that reconciles an acceptance of our mortality with an ac-
knowledgment of our quasi-immortal talents.

In terms of Horace's own capacity for action and initiative,
what we might call the theme of his *virtus*, the same pattern
emerges. 1.1 suggests his almost limitless capacities, the noble
heights to which, Icarus-like, he can soar (cf. *sublimi feriam
sidera vertice*, 1.1.36), 1.6 the extreme limitations of his powers
and the minuscule range to which he proposes to confine his
activities; the contrast between the two poems is emphasized
by 1.3, where Horace both admires and retreats from human
daring. In retrospect one suspects that this ambivalent stance
in 1.3 may owe a good bit to Horace's experience at Philippi.
The individual unsure of his own courage—and *Odes* 1–3
suggests at several points that Horace had serious qualms
about his *virtus* as a result of Philippi—both stands in awe of
others' untainted courage and, in envy, denigrates in them a
quality that he fears he lacks. Nor is it surprising to find
Horace shortly after 1.3 withdrawing from active involvement
(in 1.5) and (in 1.6) eschewing anything connected with the
battlefield: the easiest way to deal with failure or fear of failure
is to withdraw from and scorn the arena of action.

Once more the nadir comes in the total resignation of 2.6,
where Horace cares only to find a peaceful retreat in which
to grow old and die, and in 2.7, where he confronts the fact
of his *virtus fracta*. Again, however, 2.7 and subsequent poems
point the way back—2.7 and 2.11 with their emphasis on
living the present to the full, 2.13 with its confrontation of
the tree incident, 2.15–18 with their emphasis on the choices
by which one can shape the quality of one's life. By 2.19–20
Horace is pulsing with action and life, ready to take the ini-

tiative and to climb to unknown heights. This he does in the Roman Odes, only to stumble on the ambiguities of *virtus* in 3.2 and 3.5, their unexpected relevance to his own situation, the recognition of how hard it is truly to restore *virtus*, whether in the state or the individual. It is only after the testing of 3.1–6, the slow climb through 3.7–24, that Horace can in 3.29 find solace and protection in a *virtus* at once more sober and more real than the imagined autonomy of 2.20.

This rapid survey of the overall movement of these three themes highlights an important feature of the collection. While in terms of length of poems its nadir comes in the third group of Book 1 (1.20–26—see Diagram 9, page 216), its "thematic nadir" comes at the center of the collection, in the vicinity of 2.6. It is in 2.6 that Horace first openly confronts his own mortality, in 2.6 that his will to act reaches its lowest ebb, here too that he seems farthest from singing of national issues. Like other anomalies in the collection, however, this apparent inconsistency—the fact that "thematic nadir" does not coincide with "numerical nadir"—makes sense in terms of the overall movement of *Odes* 1–3. The function of Book 1 in this larger movement is to give powerful expression to the initial urge toward escape and then, at the end, to check and reverse that impulse so as to prepare Horace to plunge into the serious concerns of Books 2 and 3. The abrupt descent to the 16.57-line average of 1.20–26 graphically embodies the inclination to take refuge in the *tenue* (cf. 1.6), to retreat from serious issues, while the gradual rebuilding of magnitude in the final twelve poems (1.27–38) checks this rapid decline and suggests that slow resurgence of those impulses toward action and involvement that already in 1.13–19 are beginning to make themselves felt. In Book 2 Horace applies this renewed energy to the issues themselves, building on the final upward impulse of Book 1. It is this resurgence of initiative that enables him to push ahead to the traumatic confrontations that come with 2.6, 2.7, and 2.13, and the very act of confrontation represents a significant triumph over that inclination toward retreat which was so strong in Book 1. At the same time, however, by their very nature these confrontations of Book 2 are a plunge into the dark night of the soul, a facing of facts from which one would rather hide. In metaphorical terms, it is the descent to the underworld, a descent that in myth and ritual marks both the nadir of the hero's fortunes and also the ultimate expression of his courage. Horace's confrontations with his own inevitable death (2.6), with his flight at Philippi (2.7), and with the falling tree (2.13) represent his personal descent into the underworld, a metaphor that is consistent with the underworld imagery of 2.3, 2.13, and 2.14.[3] It is a descent that is at once the expression of his renewed vigor for the fray and also an agonizing plunge into the depths. The increased length of the poems throughout Book 2, and the frequent use of the Alcaic, suggest the magnitude of the confrontation, the heroic tenor of the descent, while the content and imagery of the poems mark the section as Horace's own Harrowing of Hell. Only the resurgence of energy accomplished by Book 1 makes possible the heroic confrontations of Book 2, but these confrontations by their very nature represent the thematic low point of the collection. One should remember also, though, that whether in initiatory patterns or in heroic legend, the confrontation of death is the necessary precondition to rebirth, and just as Book 1 provides the restoration of will necessary for the descent of Book 2, so the *katabasis* of Book 2 is a prerequisite to the rebirth that is to come (cf. the imagery of 3.4).[4] In the same way, the despair of 3.6 will serve as catalyst for the upsurge that begins, slowly, with 3.7.

The Linearity of *Odes* 1–3

We have seen that the essential configuration of the collection, with its progression through a series of ups and downs to an eventual middle course, is reflected in the movement of individual themes. The same is true of another characteristic of *Odes* 1–3, its essential linearity. Just as Book 1 provides the

---

[3] Cf. also the triumphant allusions to the underworld in 2.19.29–32 and 2.20.8.

[4] Cf. T. S. Eliot, *Family Reunion* I. ii.: "I believe the moment of birth is when we have knowledge of death. . . ." On the widespread pattern by which

impetus for the descent of Book 2, that descent the impetus for the renewed emphasis on life in Book 3, so in his treatment of individual themes Horace creates a similar sense of linearity, of progressing via a series of logically necessary steps.

In his handling of national themes, for instance, there is such a linear progression, with each stage preparing for what is to follow. The sharp opposition with which the collection opens, that between grandiose treatment of national themes in 1.2 and 1.12, total avoidance of such an approach in 1.6, is gradually mediated as Horace explores in 1.32 and 2.13 (and perhaps implicitly in Alcaean imitations such as 1.10, 1.14, and 1.37) the implications of his adoption of Alcaeus as his model. After 2.13, with its emphasis on the serious songs of Alcaeus, the way appears open for Horace to compose such songs too, as he will indeed do in 3.1–6. Before that can happen, however, another and perhaps greater obstacle must also be surmounted: in the civil wars Horace himself had opposed Augustus—how is he now freely to praise him?

That Horace was acutely aware of this potential inconsistency is strongly suggested by the *Epodes*, where he builds a sharp contrast between *Epodes* 7 and 16, two poems that bitterly focus on the tragedy of the civil wars, and *Epodes* 1 and 9, two poems that look with nascent optimism toward the new Augustan era.[5] In the course of Books 1 and 2 Horace faces and surmounts this obstacle also. As with the theme of mortality, half the battle lies in simply bringing himself to confront the problem, with the crucial confrontation coming, typically, in the middle of the collection, in 2.7, where for the first time he mentions his earlier allegiance to Brutus. As with other thematic turning points, earlier poems prepare for this critical confrontation. Both 1.2 and 1.35, like the *Epodes*, counterpose the possibility of recovery and rebirth against the trauma of the civil wars, but whereas in 1.2 Horace's evocation

---

the hero or initiate must encounter death in some form prior to rebirth, see esp. M. Eliade, *Rites and Symbols of Initiation*, tr. W. R. Trask (New York, 1958), *passim*.

[5] On the *Epodes*, see below, pp. 254 ff.

of the civil wars is veiled in the language of myth and met-
aphor, in 1.35.33–38 it is direct and hard-hitting in the manner
of *Epodes* 7 and 16. Building on this directness, 1.37 and 2.1
confront the civil wars even more openly, with the contrast
between the triumphant optimism at the start of 1.37 and the
mounting pessimism at the end of 2.1 recalling the central
thematic rift of the *Epodes*, that between 1 and 9 on the one
hand, 7 and 16 on the other. This more open treatment of
civil war themes in 1.37 and 2.1 paves the way for Horace's
first and critical reference in 2.7 to his own role in those wars,
and this open acknowledgement of his own past history is in
turn the step that must be taken before he can in 3.3 and 3.4,
albeit largely through the indirections of myth, deal with civil
war themes in such a way as to suggest in both poems that
the violent animosities of the past must be forgotten and left
behind if a more peaceful future is to be created. That Horace's
own role at Philippi is again mentioned in 3.4, in the poem
that opens the second half of the Roman Odes just as 2.7
opens the second half of the collection, underscores the anal-
ogy between the personal and the national spheres. Just as
Augustus can build Rome's future only if he will move beyond
the violence of the past (3.3 and 3.4), so Horace's open ac-
knowledgement of his own opposing role in that past, and
his willingness in 2.7 and 3.4 to move beyond that past, are
the necessary steps he must take before he can deal directly
and fully with Augustus and his new regime. And we have
already seen how the concluding lines of 3.14 both recall past
divisions between Horace and Augustus and suggest Horace's
intention of moving beyond those divisions.

Horace's gradual exploration of his Alcaean model and his
progressive confrontation with his and his country's past thus
in tandem pave the way for 3.1–6. In the same way, the Roman
Odes in turn pave the way for his subsequent Augustus poems,
3.14 and 3.24. It is the growing recognition of the degeneracy
of the present which precipitates the pessimism of 3.6, but
this same recognition, with its strong emphasis not on ex-
ternals but on inner character, provides the focus for Horace's
hard-hitting advice to Augustus in 3.24: if Rome's moral de-

cline cannot be halted, all else is for naught—a realistic assessment of the present that builds not only upon 3.6 but also upon foundations laid earlier in 2.15, 2.16, and 2.18. The Roman Odes have also suggested the essential emptiness of any easy answers—that merely beating the Parthians, erecting new temples, or deifying the *princeps* in no way strike at the heart of Rome's problems. This lesson too is not overlooked in 3.24, which boldly faces the grave problems that exist and honestly limns the toughness of their solutions, thus, Daedalus-like, steering a course between the immobilizing despair on which 3.6 ends and the too-easy optimism of other portions of the Roman Odes.

3.14 also picks up important themes introduced in the Roman Odes while avoiding their excesses. 3.3 and 3.4 have emphasized the necessity of putting an end to the civil strife of the past and focusing on the peaceful needs of the present, on stressing *lene consilium* and *vis temperata* rather than sheer force. 3.14, with a terseness that casts off the mythological baggage of 3.3 and 3.4, makes a similar point in its central stanza:

> hic dies vere mihi festus atras
> eximet curas; ego nec tumultum
> nec mori per vim metuam tenente
>   Caesare terras.
>
> (3.14.13–16)

Similarly, 3.14's portrait of Augustus as a hero who, Hercules-like, returns to his loving family and to the tasks that await him at home retains 3.3's analogy between Augustus and Hercules, with its emphasis on the need for heroic action and determination, but avoids any mention of the deification of Augustus such as that of 3.3.11–12. And 3.14's implicit focus on *human* answers to human problems in turn paves the way for 3.24's more explicit emphasis on what Rome's human leader and human denizens must do if they are to restore their city. This emphasis in 3.14 and 3.24 coheres also with the prevailing thrust of the two groups in which they appear (3.7–15, 3.16–24), which throughout tend to turn away from divine solutions, divine agents, and to emphasize what humans can do about their own lives. It is as part of this sequence that 3.14 and 3.24 succeed for the first time in placing Augustus himself in a fully human context and addressing him wholly as a human agent with tough but human tasks to confront, human rewards to reap. The distance from the stance taken toward Augustus in 1.2 and 1.12 to that taken in 3.14 and 3.24 is vast, but one can follow the logical and necessary steps by which Horace has executed the long traverse.

Horace's treatment of mortality follows a similarly linear progression in which early poems provide the necessary base camps from which subsequent poems can progress. After the despair with which Horace views death in 1.3, 1.4, 1.9, and 1.11, 1.28 and especially 1.24 place death in a broader and more philosophical context and suggest the necessity of facing death rather than evading the issue, while 1.37 pushes the argument a step farther by demonstrating that the manner in which one dies can represent a triumph of sorts. It is after this preparation that Book 2 can, in effect, focus on the theme of mortality, building a sequence of poems on the general theme (2.3, 2.11, 2.14) as the framework within which Horace can face his own inevitable death. This he does, at first with resignation in 2.6, then with more hope and initiative in 2.13 and 2.17, and finally with quite unrealistic optimism in 2.20. In the course of this confrontation with the fact of his own mortality Horace necessarily comes to terms also both with the dangers of Philippi and with the apparently traumatic tree incident.

Horace's preoccupation with death, and especially with his own death, in Book 2 is a necessary prelude to the Roman Odes. For just as in myth the hero's far-flung adventures and his descent to the underworld precede his taking on the affairs of state, so Horace's large-scale treatment of public issues in the Roman Odes, a process already incipient in 2.15, 2.16, and 2.18, can take place only after the personal confrontations of 2.6, 2.7, and 2.13, the general confrontations of 2.3, 2.11, and 2.14. The pessimistic conclusion of the Roman Odes in turn checks the unrealistic optimism of 2.20 and brings Horace back to mortal reality in 3.7 ff. Now, however, his attention is directed not toward the ultimate fact of death but toward the manifold realities of life, and the synthesis finally attained in 3.29–30 builds on everything that has preceded, with 3.30 blending 2.20's intimations of immortality with 2.6's acceptance of mortality, 3.29 retaining something both of Book 2's probing into absolutes and of Book 3's facing of present realities.

Horace's progression from the cautious timidity of 1.3 and 1.6 to the bold initiative of 3.29 and 3.30 also moves via a series of logical stages. The somewhat bemused recognition in 1.29 and 1.34 that both others and he himself are capable of surprising changes represents an early and necessary step ahead, as does the more active role assumed toward Apollo in 1.31–32, toward Tibullus in 1.33, and toward Augustus in 1.35. Above all, however, it is the Cleopatra ode, in which Horace himself appears only tangentially, that prepares for the greater initiative that he will show in Book 2. Cleopatra, who by boldly confronting defeat and disgrace wrests nobility from the jaws of ignominy, provides the model for Horace's confrontation of his own ignominy in Book 2 (cf. the way in which Horace's advice to Vergil in 1.24 provides the model for his confrontation of his own mortality in Book 2). It is shortly after the Cleopatra ode that in 2.2 he first uses the word *virtus*, a word that there carries general connotations only but that in subsequent poems will carry highly personal associations. The general use of the word in 2.2.19 prepares for its appearance at 2.7.11, where Horace relates it specifically to the flight at Philippi and places it in a context that suggests both its general and its personal relevance. 2.7's critical allusion to Philippi builds also, as we have seen, upon the several increasingly open but still general allusions to the civil wars that have appeared in 1.35.33 ff., in 1.37, and most obviously in 2.1. Thus just as the personal revelations of 2.7 open the way for Horace's more general reflections on the civil wars in 3.3 and 3.4, so the general allusions to the wars and to *virtus* in 2.1 and 2.2 open the way for the personal revelations of 2.7.

Public and private are similarly intertwined in what follows also. It is in the more general 2.15, 2.16, and 2.18 that Horace, building on foundations laid in 1.31.17–20, 1.35, and 2.2, for the first time explores ethical and philosophical issues in depth, an exploration that does not explicitly mention *virtus* but that sets human activities and aspirations in a broader context than that of the battlefield. In this broader context Horace can see his *virtus* as still intact, and a new confidence toward his own capacity for action and accomplishment is evident both in the references to himself in 2.16.37–40 and 2.18.9–11 and in his stance toward Maecenas in the intervening 2.17.

It is this surge of renewed confidence that leads into the extraordinary assertions of 2.19–20, 3.1.1 ff., and 3.4.5 ff. Already, however, opposing forces are at work, for these very odes into which Horace's new self-confidence launches him with so bold a rush contain in their references to *virtus* implications which undercut that confidence. For the *virtus* of 3.2.17 and 21 and 3.5.29 ff., as we have seen, carries strongly military connotations and is, in addition, in both instances described in terms that recall the flight at Philippi. Some years after *Odes* 1–3 Horace was to describe the impact of Philippi in terms of having his wings clipped (*Epistles* 2.2.50), and such is very much the effect of the Philippi reminiscences in 3.2 and 3.5. *virtus*, having made a start in 2.2 (cf. the flight image at 2.2.7–8), having faced up to the fact of Philippi in 2.7, and having figuratively taken flight in 2.20, comes crashing back to earth after these two passages of 3.2 and 3.5. Indeed, in the context of Horace's experience at Philippi, most of 3.2 and the entire story of Regulus in 3.5 carry potentially troubling personal undercurrents for Horace. Just as the initially optimistic Roman Odes end up suggesting the magnitude of Rome's problems, the inefficacy of pat solutions, so the bold confidence of 3.1 wanes as Horace recalls that restoring a lost *virtus*—be it that of a country or that of an individual—is also a process that defies easy answers:

CHAPTER V

neque amissos colores
lana refert medicata fuco,

nec vera virtus, cum semel excidit,
curat reponi deterioribus.
(3.5.27–30)

No doubt the personal connotations of these apparently public lines are among the factors that precipitate the pessimistic plunge of 3.6, the subsequent more earthbound course of 3.7 and the poems that follow it.

At the same time, however, both these more low-lying poems and the Roman Odes that precede them also help provide the means by which Horace will eventually come to terms with his *virtus fracta* in 3.29 and 3.30. For while the Roman Odes include these references to military *virtus* with their disturbing reminders of Philippi, as a whole these odes point away from purely military *virtus* toward broader ethical contexts. The focus of 3.1 is clearly on non-military virtues, 3.3 expressly moves away from the violence of the past, and 3.4 openly favors *lene consilium* and abjures untempered *vis*. Even 3.2 and 3.5 themselves, despite their military settings, suggest the limitations of *virtus* that is merely martial and, at their conclusions, point to inner qualities that transcend mere excellence in battle. Above all, however, it is 3.6 that is of critical importance. For just as its firm emphasis on rebuilding character rather than temples points toward the stance Horace adopts in the crucial 3.24, so its same emphasis on inner morality removes *virtus* from the military—and potentially threatening—context of 3.2 and 3.5 and thus points to its broader implications in 3.24 and 3.29. The poems from 3.7 to 3.24 build on this thrust, exploring a variety of human activities and excellences that not only make life possible but also lend it nobility—the faithfulness of husband and wife (3.7), the warmth of friendship (3.8), lovers' ability to patch up injured love (3.9), one individual's willingness out of love to brave harsh anger and cruel reprisals to save another (3.11), etc. This

series of poems climaxes in the larger ethical explorations of
3.16 and ultimately in the full-scale moral probings of 3.24.
While 3.8 and 3.14 refer to recent victories, their emphasis is
on wars successfully concluded rather than on military *virtus*
per se; moreover, several poems in this group, most notably
3.11 and 3.14, specifically emphasize qualities associated with
peace and, either explicitly or implicitly, turn away from vio-
lence. It is against such a backdrop that *virtus*, virtually un-
mentioned after its troubling appearances in 3.2 and 3.5,[6]
makes its emphatic reentry at three points in 3.24, all of them
non-military in emphasis. This broad exploration of human
activities in 3.7–24 in turn provides the foundation for the *mea
virtute me involvo* of 3.29.54–55. Viewed from this larger per-
spective, Horace's single act of cowardice at Philippi assumes
its proper insignificance as a temporary lapse from a moral
strength, a *virtus*, that elsewhere is manifest in every aspect
of his life and character. The *virtus* with which he prepares to
face the unknown in 3.29, like the *virtus* implicit in many
poems from 3.7 to 3.24, represents no more, and no less, than
the human willingness and courage to take on and deal with
the varied problems of life itself, be they the limitations in-
herent in our mortality, the tough public and private tests of
daily life, or the unexpected and undeserved blows of "the
gods" themselves. The *mea virtute me involvo* of 3.29.54–55 is
no donning of the wings of Icarus, as in 2.20, and the voyage
for which Horace is prepared in 3.29.57 ff. crosses the sea in
a small skiff rather than soaring above it on waxen wings.
The sense of restored *virtus* that animates 3.29 is thus more
solidly and broadly based than is that of 2.20; the voyage on
which Horace will embark is the more secure precisely because
it relies on a *virtus* that is thoroughly human rather than on
a flight that emulates the gods.

3.30 lends further substance to the security expressed in

[6] The one appearance of *virtus* between 3.5 and 3.24 is in the formulaic
periphrasis *prisci Catonis . . . virtus*, 3.21.11–12. Even this passing reference
fits into the larger pattern, however, in that the *virtus* described is non-martial
in character.

3.29 by reminding us that Horace's renewed sense of *virtus* has its complement in his enhanced awareness of his poetic powers. For the journey Horace charts in *Odes* 1–3 is above all that of a poet who finds himself, and that journey ends only with 3.30. It is in connection with the poet Vergil that Book 1 so incisively first broaches the question of human initiative and courage in 1.3, and it is in a poem on his own poetic ambitions (1.6) that Horace most explicitly expresses his own escapist inclinations. The triumphant confidence of 3.29 and 3.30 responds as much to these acknowledgements of doubt in 1.3 and 1.6 as it does to the lofty poetic hopes voiced in 1.1. Moreover, the qualities that distinguish Horace's *virtus* in 3.29 find voice also in 3.30, all now in association with his *poetic* activities and achievements. It is poetry that here lends him a renewed potency (*ex humili potens*, 3.30.12, cf. *potens sui*, 3.29.41), poetry that will be his secure and lasting protection (cf. the protective role of *virtus* in 3.29.55), poetry where his revivified initiative finds expression (*princeps Aeolium carmen ad Italos deduxisse modos*, 3.30.13–14). When Horace several years later looks back at *Odes* 1–3, it is this last quality that he emphasizes, this daring to plunge into the unknown—the same quality that animates the end of 3.29, and from which he feels so separated in 1.3:

> libera per vacuum posui vestigia *princeps*,
> non aliena meo pressi pede.
> (*Epistles* 1.19.21–22)[7]

Freedom, and The Gods

This daring quality of Horace's response in 3.29 and 3.30 both attests to his renewed sense of *virtus* and also distinguishes the

[7] Note how the *per vacuum* of these lines recalls *expertus vacuum Daedalus aera*, 1.3.34, and *vacuum nemus mirari libet*, 3.25.13–14. The Horace who in 1.3 shies away from the flight *per vacuum . . . aera* and who in 1.6.19 and 1.32.1 uses *vacuus* of his own freedom from serious involvements ends up in 3.25 boldly surveying the *vacuum nemus* and, in *Epistles* 1.19, priding himself on his willingness to blaze a trail *per vacuum*.

Freedom, and The Gods

stance of these poems from that of poems such as 1.6, 1.17, and 1.22. *Odes* 1–3 in one sense represents Horace's quest for freedom from the stain of Philippi, a quest to restore lost faith in himself, lost *virtus*, a quest to become whole again—*integer vitae scelerisque purus*. One route to such freedom is to avoid subjects that might touch this sore nerve—large military themes, national topics, anything that might come close to the theme of *virtus*. On a broader level this route entails a general avoidance of involvement, of risk, a general eschewing of higher aspirations, a general search for a safe haven where one can rest secure, untouched by the harsh blows of men or of gods. It is a route frequently chosen by those who, like Horace, have suffered some great blow to their self-esteem and who want at all costs to avoid risking another such blow. Such is the course Horace articulates in 1.6, in which, significantly, he speaks of his own *pudor* (9) and *culpa* (12),[8] and it is the course he follows in much of Book 1, carefully avoiding larger subjects for the most part, and absolutely avoiding any mention of either *virtus* or Philippi. The balancing 1.17 and 1.22, with their emphasis on avoidance, escape, protection, are perhaps the fullest embodiments of this sort of freedom, a basically passive freedom that we might call "freedom from."

The other road to freedom entails not avoidance but confrontation, not escape but involvement. This is the painful road Horace, drawing upon the example of Cleopatra in 1.37, and upon his own advice to Vergil in 1.24, takes in Books 2 and 3, a road that entails facing up fully to Philippi and ex-

[8] It is clear that in this passage the primary reference of *pudor* and *culpa* is to Horace's literary activities and that in this context both words suggest Horace's recognition of the nature and limitations of his own talents and his appropriate determination to work within those bounds (cf. his use of *pudor* with similar connotations at *Epistles* 2.1.258–259). Elsewhere in *Odes* 1–3, however, both words carry strong personal and moral connotations (e.g., *pudor* in 1.35.33, 3.5.38; *culpa* in 3.6.17, 3.11.29, 3.24.34). Given the larger purview of the surrounding lines in this poem (1.6.1–8, 13–16), something of these larger connotations carries over to Horace's use of *pudor* and *culpa* in the central stanza.

ploring fully the meaning of *virtus*. The freedom won by this route is no mere skirting of the issues, no passive "freedom from," but a courageous running of the gauntlet which is itself an act of *virtus* and which leads to true restoration and freedom, now an active and bold "freedom to." Horace's own Pilgrim's Progress is most readily apparent in the dramatic confrontation of 2.6, 2.7, and 2.13, but the same sort of active dealing with real issues is at the heart of his advice to others in 2.15–18 and provides the unifying thread in the varied poems of 3.7–24, with the Hypermnestra of 3.11 perhaps being the noblest embodiment of this active freedom. Such is the freedom, such the *virtus*, celebrated in 3.29 and 3.30, a *virtus* aware of human flaws but willing still to dare involvement, a freedom as weighty as the pyramids and as solid as bronze, not the airy freedom associated with Tyndaris and Lalage in 1.17 and 1.22, nor yet the irresponsible freedom of the Icarean swan in 2.20.[9]

There is also a close relationship between the route by which Horace finds personal redemption, if that is not too strong a word, and that which ultimately he sees as Rome's only road to redemption. For in *Odes* 1–3 Rome too is searching for purgation from *scelus* and *culpa*,[10] and Rome too must choose between "freedom from" and "freedom to." 1.2 and 1.12 clearly look toward "freedom from" in their pleas for god-bestowed purgation, their cries of "Get the barbarians"—both of which approaches really skirt the issue. 2.1 faces facts only again to turn away at the end, and even the Roman Odes, despite their closer look at the problems facing contemporary

[9] Horace's differing uses of *vacuus* (see note 7 above) precisely mirror his movement from the freedom of uninvolvement (*vacuus* in 1.5.10, 1.6.19, 1.32.1) to the daring freedom of involvement (*vacuus* in *Epistles* 1.19.21–22, cf. *Odes* 1.3.34, 3.25.13–14). For a powerful evocation of these two freedoms, see J.-P. Sartre, *Les Mouches* (Paris, 1947), 24 (the gossamer freedom of uninvolvement), 83–84 (the frightening, weighty freedom of action and responsibility).

[10] Cf. *scelus* in 1.2.29, 1.35.33, 3.24.50, *Epode* 7.1 and 18; *culpa* in 3.6.17, 3.24.34, *Epode* 7.14.

Rome, turn frequently to the hope of divine aid, foreign conquest, a deified Augustus. Only at the end, in 3.5 and 3.6, do they fully face harsh facts, in effect posing for Rome, as for Horace, the central questions explicit in 3.5.27 ff. and implicit throughout both poems: Can *virtus* once lost ever be restored? What is the road to renewal? As we have seen, it is the despairing realism of 3.6 that eventually points the way to the more realistic solutions offered in 3.14 and 3.24. What these poems propose is the steep and strenuous road toward active freedom, a road that for Augustus entails staying in Rome to deal with problems there (3.14.13–16) and himself showing the way toward moral purgation and rebirth (3.24.25 ff.), and that for the Romans themselves entails facing the hard choices and painful involvement of active *virtus* (cf. 3.24.45 ff.). Such alone is the road by which *culpa* can be cut back (3.24.34), *scelus* purged (3.24.50).

The movement from passive to active freedom appears also in Horace's changing attitudes toward the larger powers that shape the lives of both individuals and states—fortune, necessity, death itself. Poems early in the collection mention these looming uncertainties mainly to suggest ways of lessening their impact: "Think not of the morrow, of what it may bring, but enjoy what you can in the present." This *carpe diem* stance, articulated so powerfully in 1.9 and 1.11, is ultimately escapist in that the peace and pleasure it enjoins are to be won only by consciously ignoring the ultimate uncertainties of life. It is a stance not unlike that of 1.17, where Horace urges Tyndaris to escape the harsh realities of the world by fleeing to his protected vale. In 1.9 and 1.11, as in 1.17, the goal is "freedom from."

carpe diem is again Horace's theme in 3.29, but whereas 1.9 and 1.11 find freedom in avoiding troubling questions and concerns (*quid sit futurum cras fuge quaerere,* 1.9.13; *tu ne quaesieris, scire nefas, quem mihi, quem tibi finem di dederint,* 1.11.1–2), 3.29 actively faces the future in all its uncertainty—the caprice of Jupiter (43–45), Fortune's savage play (49 ff.), the roaring sea itself (57 ff.)—and urges its *quod adest memento*

componere aequus as an active means of dealing with these in-
scrutable realities:

> ille potens sui
> laetusque deget, cui licet in diem
> dixisse 'vixi: cras vel atra
> nube polum Pater occupato

> vel sole puro; non tamen irritum,
> quodcumque retro est, efficiet neque
> diffinget infectumque reddet,
> quod fugiens semel hora vexit.'
> (3.29.41–48)

Whereas 1.9 and 1.11 consciously turn from the future and
strive to ignore its uncertainties, 3.29 points to the folly of
fearing the future (31–32) and boldly faces its uncertainties (32
ff.).

This shift of emphasis from 1.9 and 1.11 to 3.29 is dramatic,
but as always Horace has carefully paved the way. 1.24, in
which Horace urges Vergil to face harsh facts rather than to
hope for some miraculous cure, marks one important step,
one that leads in short order to 1.28's dark reminder of our
mortality,[11] to 1.35's confrontation with Fortune, and to 1.37's
portrait of Cleopatra bravely facing disaster. Book 2 continues
to move ahead, looking with ever-increasing clarity and in-
sistence both at the grim uncertainties that surround human
life in general (2.3, 2.11, 2.14, 2.16, 2.18) and at the specific
anxieties that haunt Horace himself (2.6, 2.13, 2.17). There
is clear progress toward the active freedom of 3.29 also in the
ever-increasing confidence with which Horace faces the fact
of his own mortality in 2.6, 2.13, 2.17, and 2.20; and the
movement from the basically escapist stance of 2.3 and 2.11
to the clear-eyed facing of the future in 2.16 reflects in mi-

---

[11] Note the important forward step in 1.28: it is another human, the *nauta*
of 23, who has the power to free the spirit of the speaker by conferring the
boon of burial.

crocosm the movement of the collection as a whole from the stance of 1.9 and 1.11 to that of 3.29.[12]

In the course of discovering a more active freedom and a more balanced stance toward the great uncertainties of life, Horace arrives also at a more balanced and independent stance toward the gods. In brief, the movement is from the *permitte divis cetera* of 1.9.9 to the bold independence of 3.29 and 3.30. Whereas, for instance, 1.2 and 1.12 suggest that freedom for Rome must come from the gods, the final poems of the collection suggest that true freedom, whether for the state (cf. 3.24) or for the individual (cf. 3.29) can come only from humans themselves.[13] 1.3 seeks freedom from divine wrath in the avoidance of bold ventures and soaring ambitions, while 3.29 and 3.30 find in human daring and initiative a freedom that enables us to withstand the caprice of the gods and to rise above our mortality. Early poems often place their hopes in humans who become divine, whether it be the Augustus who will attain divine status (e.g., 1.2.45 ff., 3.3.11–12, 3.5.2) or the Horace who himself will mingle with the gods (1.1.29 ff.). The final poems of the collection, in contrast, rest their hopes on human agents, human actions, human recognition. These poems suggest both the degree to which humans are limited in their powers and also the degree to which they remain free to shape and control what really matters, thus steering a course between the reckless presumption that supposes humans can become gods and the demeaning self-effacement that supposes that because humans are not gods they are nothing. Horace may in 3.30 rise toward divine status, but he does so as a result of his own poetic accomplishments (cf. 3.30.14–15) and without for a moment forgetting that he is mortal. Augustus may be destined in 3.25 for insertion in

[12] Note also as part of this progression toward autonomy and freedom of choice the fact that 2.10, in so many ways a crucial poem, offers Murena a clear choice between two alternatives.

[13] Cf. the reflection of this same movement in the progression from 3.27 to 3.29. In 3.27 freedom and salvation are conferred by the gods, in 3.29 won by humans despite the gods.

the stars and the council of Jupiter, but the boon will be conferred by a human poet and will but complement the purely human honor bestowed by his own people in recognition of his human accomplishments (3.24.25 ff.).

Poetry

We come finally to poetry itself, a theme touched upon at several points in this chapter but not yet fully discussed. The same features that distinguish Horace's treatment of other themes appear here also—the same sense of sequential build, the same movement from uncertainty toward assurance, from oscillation between extremes toward a middle course.

The start of the collection creates a powerful illusion of a poet in search of his proper voice. The opening odes parade in reckless profusion a seemingly indiscriminate array of meters, genres, and themes, violently juxtaposing materials of the most diverse tenor in a manner not unlike that of a Feydeau farce. The theme of searching for one's proper role is prominent in the very first ode, with its parade of different vocations, and while in 1.1.29–36 Horace seems certain at least of his calling, in the poems that follow, the sharp clash between odes 1.2 and 1.12 and ode 1.6 suggests that he is unsure of where that calling will lead him. Is he to be, as 1.6 professes, the poet of the *tenue*, crafting superbly polished Callimachean poems on sympotic and erotic themes, leaving weighty, serious themes to others while himself retaining always a *levitas* (cf. *non praeter solitum leves*, 1.6.20) that implies both lightness of touch and the airiness of uninvolvement? Or is he, as 1.2 and 1.12 by their very existence suggest, to be the poet of grandiose poetry that deals with substantial subjects and that dares to become involved? 1.3, of course, with its ambivalent stance toward human enterprise and initiative, half admiring, half depreciating such daring, further emphasizes this central thematic rift.

Even 1.1 itself contains hints of this basic dichotomy, for while in 1.1.29–36 Horace expresses poetic ambitions that in

their lofty sweep foreshadow 1.2 and 1.12, in 1.1.19–22 he
evokes a picture more akin to the low-lying goals of 1.6:

> me doctarum hederae praemia frontium
> dis miscent superis, me gelidum nemus
> nympharumque leves cum Satyris chori
> secernunt populo, si neque tibias
> Euterpe cohibet nec Polyhymnia
> Lesboum refugit tendere barbiton.
> quodsi me lyricis vatibus inseres,
> sublimi feriam sidera vertice.
> (1.1.29–36)

> est qui nec veteris pocula Massici
> nec partem solido demere de die
> spernit, nunc viridi membra sub arbuto
> stratus, nunc ad aquae lene caput sacrae.
> (1.1.19–22)

The *est qui* of the latter passage is not, of course, identified,
but several aspects of the passage point toward Horace him-
self—or at least toward one side of him. The picture conjured
up, with its leisurely delight in the green shade and the sacred
spring, corresponds closely to pictures Horace paints of him-
self elsewhere,[14] and the Massic wine of line 19 appears else-
where in *Odes* 1–3 only in 2.7.21 and 3.21.5, two passages
where Horace himself chooses this particular wine to celebrate
special occasions. In addition, the details of the picture are
without exception those regularly associated, both tradition-

---

[14] With *nec . . . spernit*, 1.1.20–21, cf. 2.7.6–7; with *nunc . . . stratus*, 1.1.21–
22, cf. 2.7.18–19, 2.11.13–14, *Epistles* 1.14.35; with *nunc . . . sacrae*, 1.1.22,
cf. 3.16.29, *Satires* 2.6.2, and Horace's constant association of himself and
his poetry with sacred springs. With the whole picture created in 1.1.19–22,
cf. Horace's description of his villa in 1.17. On the way in which the whole
passage closely recalls Horace himself, see A. J. Pomeroy, "A Man at a Spring:
Horace, Odes 1.1," *Ramus* 9 (1980): 42 ff.; also H. Musurillo, "The Poet's
Apotheosis: Horace, *Odes* 1.1," *TAPA* 93 (1962): 233, 237–239; M.C.J. Put-
nam, "Horace C. 3.30: The Lyricist as Hero," *Ramus* 2 (1973): 16–17.

CHAPTER V

ally and in Horace's works, with poetic inspiration and cre-
ation—wine, the shade of the green tree, the gentle spring of
sacred water.[15] Two other features are noteworthy also, the
location of the *est qui* passage at precisely the start of the second
half of the poem, a position to which Horace regularly attaches
special importance in the construction both of individual
poems and of books,[16] and the absence in the passage of any
of the negative or satiric touches that color the surrounding
vignettes (lines 3–18, 23–28). It is clear that Horace has a
special affection for the *est qui* of lines 19–22, an affection that
he does not feel toward the other types pictured, and given
the other hints that link this passage to poetry and to Horace
himself, it is hard not to assume that these lines evoke one
side of Horace, that same side which finds expression above
all in 1.17, with its emphasis on the reflective leisure of Hor-
ace's secluded vale, its distance from the pressures and hazards
of the real world—and also with its *arbutus* (1.17.5, cf. 1.1.21),
its shade (1.17.22), its wine (1.17.21), and, in the *manabit* of
1.17.15, its own metaphorical sacred spring (cf. 1.1.22). In-
deed, the secluded uninvolvement of 1.1.19–22 is underscored
by its contrast with the hyperactive hustle and bustle, the
slightly sordid ambitiousness, of the vignettes that surround
it. Moreover, the gulf between these near-central lines, which
seem to suggest Horace, and the concluding lines, which ex-
plicitly refer to him, precisely captures the split within himself
as to his poetic ambitions—a split that has its obvious kinship
to that earlier discussed between active and passive freedom.

[15] On the traditional association of these motifs with poetry, see esp. I.
Troxler-Keller, *Die Dichterlandschaft des Horaz* (Heidelberg, 1964), *passim*,
esp. 70 ff. For these motifs in association with Horace's own poetry, see
1.1.29–30, 3.4.6–8, 4.2.29–31, 4.3.10–12, and 3.13 *passim*. On the positive
connotations of 1.1.19–22, see Cody, *Horace and Callimachean Aesthetics*, 63–
71.
[16] See, e.g., the key phrases that begin the second half of several Roman
Odes: 3.1.25, 3.2.17 ff., 3.4.41–42, 3.5.29–30; or the crucial importance of
1.20 and 3.16, which begin the second halves of Books 1 and 3, and of 2.7,
which begins the second half of the collection. Cf. the importance of *Satire*
1.6 within *Satires* 1.

The peaceful 19–22, with its escapist overtones, nicely suggests that side of Horace which inclines to a poetry whose hallmarks are a refinement, a balance, a perfection of craftsmanship so exquisite as to require one to work on a small scale, to rule out larger, more passionate involvement, while the soaring ambitions of 29–36, with their hint of Icarean flight, suggest that side which longs to fashion a new form of Roman lyric that would dare to deal with serious topics—national, personal, philosophical—with eloquence and passion. In the poems that immediately follow, this central split within 1.1 receives dramatic reinforcement in the ambivalence of 1.3 and in the dramatic contrast between 1.6 on the one hand, 1.2 and 1.12 on the other.

From the near-schizoid extremes of 1.1–12 Horace moves gradually but steadily toward what we might call "Alcaean gravity."[17] We have seen that Horace himself emphasizes this movement by the increasingly specific manner in which he speaks of his poetic allegiance. In 1.1.34–35 he speaks merely of his hope to be included among the lyric bards and of his general allegiance to the Lesbian lyre, and the profusion of poets he imitates or echoes in Book 1—Pindar, Bacchylides, Anacreon, Simonides, Stesichorus, Sappho, Callimachus, in addition to Alcaeus—underscores the broad purview and the lack of specificity of this opening statement. Indeed, while the collection will in fact eventually focus in on the Alcaic meter as Horace progressively sharpens the implications of *Lesboum . . . barbiton*, the opening poems seem calculated instead to suggest a leaning toward the Sapphic. The Sapphic appears three times in the opening twelve odes and is, as we have seen, the only meter repeated within this group. Moreover, the poem that immediately follows these "Parade Odes," 1.13, is colored throughout by clear reminiscences of what is perhaps Sappho's most famous poem, φαίνεταί μοι κῆνος (Lobel-Page, *Poetarum Lesbiorum Fragmenta*, 31). At the same

[17] For an excellent treatment of the significance of Alcaeus to Horace, see Reckford, *Horace*, 45–69, a chapter from which I have learned much.

time, however, the clear imitations of Alcaeus in early poems such as 1.9, 1.10, and 1.14 foreshadow Horace's explicit focusing on Alcaeus in 1.32, a focus he further refines in 2.13, where he places special emphasis on Alcaeus's political poems, obviously in preparation for the Alcaic climax of the Roman Odes.

We have seen also that the very shape of *Odes* 1–3 embodies this gradual movement toward "Alcaean gravity" in its progressions toward more serious themes, toward longer poems, toward increasing consistency of length and of tone, and toward a predilection for the Alcaic meter. Already by the last section of Book 1 serious themes are beginning to predominate, poems to lengthen, the Alcaic meter to be preeminent. The poems of Book 2 are largely serious in tone, with erotic and sympotic poems notably less frequent than in Book 1, philosophical themes increasingly in evidence. Average length continues to increase in the book as a whole, consistency of length and meter to become more pronounced, the Alcaic to dominate. These progressions all climax in the almost unbroken gravity of the Roman Odes, their consistently large scale, and their uniform use of the Alcaic. As in so many other areas, however, the climactic quality of the Roman Odes proves misleading, their gravity and consistency not the ultimate goals toward which Horace is to move in his search for his poetic calling. The remainder of Book 3 abruptly turns back toward the model of Book 1—toward a lighter manner and smaller compass, toward variety rather than consistency of meter, theme, and tone, and toward radical variations in length, with 3.7–15 containing poems that vary from twelve to fifty-two lines in length, 3.16–24 poems from eight to sixty-four lines long, and 3.25–30 poems from twelve to seventy-six lines long. At the same time, however, there is again a steady rise in length as Horace moves toward the final group, and the Alcaic meter, absent in 3.7–15, begins to reassert itself.

In the progression we have charted one can again distinguish both the characteristic stages of Horace's journey and also its essential linearity. Book 1, after suggesting in its opening groups the possible extremes, settles largely for the "low road" of light, erotic poetry, and its mention of Alcaeus in 1.32 expressly identifies him as Horace's model for *this* sort of verse. Book 2, after its initial descent toward the resignation of 2.6, increasingly rises toward the daring heights of 2.20, an ascent accompanied by the growing predominance of the Alcaic meter in 2.13–20 and by the increasing scale and seriousness of the poems in this same group. The poem that opens this final group, 2.13, appropriately places special emphasis on Alcaeus's serious public poetry and expressly marks its superiority to the lighter verse of Sappho. Following the temporary high point attained in the Roman Odes, Book 3 gradually works toward a conclusion, 3.25–30, which combines elements of the lighter, more personal side of Alcaeus stressed in 1.32 with elements of the more serious Alcaeus stressed in 2.13. As with other themes in the collection, this eventual middle course alone can provide a satisfactory conclusion. Just as the first poem of the collection points toward two contrasting sides of Horace, both the easygoing figure of lines 19–22 and the soaring *vates* of 29–36, so the collection as a whole suggests that Horace is the poet both of the *tenue* and of the *grande*, that both sides are essential facets of his genius, each incomplete without the other. For just as the central portions of Book 1 scarcely suggest the sustained grandeur to which Horace can rise, so the consistent magnitude and solemnity of the Roman Odes fail fully to convey his flashing wit, his mordant irony, his penchant for poetic play. The full discovery of this poet's distinctive voice comes only in the last six poems of the collection, with their profusion of surprises, their sharp juxtapositions, their kaleidoscopic shifts of genre and tone. The middle course of these final poems reverts in many respects to the character of the opening six poems of the collection but infuses that model with a new spirit that retains something of the daring flight of 2.20 and the passion of the Roman Odes. For just as 3.25–30 recall 1.1–6 but in reverse order, so they echo the themes of the opening poems but invert them, substituting the poetic confidence of 3.25 and 3.30 for the poetic caution of 1.6, the daring voyage of 3.29 for the shore-bound fears of 1.3, the invitation to love in 3.26–28 for the withdrawal from love in 1.5, the call to new life, to an unknown future throughout 3.25–30 for the emphasis on death in 1.3 and 1.4, the retrospective gaze of 1.5. It is a conclusion that recaptures something of the magical grace of Pyrrha, something too of the secluded vale to which Horace invites Tyndaris, but that blends in the honest realism of the poems that stretch from 3.5 through 3.24 and that substitutes for the urge to escape the willingness to dare involvement. Both 3.29 and 3.30 retain something both of the *est qui* of 1.1.19–22 and of the *vates* of 1.1.29–36—something of the former's delight in his peaceful refuge as well as of the latter's zeal for high accomplishment. But whereas in the whole opening group these two inclinations are at cross purposes—witness not only the contrast between these passages of 1.1 but also the central ambivalence of 1.3, the clash between 1.2 and 1.12 and 1.6, in 3.29 and 3.30 these contrasting inclinations work in concert with each other. In 3.30 the poetry that is the fruit of Horace's high aspirations, his willingness to dare uncharted waters, itself provides a secure and unassailable refuge; and in 3.29 the haven to which Horace invites Maecenas, a haven that with its wine (2), its summer shade, and its gentle streams (cf. 21–24) recalls 1.1.19–22, is now the refuge where Horace can clothe himself for action, donning the *virtus* that is his *aes triplex* for the bold voyage. His stance in these final poems blends active and passive freedom and embodies the realization that true "freedom from" can spring only from the willingness to dare that is the hallmark of "freedom to." It is a stance that aptly captures Horace's unique *virtus* both as a poet and as a person, and as such is an appropriate *telos* for the collection.

One can trace the ups and downs by which Horace at length discovers his poetic voice also by following his use of two key words, *tenuis* and *parvus*. In 1.6.9 Horace's use of *tenuis* clearly aligns him with the λεπτότης of Callimachus and his followers and points toward his quest for their elusive refinement and toward his consequent abandonment of larger themes, subjects, and forms.[18] In 2.20.1–2, by contrast, as he is borne aloft *nec tenui . . . penna*, he as clearly lays aside this allegiance to the Callimachean esthetic, an apt introduction to his large-scale treatment of public themes in the Roman Odes that are immediately to follow. Horace does not use *tenuis* again in the collection,[19] but the synthesis he arrives at in 3.25–30 clearly combines the *tenuis* and the *non tenuis* sides of his genius evoked in 1.6 and 2.20. This eventual synthesis is foreshadowed in 2.16, where Horace uses *tenuis* twice, once in connection with his self-imposed simplicity of life (14), once in connection with his poetry (38). The very fact that in the first passage *tenuis* can take on ethical overtones suggests a clear progression beyond the limited, amoral world of 1.6, and this enlarged reference of *tenuis* is further emphasized by the fact that in the last stanza Horace uses the word of a Muse who in this very poem has led him to treat substantial themes in a substantial manner. Indeed, in many ways 2.16 briefly embodies the synthesis at which Horace will arrive in 3.25–30—poetry that deals seriously with themes which have both public and private significance, but poetry that never loses Horace's distinctive elegance and lightness of touch and that explicitly reminds us of the importance of laughter (2.16.26–27). By the time Horace reaches 2.16, however, he is already beginning the swift ascent that will carry him aloft to 2.19 and 2.20 and the Roman Odes, only then to plunge him back downwards, and it is not until the final poems of the collection that he fully grasps the synthesis of which 2.16 offers a fleeting glimpse.

In a sense *parvus* picks up where *tenuis* leaves off. For if 2.16 marks the climax in Horace's use of *tenuis*, it marks also an important starting point in his use of *parvus*. Just as in 2.16

[18] Cf. the use of *tenuis* in 1.33.5 in just such a context as described in 1.6. 17–20.

[19] Cf., however, the related verb *tenuare* in 3.3.72, a passage where Horace is clearly reverting toward the ideal of 1.6.

tenuis carries enlarged connotations that move far beyond its limited range in 1.6, so in the same poem *parvus* takes on ethical overtones and comes to denote not deficiencies but strengths. The ability to live "on little" (*vivitur parvo bene*, 2.16.13) is now seen as a key to survival, and the *parva rura* of 2.16.37, like the *spiritum . . . tenuem* of the next line, are the gift of a Muse that is already soaring toward the heights of the Roman Odes (cf. the *malignum spernere vulgus* of 2.16.39–40 with the *Odi profanum vulgus* with which the Roman Odes open).

The passage with which 3.3 ends seems at first no more than a passing reminder of 1.6, a momentary downdraft to the swan's relentless surge:

> non hoc iocosae conveniet lyrae:
> quo, Musa, tendis? desine pervicax
>   referre sermones deorum et
>   magna modis tenuare *parvis*.
>   (3.3.69–72)

In fact, however, these words, with their emphatic concluding use of *parvus*, foreshadow what is soon to come, for in 3.7 Horace does relinquish the speeches of gods, does abandon large measures for small. By the time he reaches 3.29, though, he is on the rise again, and once more, as in 2.16, *parvus* takes on connotations of strength rather than of weakness, of solace rather than of shame:

> plerumque gratae divitibus vices
> mundaeque *parvo* sub lare pauperum
>   cenae sine aulaeis et ostro
>   sollicitam explicuere frontem.
>   (3.29.13–16)[20]

---

[20] Just as *parvus* comes to connote strength rather than weakness in the course of *Odes* 1–3, so Horace's allegiance to the light and humorous (cf. *non praeter solitum leves*, 1.6.20, *leviore plectro*, 2.1.40; *ne relictis . . . iocis*, 2.1.37, *iocosae . . . lyrae*, 3.3.69) takes on larger, more serious significance in 2.16.26–27: *et amara lento temperet risu*. Cf. above, notes 7 and 9, on the comparable movement of *vacuus*.

The point is extended when at the end of the poem Horace emphasizes that his very poverty can be a source of his strength (3.29.55–56, cf. 2.18.10)[21] and where he deliberately sets out in a *small* boat (*biremis . . . scaphae*, 62).

Horace's use of *tenuis* and *parvus* thus again charts his search for, and his eventual discovery of, a middle course. The position at which he ultimately arrives is one that, with respect both to his way of life and to his poetry, resolutely retains the best of his allegiance to that which is *tenue* and *parvum*—small, modest, temperate, delicate, refined—but extends the range of these terms so that no longer do they rule out serious concerns, significant themes, and daring initiative. Such is the context in which one must view the *virtus* in which Horace wraps himself in 3.29, such the backdrop to his description of himself at 3.30.12 as *ex humili potens*, a phrase that perfectly captures his midway stance.

At a relatively early stage in the collection Horace prays to Apollo, *frui paratis . . . Latoe, dones* (1.31.17–18). In a sense both Horace's recovery of his lost *virtus* and his discovery of his unique poetic voice represent the fulfillment of this apparently modest prayer. As Book 3 unfolds, *virtus* increasingly emerges as a many-sided quality, one that comprehends far more than mere courage in battle, and in that context Horace can see his *virtus* as fully alive, and indeed, as a source of pride and protection. In the same way, as Book 3 unfolds, Horace moves back toward the poetic characteristics that mark Book 1, but now in a more positive, more confident frame of mind. And the poetic synthesis at which he arrives in 3.25–30 in effect represents no more than making full use of what he has: *frui paratis*. For the qualities that he praises in 1.6, those that

---

[21] Note also how the reference to *pauperies* near the end of 3.29, in a peaceful, personal context, recalls and transforms the reference to *pauperies* at the start of the balancing 3.2, where the word appears in a military and public context; also how the negative *pauperies* of 3.16.37 and 3.24.42 becomes positive in the climactic 3.29.56 (the motif is introduced in 1.1.18). On the way Horace similarly lends a positive coloring to the *pauperies* motif at the end of Book 2, see above, pp. 141 ff.

he strives for in the Roman Odes, are clearly among his native gifts, his *parata*, be they the lightness of touch, the elegance and refinement, the vein of irony and humor that he so admires in the Alexandrian poets, or the passionate public concern and the grandeur of diction that he praises in the Alcaeus of 2.13. Such qualities are clearly his already; he need merely draw upon them in that unique manner which is his *virtus*. It is again no more than giving an active, positive cast to the *carpe diem* theme, and applying that theme to his poetry: *quod adest memento componere aequus* (3.29.32–33).

Conclusion

Just as *tenuis, parvus,* and *frui paratis* take on expanded significance as Horace's collection unrolls, so in the course of *Odes* 1–3 he gives a new and active life to the familiar and potentially static notion of the Golden Mean. The theme of *aurea mediocritas* is traditional, almost a cliché by Horace's time, and Horace's treatment of it in 2.10 (appropriately near the middle of the collection!) is memorable for its felicity of diction and structure, its subtle aptness to its addressee, rather than for its philosophical penetration or originality.[22] What gives 2.10 its special significance in *Odes* 1–3 is the fact that the theme it presents, the search for the course between the too low and the too high, the too cautious and the too daring, becomes a central metaphor through which Horace explores all the major themes of the collection, in each instance probing both extremes and only at the end finding something of a mean between them. Most important of all, the very shape of the collection, whether in terms of length of poems, of

---

[22] On the traditional theme of the Golden Mean, see Nisbet-Hubbard, *Commentary on Horace, Odes II,* 160–161 (the oxymoron *aurea mediocritas* may well be Horace's own creation). On the relevance of 2.10 to its addressee, see Nisbet-Hubbard, *Commentary on Horace, Odes II,* 151–158. In terms of actual number of lines, the midpoint of the collection comes between lines 34 and 35 of 2.13, where Horace is dealing with the power of poetry to bring peace even to the tortured creatures of the underworld: an appropriate turning point.

gravity of theme, or of metrical consistency, reveals the same exploration of extremes, now too high, now too low, and, at the end, the same striking of a proper balance. The search for *aurea mediocritas* thus literally comes alive in that the collection, both in its thematic movement and in its shape and structure, acts it out, turning *logos* into *ergon, topos* into *poiēma*. It is typical of Horace, however, that even the middle course of 3.25–30 remains relentlessly active, no static coming to rest but a delicate and mobile equilibrium of opposed thrusts, dissimilar entities, contrasting movements—the breathless *quo me, Bacche, rapis* of 3.25 pitted against the solidity of *exegi monumentum*, Europa's Jupiter-attended arrival against Horace's *Pater*-flaunting embarkation, the large 3.27 and 3.29 interwoven with the brief 3.26 and 3.28. But in this daring finale Horace resolves the dissonances on which the collection opened, forging harmony out of opposites that nonetheless retain their individuality. In the concluding poems, intensely personal concerns can be treated in the large-scale Alcaic format hitherto reserved for national issues (3.29), the leader of state can be approached with a directness formerly reserved for close friends (3.24), and a love poem can burgeon into a mini-epic (3.27). The contrasting thrusts of 1.1 and 1.3 are reconciled in a similarly restless counterpoint. 3.25 has Horace at once moving into the secluded groves of poetry (cf. 1.1.19–22) and outward toward the world of action (cf. 1.1.29–36), and 3.26 has him both celebrating his withdrawal from the field of love and anticipating his imminent return to the fray. 3.27 begins with the dangerous departure of Galatea but ends with the safe arrival of Europa, while 3.29, reversing this movement, begins with Horace inviting Maecenas to his safe haven but ends with him setting forth upon the dangerous deep. And 3.30, with its emphasis both on the eternal refuge of poetry and on the ongoing life of poetry, both on bold poetic departures (cf. 13–14) and on the satisfaction of arrival, provides the final cadential resolution.

We have spoken of Books 1–3 through the metaphor of a journey, an image Horace himself suggests in a number of crucial poems. One should not push the image too far—this is a collection of individual and in many ways self-contained poems, not a continuous narrative. As we have seen, however, its basic outlines do suggest the familiar pattern of the heroic journey, both for Horace and for Rome. There is a movement from a world polluted toward a world that is purged. There is a movement from a preoccupation with death to a focusing on life. Above all, there is a progression from impotence, failure, circumscribed powers, loss of initiative to recovery of lost *virtus*, renewed vitality, rebirth of confidence. There is even at a crucial point a clear hint of that central feature of so many heroic journeys, the descent to the underworld, the confrontation of death that must precede rebirth—Horace's imaginary descent to Hades in 2.13 (with supporting underworld imagery in other poems of Book 2).[23]

Nor, in view of the many evidences of Vergil's influence on Horace, may it be too far-fetched to suggest a rough analogy between *Odes* 1–3 and the *Aeneid*. Both works strongly emphasize journeying by sea, both contain a central descent to the underworld, both rise too high in their hopes following that descent only subsequently to fall into renewed despair. And both surely deal with the quest for rebirth out of death, for purification out of pollution, for renewed initiative out of stagnation. That Horace assigns Vergil a prominent place in an early poem—a poem, moreover, that follows the highly Vergilian 1.2 and that concerns the hazards and the glory of seafaring—is, given these other similarities, scarcely accidental.[24] Nor is it accidental that the collection's two Vergil poems, 1.3 and 1.24, both mark crucial stages in Horace's journey (cf. the critical role Vergil plays in the journey to Brundisium and the introduction to Maecenas, *Satires* 1.5–6), or that the Alcaeus of 2.13's underworld, the figure who in

---

[23] See 2.3.24–28, 2.18.30, 2.19.29–32, 2.20.8, and esp. 2.14.6–12, 17–20.

[24] Note also the echo of *Eclogue* 9.29 in 1.1.36, an early indication of the Vergilian cast of much that is to come. Cf. Santirocco, *Arethusa* 13 (1980): 51. On the Vergilian character of 1.2, see C. F. Saylor, "Horace, *C.* 1.2 and Vergil's Storm (*Aen.* 1.81 ff.)," *Vergilius* 25 (1979): 20–25; also Fraenkel, *Horace*, 243 ff.; Nisbet-Hubbard, *Commentary on Horace, Odes I*, 16–17.

252

Conclusion

so many ways points the way back to life for Horace, is clearly identified with Orpheus, a figure strongly associated with Vergil's underworld, and one who figures prominently in Horace's second ode to Vergil, 1.24.

One could push the parallel between the *Aeneid* and *Odes* 1–3 farther—to the analogy between the deaths of Dido in *Aeneid* 4, of Cleopatra in *Odes* 1.37, both crucial, emotion-charged events in the unfolding narratives, both marking the end of the first third of the journey; to the similarities between Vergil's underworld in *Aeneid* 6 and Horace's in 2.13, both located near the center of the work, both divided between a sense of tragic loss and a sense of new possibilities, both marking the transition from obsession with the past to readiness for the future; to the possible analogies between the shield in *Aeneid* 8 and the Roman Odes, both weaving a complex and many-hued web of past and future, of hopes and fears, and both located approximately two-thirds of the way through the narrative; above all, to the fascinating contrast between the resolutions of 3.25–30, the lack of resolution at the end of the *Aeneid*, a contrast that may owe something to the unfinished state of the *Aeneid* but that probably suggests also a basic divergence of attitude between the two poets. These subjects, however, deserve their own book; for now it is sufficient to recall that the Vergilian qualities of *Odes* 1–3 are followed by the numerous Vergilian touches of *Odes* 4,[25] the Vergilian voyage of *Odes* 1–3 by the nautical reference on which Book 4's Vergil poem opens:

> Iam veris comites, quae mare temperant,
> impellunt animae lintea Thraciae;
> (4.12.1–2)

The wind and the sea again, and friendship (*comites*—the same word Horace uses of the life's journey he will make with Maecenas, 2.17.12), and, as in 1.3, the impetus to set sail once more.

[25] See Duckworth, *TAPA* 87 (1956): 313–316.

THE LARGER CONTEXT: *EPODES,*
ODES 1–3, *ODES* 4

In conclusion we may briefly view *Odes* 1–3 in the larger context of Horace's total lyric output. In composition and publication the collection falls chronologically between the *Epodes*, which Horace completed around 30 B.C., and *Odes* 4, which Horace completed probably in 13 B.C., and we shall see that *Odes* 1–3 stands midway between these two other collections also in theme, tone, and movement. Since our purpose here in looking at these two other collections is only to suggest what light they cast on *Odes* 1–3, we shall examine them briefly and focus on one aspect only, their larger thematic movement.

The *Epodes* and *Odes* 4[1]

Central to the architecture of the *Epodes* are four poems. Two poems to Maecenas, comparable in length and both dealing with the campaign against Antony and Cleopatra, open the two halves of the book—Epodes 1 and 9. Balancing this pair of Maecenas poems are two epodes, 7 and 16, that focus on the ravages of the civil wars. The balanced opposition between

---

[1] This section of the Epilogue represents a revised version of portions of my Horace article in T. J. Luce, ed., *Ancient Writers: Greece and Rome*, vol. 2 (New York, 1982), 703–731. Excerpt is reprinted with the permission of Charles Scribner's Sons. On the architecture of the *Epodes*, see esp. Carrubba, *The Epodes of Horace*, 22–83. On *Odes* 4, see W. Ludwig, "Die Anordnung des vierten Horazischen Odenbuches," *MH* 18 (1961): 1–10, and D. H. Porter, "The Recurrent Motifs of Horace, *Carmina* IV," *HSCP* 79 (1975): 189–228.

these interlocked pairs, 1 and 9 on the one side, 7 and 16 on the other, provides the focal tensions for the book: 1 and 9 look with hope toward a restoration of Rome, whereas 7 and 16 emphasize Rome's decline and the impossibility of recovery. From the standpoint of mood, the remaining epodes fall somewhere between the polar extremes established by these two pairs; more important, in both halves of the book (1–8, 9–17) we progress from the hope and affection of the Maecenas poem to the despair and alienation of the civil war poem.

This movement is especially marked in the first half of the book. Epode 1 exudes affection, hope, and confidence mixed with concern. Epode 2 maintains this bright mood in its idyllic reverie on country life, its picture of a world of peace and fellowship. There are, however, jarring notes in both poems. Hanging over Epode 1 is the fact that Horace and Maecenas must part, that Maecenas is off to the scene of dangerous wars; and the tone of Epode 2 changes radically when we discover at the end that the whole reverie is just that—the idle dream of a man who, whether he likes it or not, is bound to the sordid realities of Rome. Epode 3, again to Maecenas, remains basically cheerful throughout. Horace's exaggerated outrage over some garlic he has eaten is obviously in jest, and it is clear that a warm and open friendship of poet for patron lies behind the poem. Epode 3 does, however, introduce a number of motifs that will become more sinister in subsequent poems—interfamily strife, poison, blood, the witches Canidia and Medea, substances that burn and seethe. The tone of Epode 4 is both harsher and more unpleasant. The *discordia* (2) on which it focuses is elemental, of a piece with that which obtains between lambs and wolves, and its source is no passing jest. This discord carries overtones of class strife, a contrast to the easy friendship of Horace and Maecenas in 1 and 3, that of the farmer and his slaves in 2; and whereas 3 ends with a smile, 4 ends with a clear reference to recent wars.

Epode 5, the longest of the *Epodes* and the longest of Horace's three poems on Canidia, is on one level merely a brilliant example of Horatian play, a virtuoso exercise within a popular

genre, the witch poem. Horace works into this poem, how-
ever, numerous motifs that are significant elsewhere in the
book, and the overall coloration of Epode 5 is anything but
light. Witches and poisons, introduced in Epode 3, become
ubiquitous in 5, but whereas in 3 they were touched upon
humorously, here the poisons are violent and virulent, the
witches a sinister coven worthy of *Macbeth*. And if Epode 4
began with a comparison of the human to the animal world,
in Epode 5 the bestial has taken over the human at every point.
This is a world of savage, predatory, destructive creatures,
and adding to its terror is the fact that humans are working
with, not against, these unleashed animal energies. Discord,
hatred, wrath, lust for revenge, unbridled passions are the
forces that rule; the fiery garlic of Epode 3 has become a host
of substances that burn out of control. Above all there is the
horror of the basic situation—a young boy all but buried alive,
tortured, his body mutilated. The genre in which Horace is
working is by nature grotesque, but Horace goes far beyond
generic requirements. What remains with us from the poem
is not black humor, the fascination of a chilling gothic tale,
but the pathos of a young child made victim to such evil
forces and, in the end, himself transformed into a curse-
mouthing creature like his tormentors.

Epode 6, though briefer than 5, picks up some of the same
motifs. Most notable again is the pervasive comparison of
humans to predatory animals, once more with a clear hint of
the passions that turn humans into beasts. The poem, with
its sneers at a cowardly blackmailer and its threat of poetic
revenge, is lighter in tone than Epode 5, but like Epode 4 it
has an underlying ugliness of tone; it is a poem with a snarl.

Epode 7 makes clear where the previous poems have been
leading. Epode 7 throughout focuses on the civil wars, ap-
plying to this theme the motifs that have been introduced in
the previous epodes. The poison of Epodes 3 and 5 now
becomes the Roman blood spilled on land and sea, an irrev-
ocable stain on later generations. The hints of internecine strife
in Epode 3 and the child tortured in 5 lead in 7 to the murder

of Remus by his brother, and the cursing motif so common in the previous four poems becomes the everlasting curse born of this fratricide. Like the humans in Epodes 4–6, the Romans of Epode 7 turn against each other, driven by evil forces beyond their control; terror marks their faces as it did the face of the young boy in Epode 5. The animal motif is again present, though here with a cruel twist: even animals, unlike the Romans, do not turn against their own kind (11–12). Thus the themes and motifs of the previous epodes, handled there always with at least a touch of humor, return in Epode 7 in complete earnest, capping the inevitable march from the hope and harmony of Epodes 1 and 2 to the black despair of 7. The hints of separation and war introduced in Epode 1 move through a crescendo of antagonism in Epodes 3–6 to the all-encompassing civil strife of Epode 7; in the same way, Alfius's idyllic vision in Epode 2, a vision revealed as merely utopian by the end of that poem, recedes even farther into the distance as we move in 3–6 increasingly into a world dominated by substances and forces beyond human control and arrive, in 7, in a world where blind madness, ancestral guilt, and the curse of fraternal murder reign supreme.

Epode 8 serves two functions in the larger structure of the collection. By its sheer ugliness and its use of numerous motifs familiar from the previous poems (disease, animal-human comparisons, distaste of one person for another, etc.), it underscores the progression from the fellowship and harmony of 1 and 2 to the separation and violence of 7. It serves also, however, as transition to Epode 9, for its vulgarity is so overdone, its conclusion so clever in its very obscenity, that one can scarcely take it seriously. The very ugliness that makes it an appropriate companion to Epode 7 thus provokes the laughter needed as antidote to 7 and as preparation for 9.

The second half of the book follows a similar progression, though its movement is less regular, the overall tone somewhat less dark. There is no need to chart this progression in detail. Again we begin with Horace and Maecenas, with hope, companionship, joy, with escape from danger and disease and war (though, as in 1, not without occasional off-key notes, such as the mention of recent Roman disgrace in line 11 ff., the reference to *nausea* in line 35). Again we move from here to a deeply pessimistic poem about civil war, Epode 16, a poem that picks up many specific motifs from Epode 7 (compare *ruit*, 16.2, with *ruitis*, 7.1; the animal motif in 16.10 with similar motifs in 7.11–12). And again the intervening poems mediate between these two poles, effecting a transition, here somewhat jerky, from one to the other. Epode 10 reintroduces various motifs familiar from 3 to 7—rage, separation, thirst for revenge, curses on an antagonist, predatory animals, the pallor of terror, etc. In 11 and 14, both love poems, Horace treats passion as something that invades the individual, leaving him helpless, burning, tortured, wounded, stricken out of his senses.[2] Epode 12 is an obvious throwback to Epode 8 in mood, tone, and theme, with the typical elements—rage, disease, animals—treated with perhaps even greater venom and virtuosity than in 8. Epode 13 begins with a violent, earth-shaking storm and ends with war, separation, death, and, metaphorically, the disease of living (17–18); and 15, though not without irony and humor, focuses on division and passion—on anger, hatred, revenge. Like its structural counterpart, Epode 6, it ends with teeth bared, an effective preparation for 16, as 6 is for 7.

The progression from 9 to 16 is thus clearly less measured than that from 1 to 7. At first glance this second half also seems somewhat more optimistic in tone than is the first. For one thing, 1 has as its occasion the departure of Maecenas for the uncertainties of the campaign against Antony and Cleopatra, while 9 celebrates the victory at Actium and looks ahead to Maecenas's return. Epodes 11 and 14 deal with possession by passion, but the passion is love, not the hatred of 4 and 6. And 13, despite the presence of storm, destruction, and death, projects an attractive and typically Horatian *carpe diem* response to these givens of the human condition. Above all, 16,

---

[2] Cf. the similar thrust of 1.13, 1.16, 1.17, and 1.19.

while painting the horrors of civil war almost as vividly as does 7, at least raises the possibility of escape to the Blessed Isles. This famous and beautiful vision of a better life in a better world picks up and rights many of the motifs we have met earlier in the book: this is a world free from poison, a world where animals normally antagonistic are friends, a world free from human villainy and antagonism, a world of peace and plenty.

It is clear, however, that we are not meant to accept this vision too completely; as always, Horace jiggles the kaleidoscope. For one thing, in the architecture of the *Epodes* there is a clear balance between 16 and 2, the one standing second in the collection, the other next to last (cf. the complementary relation of 1.2 and 3.29 within *Odes* 1–3). In addition, the poems are of approximately the same length, and both project a lovely but unrealistic vision of a better world—if only one could get there! The ending of 2 makes it clear that Alfius will never attain his vision. Epode 16 stops at line 66, the line parallel to the end of Alfius's speech in 2, but it is clear that here too Horace's vision is a utopia, a "no-place." As if to underline his point, Horace proceeds to end his book with a return to Canidia. Epode 17 is in form a recantation, with Horace pretending to retract the ugly things he has said of Canidia in earlier poems. In keeping with the generally brighter tone of the second half of the *Epodes*, 17 is less ugly than 5, but it nonetheless reinforces some of the darker themes from the rest of the book. Again we are plunged into a world of hatred and wrath, of flame and blood and poison and destructive beasts, of humans confronted with forces and emotions beyond their control. Significant above all is the fact that Horace's plea is rejected: Canidia's perverted passions are the note on which the *Epodes* end.

The structure of the *Epodes* thus consists of two varied but complementary progressions from order, peace, and harmony to chaos, antagonism, and discord. The rhythms of *Odes* 4, again on several mutually complementary levels, move in precisely the opposite direction. This overall movement of *Odes*

4 is most easily approached through the contrast between the outside poems, 4.1 and 4.15. 4.1 opens the book with war, separation, and loss. By the time Horace comes to 4.15, he is singing of peace, plentiful sharing, and poetry. The completeness of this about-face becomes fully apparent if we juxtapose key passages from each poem. The opening lines of 4.1 lament the resumption of wars (albeit the wars of Venus); 4.15.4–9 rejoices in the coming of peace. *Odes* 4.1.29–32 proclaims Horace's separation from others, from the joys of feast and symposium, from poetry and song; 4.15 ends with Horace joining others in symposium and song, joyful concerns that seem far removed from the resumption of wars with which the book began. And in yet one more of the motivic links that tie these poems together and simultaneously underscore the tonal gulf between them, Venus the *mater saeva* at the start of 4.1 yields to Venus the *alma mater* at the end of 4.15, Venus the instigator of new wars (4.1.1 ff.) to Venus the subject of peaceful song (4.15.25–32). These final eight lines unite young and old, man and god, the ancient and the new, male and female, in joyous communal song and festivity; there is no hint of the barriers that isolated Horace so completely in 4.1.

Contributing to this movement from separation to union, war to peace, silence to song, a movement present at many levels of *Odes* 4, are several actual events. On the political front, the years during which Horace was composing *Odes* 4 witnessed a literal movement from war and separation to peace and return. In 16 B.C. Roman forces under Lollius suffered a major defeat on the northern frontier, and in the years immediately following this defeat both Augustus and his stepsons, Drusus and Tiberius, became actively involved in the Germanic campaigns, with Augustus himself not returning to Rome until 13 B.C. Augustus's absence from Rome is openly and emphatically mentioned in 4.2.33 ff. and 4.5.1 ff., passages that gain poignancy in light of 3.14.14–16, and one suspects that Augustus's return in 13 B.C., a return celebrated by the erection of the *Ara Pacis*, lies behind the fulfilled joy of 4.15 and its emphasis on union, peace, and return.

Horace in this period had experienced separation on the personal front as well. Vergil, the poet who plays so important a role in *Odes* 1–3, had died in 19 B.C., and Tibullus, to whom Horace had addressed *Odes* 1.33 and *Epistles* 1.4, had died around the same time. There are also hints at this time, especially in *Epistles* 1.7, of some tensions between Horace and Maecenas.[3] Finally, Horace alludes in 4.13 to the death of Cinara, the woman mentioned four times, always with feeling, in his late poetry. Although we know nothing more about Cinara than what these passages tell us, there is about her a reality lacking in most of the women Horace mentions, and her appearances are always tinged with melancholy. From these several separations there could be no complete recovery, no literal return that, like Augustus's return to Rome, would fully restore what had been lost. But several poems toward the end of *Odes* 4 suggest some sense of healing. Horace's poem on Maecenas, 4.11, certainly bespeaks warm reunion as well as underlying sadness, and his poem to Vergil, 4.12, seems best interpreted as an immortalizing through poetry of the close friendship the poets had once shared.[4] And although 4.15 does not explicitly mention Vergil, it is significant that the song on which *Odes* 4 ends is one with decidedly Vergilian overtones and that, almost alone of *Odes* 4, this final poem carries no reference to the ultimate separation of death.

The years preceding the composition of *Odes* 4 had, in addition, witnessed Horace's literal return to lyric poetry. There is some reason to believe that Horace had been dis-

---

[3] Fraenkel's excellent analysis of *Epistle* 1.7 (in *Horace*, 327–339) rightly argues that there was no permanent cooling of the friendship between Horace and Maecenas. I tend to agree, however, with those who sense some degree of tension at the time of *Epistles* 1 and especially in *Epistle* 1.7: see E. Courbaud, *Horace. Sa vie et sa pensée à l'époque des Épîtres* (Paris, 1914), 62–64, 281–301; J. H. Gunning, "Der siebente Brief des Horaz und sein Verhältnis zu Maecenas," *Mnemosyne* 10 (1941): 303–320; K. Meister, "Die Freundschaft zwischen Horaz und Maecenas," *Gymnasium* 57 (1950): 19–26; K. J. Reckford, "Horace and Maecenas," *TAPA* 90 (1959): 204–208; W. Desch, "Horazens Beziehung zu Maecenas," *Eranos* 79 (1981): 41–43.

[4] See my articles in *Latomus* 31 (1972): 71–87 and *CB* 49 (1973): 57–61.

appointed by the reception accorded *Odes* 1–3 upon their publication in 23 B.C. and that this disappointment may well have been what turned him from lyric poetry to the writing of *Epistles* 1 in the years immediately following. Whatever the reason, *Epistles* 1.1 declares Horace's abandonment of the *ludus* of lyric, and we can date no lyric poem surely to the years 23–17 B.C. In 17 B.C., however, Horace was selected to compose the *Carmen Saeculare*, and it seems that his selection to compose this national ode, and the enthusiastic reception accorded it, played a major role in his decision to return to lyric poetry in the years 17–13 B.C., a return that culminates in the publication of *Odes* 4 in 13 B.C.[5]

We have seen that 4.1 and 4.15 represent the polar extremes of *Odes* 4. The intervening thirteen poems move between these poles, though in no precisely modulated sequence—there is the same easy flexibility that characterizes the structure of *Odes* 1–3. By the time we get to 4.8 and 4.9, for instance, the theme of poetry is already sounding loud and clear, and poetic immortality is being held up as an answer to death; similarly, the alienation Horace feels in 4.1 is clearly breaking down by the time we reach 4.5 and 4.6. There is, however, something of a steady progression in that not until we reach 4.15 do we complete the movement toward peace, poetry, harmony, life: in all of the intervening poems something remains, albeit in varying degrees, of the wars, the separation, the loss sounded in 4.1.

Ode 4.2, for instance, brings Horace closer to other people, closer to poetry, and it looks forward to Augustus's return and to the joy and peace (cf. *forumque litibus orbum*, 43–44) that will attend his return. On the other hand, war, violence, and death still loom large, and Augustus's return is still only

[5] On the sequence of events that led to Horace's abandonment of lyric in 23–17 B.C., his resumption of lyric in 17–13 B.C., see Fraenkel's comments on *Epistles* 1.19 and the *Carmen Saeculare*: *Horace*, 339–350, 364–382. For a different view, see D. R. Shackleton Bailey, *Profile of Horace* (London, 1982), 49 ff.; also R. Kilpatrick, "Horace on His Critics: *Epist.* 1.19," *Phoenix* 29 (1975): 117–127.

a hope; the poem focuses on the gulfs that divide Horace from Pindar and from Antonius, and it ends poignantly in the death of the young animal taken from its mother. 4.3 suggests Horace's renewed sense of poetic power and achievement, but there remain many hints of separation: the distinctions, sharply drawn, between Horace and other men; the reference to envy, diminished but still present; the definition of poetic acceptance in terms of the fingers that now point Horace out as someone different, a far cry from the communal poetry in which he will participate at the end of 4.15. 4.4 may celebrate the union of human and divine, of father and stepson, of new and old, but what dominates the poem is war—war from which Horace stands noticeably apart and which he describes in the most violent terms. The poem may speak of new life out of old, but we retain more its ubiquitous images of death, destruction, and separation. Ode 4.5, like 4.15, stresses Augustus's peaceful rather than his military accomplishments, and like 4.15 it ends with Horace joining other Romans in praise of Augustus. It differs from 4.15, however, in that its most memorable passage, the comparison of Rome's longing for Augustus to a mother's longing for her son, emphasizes separation. The joyful union envisioned at the end of 4.5 remains only a vision, a hope shadowed by the pain, the sadness, and the sense of distance evoked by this beautiful image.

Ode 4.6, standing near the center of the collection, is literally split down the middle by the movement that characterizes the book as a whole. In the first twenty lines we have war, violence, death, and separation; in the final twenty, gentleness, new life, and, above all, poetry (the central four lines, 21–24, provide a deft transition between the contrasting outer panels). The Apollo of the second half is similar to the Apollo at the beginning of 4.15, the Horace at the end of 4.6, happily directing his young singers, similar to the Horace at the end of 4.15. But how different is the violent Apollo at the start of 4.6, and how different from the peaceful world of the final twenty-four lines is the hell that gapes in the first twenty. Ode 4.7 sings of springtime and the return of new life in

nature, but it emphasizes that for us there is no second spring-
time, no return, only the final separation; and although it ends
on a note of friendship—man for man, goddess for man—it
is friendship that fails to overcome death and separation. Odes
4.8 and 4.9 emphasize poetry and its power to confer on
humans the second springtime that 4.7 denies, but both poems
contain also ample reminders of war, violence, separation,
and death. Again in 4.8, as in 4.3, Horace describes his poetic
vocation in terms that stress the differences between him and
other men, and again he explicitly alludes to the dividing force
mentioned in 4.3—envy. This same force reappears in the
lividas obliviones of 4.9.33–34, and the praise of private mo-
rality with which 4.9 ends emphasizes that the man of integ-
rity must face isolation, hostility, even death.

The mixture of separation with union, death with life, in
4.10–13 is readily apparent. Odes 4.10 and 4.13 both begin
with Horace standing apart from Ligurinus and Lyce, enjoy-
ing their suffering, but both odes move from this separation
to a sense of sharing and of sympathy; 4.11 and 4.12 look
forward to shared joys, to the renewed springtime of song,
but both do so with numerous reminders of separation, death,
and violence. In addition, behind 4.11 may well lie the tensions
that had divided Horace from Maecenas, and behind 4.12
almost certainly is the fact of Vergil's death. Finally, 4.14, like
4.4, balances its hints of togetherness, peace, and immortality
against its explicit mentions of violence, war, division, and
death.

Our analyses of these two collections reveal underlying
rhythms that are highly contrasting: a persistent downward
pull toward war, violence, disintegration in both halves of the
Epodes, a persistent upward pull toward union, peace, poetry
in *Odes* 4. One suspects that the downward drift of the *Epodes*
owes much to Horace's experience of the civil wars, to his
initial uncertainties about Augustus, and to his own still-ten-
uous position in the literary life of Rome. One feels less hes-
itation in seeing behind *Odes* 4 a poet increasingly at peace

with Augustus, with Maecenas, with the fact of Vergil's death, and, above all, with himself and his own advancing years.

Conclusion

In tone, theme, and movement as well as in time, *Odes* 1–3 clearly stands midway between these two other lyric collections. Its overall movement is upward, a movement retained in the upward surge on which it ends, but it is a movement checked at many points by the downward pull of doubt, despair, and frustration. The *Epodes* end with Rome abandoned (16), reconciliation blocked (17), *Odes* 4 with Rome restored and society united in communal celebration. The ending of *Odes* 1–3 again finds a middle position. In 3.24 Horace holds forth the possibility of Rome's salvation, and in 3.26–29 he reaches out toward others—Chloe, Galatea, Lyde, Maecenas—in love and friendship. The overall tone of 3.24 remains shadowed, however, its hopes for renewal more a vision of what might be than a celebration of what is. And while in 3.26–29 Horace warmly expresses his affection for other humans and in the *nos* of 3.24.45 groups himself among the citizens of Rome,[6] in the dramatic conclusion of 3.29 he emphasizes his willingness and his ability to go it alone, and 3.25 and 3.30, the balancing outside poems of the final group, extend this sense of his ultimate self-sufficiency.

The midway stance of *Odes* 1–3 is apparent also with respect to the themes of escape and involvement. The *Epodes* begin with Horace taking the initiative toward Maecenas, expressing his willingness to share in the dangers and burdens of public responsibility, and implicitly supporting the Augustan cause; even Epode 2's urge toward escape culminates in Alfius's return to Rome! At the end of the *Epodes*, however, Horace's only hope lies in abandoning Rome, and his initiative is di-

---

[6] With the *nos* of 3.24.45 compare the outward-bound *nos* of Epode 16.41 (*nos manet Oceanus circumvagus*), the communal *nos* of Ode 4.15.25 (*nos . . . rite deos prius apprecati . . . canemus*).

rected entirely toward escape, be it from Rome or from Ca-
nidia. Indeed, given the virulent forces toward whose ascen-
dency both halves of the *Epodes* move, escape must be the
primary preoccupation at the close of the collection, and it is
no wonder that several epodes late in the book find Horace
resisting involvement and treating passion as a violent, un-
welcome incursion in a manner not unlike that of Odes 1.13,
1.16, 1.17, and 1.19. In contrast, Book 4 begins with Horace
resisting involvement, seeking escape from Venus's renewed
attentions, and lamenting that he is again being drawn into
the fray. It ends, however, with his directing his attention
toward society, actively participating in rites that both bring
him satisfaction and contribute to the public weal, and man-
ifestly welcoming the place of Venus in the communal songs
of which he is now a part. Books 1–3 pursue a long course
that weaves between flight and involvement, and the balance
struck at the end preserves both the willingness to be involved
and the ability to find one's own way, both a sense of what
human initiative can accomplish and an awareness of its in-
herent limitations.

The distinctive stance of *Odes* 1–3 can perhaps most effec-
tively be approached through the by-now familiar motif of
the journey, a motif prominent in the *Epodes* and in *Odes* 4 as
well as in *Odes* 1–3. The thrust of the *Epodes* is consistently
outward, toward danger and the unknown, a movement set
up in the very first words of the book (*Ibis Liburnis inter alta
navium, amice, propugnacula, paratus omne Caesaris periculum su-
bire, Maecenas, tuo*, 1.1–4) and culminating in Epode 16's as-
sertion that the only hope for true Romans is *ire pedes quo-
cumque ferent, quocumque per undas Notus vocabit aut protervus
Africus* (21–22). The same thrust receives support at other
points in the *Epodes* as well, whether in the *Quo quo scelesti
ruitis* with which Epode 7 begins, the dire omens and harsh
threats which accompany Mevius's outward voyage in Epode
10, or the *tardiora fata* (17.62) toward which Canidia beckons
Horace in the final speech of the collection. And although
Epodes 1 and 9 move toward the hope of a better future at

Conclusion

Rome, Epode 7 undermines that hope with its reminder of the curse that lies heavy upon the city, Epode 16 portrays Rome's plight as incurable and finds its only hope in what is, after all, a "no place," and Epode 17 sounds the final death knell. Here no journey toward purgation, reconciliation, rebirth, renewed initiative—only the ultimate plague of *scelus*, separation, hatred, and impotence.[7]

Book 4 also specifically deals with journeys, but now the dominant thrust is homeward, not outward, toward return rather than toward departure. From the *abi* that Horace addresses to Venus in 4.1.7, the daring flight of the Pindaric swan in 4.2.25–27, and the absence of Augustus in 4.2 and 4.5 (note especially 4.5.4), the book moves toward the returns of 4.15—the return of peace (lines 8–9), the return of crops to the fields and of the Roman *signa* from the Parthians (4–8), the return of Rome to older and better moral standards (9–14), and, implicitly, the return of Augustus to Rome after his long absence on the northern frontier. Moreover, the journeys of Book 4, in contrast to those of the *Epodes*, are destined to reach their destinations. By its verbal echoes of 3.24 and 3.25, Book 4 marks, as we have seen, the completion of the public journey that Horace had urged upon Augustus and Rome in 3.24 in that objectives there mentioned as distant goals can now be hailed as actual accomplishments of the Augustan era. Horace can now in good conscience confer upon Augustus the sort of praise that was but an unfulfilled hope in 3.25.[8] On a personal level too, Book 4 celebrates accomplishment and completion through the sense of poetic arrival that emanates from 4.3, 4.6, 4.8, and 4.9. Even in the mellow, melancholy acceptance that sounds in 4.11–13 there is recognition of a journey completed. In a manner reminiscent of 3.26, the surprise ending of 4.1 sings of new love beginning, and 4.10 still looks to the future, albeit already with a touch of autumnal

[7] Note how Epode 2, albeit with a light touch, foreshadows the pattern of the collection: at first, the search for salvation, for a new and better life, but at the end, the recognition of the impossibility of change.
[8] See above, pp. 197–198.

sadness, but in 4.11 Horace calls Tyndaris *meorum finis amorum* and specifically says *non enim posthac alia calebo femina* (31–34), and 4.13 looks back on loves lost and ended. The intervening poem, 4.12, is even more retrospective, for it represents a recreation in verse of the bygone youth of Horace's friendship with Vergil. Just as 4.11, perhaps in response to the rift of the *Epistles* 1 period, now invites Maecenas to Horace's house, so 4.12, in response to Vergil's death, through poetry now brings Vergil home to Horace once more (cf. the departure of 1.3). The opening of 4.15 metaphorically signals the journey's end toward which the whole book has been moving:

> Phoebus volentem proelia me loqui
> victas et urbis increpuit lyra,
>   ne parva Tyrrhenum per aequor
>   vela darem.
>   (4.15.1–4)[9]

Books 1–3, in contrast, end on an ambivalent note. There is in 3.30 an undeniable sense of completion—*Exegi monumentum*—but this contrasts sharply with the image on which 3.29 closes—Horace setting sail in his small skiff into the unknown, the mirror inversion of the *ne parva Tyrrhenum per aequor vela darem* on which 4.15 begins. The preceding poems of the final group foreshadow this tension between 3.29 and 3.30. 3.25 unmistakably celebrates Horace's poetic arrival, but its breathless opening questions look to a still-uncharted future, its most memorable image is of the bacchante standing awed before new vistas, and it ends on the ambivalent oxymoron *dulce periculum*. 3.26, like 4.1, sings both of the abandonment and of the resumption of love, but here no melancholy retrospective poems in the manner of 4.11–13 follow to damp the sense of new beginning; indeed, 3.26's counterpart in the last group, 3.28, also ends on a note of erotic anticipation. And

---

[9] With this closing injunction not to set sail, compare the image used of Augustus at 4.5.9–14. With *ne . . . vela darem*, 4.15.3–4, cf. also *nunc retrorsum vela dare*, at precisely the same place in 1.34.

Conclusion

the intervening 3.27 balances Europa's completed journey against Galatea's imminent setting-out.

The close of Books 1–3 lacks 4.15's aura of rounded, satisfied completion, but it nonetheless marks the completion of one journey as well as the readiness for another. Moreover, the journey completed has, to some degree, brought a purgation and renewal that are absolutely denied at the end of the *Epodes*. The vision for Rome's future may remain still clouded in 3.24, but hope is there; the voyage on which 3.29 ends may be lonely, but Horace is fully prepared for it, and the future lies in his own hands, not in Canidia's. And if, in contrast to 4.15, 3.30 does not mention Augustus and his accomplishments, at least, in contrast to Epode 16, it clearly locates Horace's own future in Rome and even links it specifically to the ongoing public ceremonies of the Capitol.

The journey of Books 1–3 thus stands midway between those of the *Epodes* and *Odes* 4, retaining some of the *Epodes'* sense of lonely, perilous quest but holding also a hint of Book 4's sense of arrival and completion. The Horace of 1–3 is still ready to set sail or change course, but he also has a sense of how far he has come and of the positive possibilities of both his future and Rome's. The end of Books 1–3 lacks the bleak despair, the grasping at straws, the utter frustration on which the *Epodes* end, but there is still a restless surge toward the unknown, a continued striving for better things, a renewed energy that contrasts sharply with the mellow acceptance on which Book 4 ends.[10]

The movement of both the *Epodes* and *Odes* 4 is comparatively simple—downward in two clear and parallel thrusts in the *Epodes*, gradually upward in a single long arc in *Odes* 4—while that of *Odes* 1–3 is complex, a series of descents and ascents that sinks to the depths in both Book 1 and Book 2, rises to the heights of 2.19–20 and the Roman Odes, then

[10] The difference of tone between *Odes* 1–3 and *Odes* 4 strikes me as similar to that which Longinus notes between the *Iliad* and the *Odyssey* (*De Sublimitate* 9.13).

plunges downward again only to find a measure of repose, some sense of arrival, in 3.25–30, a series of poems in which again, however, contrast remains a dominant feature, surprise the governing mode. One can easily grasp the patterns of the *Epodes* and *Odes* 4, while that of *Odes* 1–3 is initially bewildering in its perpetually restive flux. The very complexity that renders the structure and movement of Books 1–3 hard to grasp is also, however, a major source of the endless fascination of this Protean collection. We easily comprehend the doomed voyage of the *Epodes*, its movement toward pollution, death, separation, and despair, and we readily grasp the safe harboring celebrated in *Odes* 4, its movement toward purgation, renewal, reunion, and hope. But it is above all *Odes* 1–3 that holds our attention, that draws us "back and back,"[11] and it does so precisely because we cannot pin it down. Poised between voyage out and voyage back, between upward thrust and downward drag, it remains questing, looking forward even at the end, its final synthesis at best a precarious balancing of contrarieties.

Adding to its complexity, its fascination, and its verisimilitude, is the role the unexpected plays in this poetic journey. For in *Odes* 1–3, as on all significant journeys, roads that seem to lead in one direction turn out to lead in another, detours taken of necessity or on a passing whim lead to places we would not have wanted to miss, seeming through-roads turn into deadends, back roads into major highways. On some occasions delight inexplicably dissolves into despair, while at other times weariness miraculously blossoms into exhilaration. Thus a poem wishing Vergil a safe voyage suddenly turns into a dark meditation on the evils humans bring upon themselves, a poem glorifying Pollio's projected history into a tragic dirge on Rome's tormented past. A poem that begins by gloating over Cleopatra's defeat ends up praising her courage, one that begins by recalling Horace's narrow escape from

---

[11] Cf. V. Woolf, "On Not Knowing Greek," in *Collected Essays*, ed. L. Woolf, vol. 1 (London, 1966), 4.

Conclusion

death ends up singing of poetry's power to survive death. The
passing advice that Asterie lock her home at night sets off a
motivic chain-reaction that leads to the *reiectaeque patet ianua
Lydiae* of 3.9.20, to the lover stretched before the door in 3.10,
to Mercury's and Hypermnestra's ability to open doors in
3.11, to Horace's ability to overlook a closed door in 3.14 (cf.
3.10!), and, after a passing wave in 3.15.9, to the open-door
variations on which 3.16 begins. The speaker's hope in 1.28
that the *nauta* may release him from his dreary round unex-
pectedly opens the door for a repeated emphasis on change
in the poems that follow—Iccius's sudden change in 1.29,
Venus's change of abode in 1.30, Horace's change of course
in 1.34, the mutability of all before *Fortuna* in 1.35—and the
theme climaxes in Cleopatra's ability to transform even defeat
in 1.37 (cf. Horace's ability to control his life in the quiet
coda, 1.38).

Horace's despairing thoughts on the civil wars in 2.1 lead
him to abandon national issues for the time, but the same
thoughts are part of a chain of references to the civil wars (in
1.35, 1.37, 2.1) that prepare for Horace's confrontation of his
own role in those wars in 2.7. Conversely, the largely private
questings of Book 2 develop in such a way as to lead directly
into the public odes of Book 3. After a brave start, these public
odes unexpectedly decline into despair, but the very facing of
facts that evokes the despair of 3.6 provides the keynote for
3.7–24, a group of largely private poems that unexpectedly
pave the way for the cautious hopes of the public poem on
which they end, 3.24. And while the exploration of public
virtus in 3.2 and 3.5 unexpectedly recalls Horace's own *virtus
fracta* and helps precipitate the decline on which the Roman
Odes end, the exploration of public *virtus* in 3.24 provides the
starting point for the final surge on which the collection ends
and the springboard for the *virtute me involvo* of 3.29.55, a
personal climax that Horace, with keen dramatic instinct,
saves for the end of this tortuous road.

As with an actual journey, it is only in retrospect that one
for the first time clearly sees the larger shape of the journey

now completed, fully understands the crucial importance of certain changes of course that, at the time, may have seemed insignificant. Only in retrospect do we, for instance, understand the importance of Horace's advice to Vergil in 1.24 and his portrait of Cleopatra in 1.37 as indicating the way by which he himself must in succeeding poems confront and deal with irrevocable evil, be it the evil of Rome's past, of his own experience at Philippi, or of death itself. Only in retrospect do we see that Horace's apparently casual mentions of Alcaeus in 1.32 and 2.13 are in fact crucial signposts for his own poetic journey; that his advice to Murena in 2.10 and his passing references to the story of Icarus and Daedalus in 1.3 and 2.20 set the program for his own quest in the collection for a middle course; or that Horace's poetic power over the wolf in 1.22 prepares for the Orpheus-like Alcaeus and Bacchus of 2.13 and 2.19.

It is typical of Horace's structural sense, and of his subtlety, that in 3.25–30, the concluding section of *Odes* 1–3, he stresses the element of surprise and the unexpected, thus reminding us of the importance of this element throughout the collection and perhaps inclining us to think back over the journey just taken, to identify the crucial turning points that at the time seemed unimportant, to notice the unremarkable beginnings of paths that turned out to be significant, to recognize the seeming detours that proved to be direct routes. This final section is important also in that by its exuberant fantasy, by its kaleidoscopic variation of theme, tone, genre, and motif, by its ever-shifting mix of past and present, myth and reality, public and private, *tenue* and *grande*, it reminds us constantly that the journey of which it marks the conclusion is, despite its many allusions to Horace's own life, not fact but fiction, not autobiography but poetic construct, a journey that takes place within the imagination of Horace and his reader, a journey as much ours as his. That this "fiction" should balance the illusion of symmetrical architectural solidity with the illusion of forward-moving, ever-changing fluidity is appropriate, for in the journey of *Odes* 1–3 the poet celebrates and embodies both completed journey and continued quest, both the human capacity to order the universe and the restless impulse to plunge anew into the chaos of experience. That Horace associates this quest with Daedalus is also appropriate, for Daedalus too was both the creator of labyrinthine solidity and the contriver of daring, untested flight. And that Horace's final middle course is itself compound of high and low is but necessary, for even Daedalus in his middle course, en route to his destination, must have reveled in the freedom of his self-wrought wings, as Vergil himself, in a passage Horace may well have known when he composed 1.3, reminds us:

Daedalus, ut fama est, fugiens Minoia regna,
praepetibus pinnis ausus se credere caelo,
insuetum per iter gelidas enavit ad Arctos
Chalcidicaque levis tandem super adstitit arce.
(*Aeneid* 6.14–17)[12]

[12] Cf. E. M. Forster, *Howards End* (New York, 1921), 195: " 'Yes, I see, dear; it's about halfway between,' Aunt Juley had hazarded in earlier years. No; truth, being alive, was not halfway between anything. It was only to be found by continuous excursions into either realm, and though proportion is the final secret, to espouse it at the outset is to insure sterility."

BIBLIOGRAPHY

BIBLIOGRAPHICAL NOTE

The notes to this book, and the selected sources that follow this brief bibliographical note, adequately document my specific debts in the writing of this study. Anyone familiar with critical trends in the last generation will, however, immediately detect in this book another set of debts, less specific, perhaps, but even more crucial in shaping my whole approach to literature; and it is a pleasure to acknowledge these long-term debts in this brief note. Like so much else in this book, these remarks will have a decidedly personal cast, for they represent an attempt not to give a summary of the critical trends of the past three decades but honestly to acknowledge particular persons and studies that have had a special impact on my thinking.

My initial critical approach was heavily indebted to the "New Criticism" of the 1940s and 1950s—to works such as Cleanth Brooks's *The Well Wrought Urn* (New York, 1947), Robert Heilman's *This Great Stage* (Baton Rouge, 1948), and, in a slightly different vein, Francis Fergusson's *The Idea of a Theater* (Princeton, 1949). The 1950s saw the first successful attempts to apply this approach to the study of the classics, most notably in Robert Goheen's *The Imagery of Sophocles' Antigone* (Princeton, 1951) and "Aspects of Dramatic Symbolism: Three Studies in the *Oresteia*," *AJP* 76 (1955): 113–137, and Bernard Knox's "The Serpent and the Flame: The Imagery of the Second Book of the *Aeneid*," *AJP* 71 (1950): 379–400, and *Oedipus at Thebes* (New Haven, 1957). My closest contact with this approach came through R. D. Murray, whose *The Motif of Io in Aeschylus' Suppliants* (Princeton, 1958) came out shortly after I had entered graduate study, but whose profound impact on me, and indeed on a whole generation of graduate students, came above all through his teaching. These pioneering efforts did much to shape my critical approach to all literature, as did a number of subsequent studies, largely on the language and imagery of Greek tragedy—e.g., J. J. Peradotto's "Some Patterns of Nature Imagery in the *Oresteia*," *AJP* 85 (1964): 378–393; C. P. Segal's "Sophocles' Praise of Man and the Conflicts of the *Antigone*," *Arion* 3, 2 (1964): 46–66; F. I. Zeitlin's "The Motif of the Corrupted Sacrifice in Aeschylus' *Oresteia*," *TAPA* 96 (1965): 463–508; and Anne Lebeck's *The Oresteia. A Study in Language and Structure* (Cambridge, 1971).

At the same time as R. D. Murray was introducing his Princeton students to the possibilities of close analysis of language and imagery, G. E. Duckworth was stressing the importance of literary structure. While I remained skeptical about his work on the Golden Section in Vergil, I was tremendously influenced by his two studies on the structure of the *Aeneid*, "The Architecture of the *Aeneid*," *AJP* 75 (1954): 1–15, and "The *Aeneid* as a Trilogy," *TAPA* 88 (1957): 1–10. Duckworth's teaching in turn led me to other studies that also emphasized structure, most notably to Cedric Whitman's *Homer and the Heroic Tradition* (Cambridge, 1958).

With reference specifically to Latin poetry, I was strongly influenced in the late 1950s by my first contact with Viktor Pöschl's *Die Dichtkunst Virgils* (Vienna, 1950) and by the appearance of Eduard Fraenkel's *Horace* (Oxford, 1957). Of the many other scholars whose work on Horace helped shape my own early efforts, four deserve special mention: Steele Commager, whose *The Odes of Horace* (New Haven, 1962) brilliantly demonstrated the rich insights to be won from applying the New Criticism to Horace; Kenneth J. Reckford, whose many sensitive articles on Horace and whose *Horace* (New York, 1969) brought me close to the person as well as to the poet; Walther Ludwig, whose concise and provocative studies of the structure of Horace's collections ("Zu Horaz, C. 2, 1–12," *Hermes* 85 [1957]: 336–345, and "Die Anordnung des vierten Horazischen Odenbuches," *MH* 18 [1961]:1–10) tied in closely with the approach Duckworth had taken; and Carl

Bibliography

Becker, whose *Das Spätwerk des Horaz* (Göttingen, 1963) appeared soon after I had myself begun work on *Odes* 4.

In recent years, as the present book obviously suggests, I have been strongly influenced by those scholars who, building on what we know of the ancient *volumen*, have stressed the importance of reading ancient poetry collections as gradually unrolling or evolving creations. It was an approach with which I had been experimenting for some time, but an APA panel and the subsequent publication of that panel's papers in *Arethusa* 13 (1980) provided the immediate impetus to apply this approach in earnest to *Odes* 1–3.

M. S. Santirocco's *Unity and Design in Horace's Odes* (Chapel Hill, 1986), which traverses some of the same ground as does my study, unfortunately reached me only after this book had gone to press.

SELECTED SOURCES

Babcock, C. L. "Horace *Carm.* 1.32 and the Dedication of the Temple of Apollo Palatinus." *CP* 62 (1967): 189–194.

Boyle, A. J. "The Edict of Venus: An Interpretative Essay on Horace's Amatory Odes." *Ramus* 2 (1973): 163–188.

Carrubba, R. W. *The Epodes of Horace. A Study in Poetic Arrangement.* The Hague, 1969.

Clausen, W. "Callimachus and Latin Poetry." *GRBS* 5 (1964): 181–196.

Cody, J. V. *Horace and Callimachean Aesthetics.* Brussels, 1976.

Commager, S. *The Odes of Horace.* New Haven, 1962.

Duckworth, G. E. "*Animae Dimidium Meae*: Two Poets of Rome." *TAPA* 87 (1956): 281–316.

———. *Structural Patterns and Proportions in Vergil's Aeneid.* Ann Arbor, 1962.

Fraenkel, E. *Horace.* Oxford, 1957.

Johnson, W. R. *The Idea of Lyric.* Berkeley, 1982.

Kiessling, A., and R. Heinze. *Q. Horatius Flaccus. Oden und Epoden.* Berlin, 1960.

Klingner, F. *Q. Horati Flacci Opera*. Leipzig, 1950.

Ludwig, W. "Zu Horaz, C. 2, 1–12." *Hermes* 85 (1957): 336–345.

Mutschler, F. H. "Beobachtungen zur Gedichtanordnung in der ersten Odensammlung des Horaz." *RhM* 117 (1974): 109–132.

——. "Kaufmannsliebe. Eine Interpretation der Horazode 'Quid fles Asterie' (c. 3, 7)." *SO* 53 (1978): 111–131.

Newman, J. K. *Horace and the New Poetry*. Brussels, 1967.

Nisbet, R.G.M., and M. Hubbard. *A Commentary on Horace: Odes, Book I*. Oxford, 1970.

——. *A Commentary on Horace: Odes, Book II*. Oxford, 1978.

Pöschl, V. *Horazische Lyrik. Interpretationen*. Heidelberg, 1970.

Reckford, K. J. *Horace*. New York, 1969.

Salat, P. "La composition du livre I des Odes d'Horace." *Latomus* 29 (1968): 554–574.

Santirocco, M. S. "Horace's *Odes* and the Ancient Poetry Book." *Arethusa* 13 (1980): 43–57.

——. "The Maecenas Odes." *TAPA* 114 (1984): 241–253.

Seidensticker, B. "Zu Horaz, C. 1.1–9." *Gymnasium* 83 (1976): 26–34.

Silk, E. T. "Bacchus and the Horatian *Recusatio*." *YCS* 21 (1969): 195–212.

Vaio, J. "The Unity and Historical Occasion of Horace *Carm*. 1.7." *CP* 61 (1966): 168–175.

West, D. *Reading Horace*. Edinburgh, 1967.

Wili, W. *Horaz und die Augusteische Kultur*. Basel, 1948.

Williams, G. *The Third Book of Horace's Odes*. Oxford, 1969.

Wimmel, W. *Kallimachos in Rom*. Wiesbaden, 1960.

Witke, C. *Horace's Roman Odes. A Critical Examination*. Leiden, 1983.

Zetzel, J.E.G. "Horace's *Liber Sermonum*: The Structure of Ambiguity." *Arethusa* 13 (1980): 59–77.

INDEX TO POEMS DISCUSSED

Index

LIBRARY OF CONGRESS CATALOGING-IN-PUBLICATION DATA

PORTER, DAVID H., 1935—
HORACE'S POETIC JOURNEY.

BIBLIOGRAPHY: P.
INCLUDES INDEX.
I. HORACE. CARMINA. 2. ODES—HISTORY AND
CRITICISM. I. TITLE.
PA6411.P58   1987   874'.01   86-43136
ISBN 0-691-06702-3 (ALK. PAPER)